COMPLEX JUSTICE

The Case of **Missouri v. Jenkins**

THE UNIVERSITY OF NORTH CAROLINA PRESS CHAPEL HILL

COMPLEX JUSTICE

JOSHUA M. DUNN

© 2008
The University of North Carolina Press
All rights reserved
Manufactured in the United States
of America
Designed and typeset in Arnhem and
The Sans by Eric M. Brooks

The paper in this book meets the
guidelines for permanence and durability
of the Committee on Production Guidelines
for Book Longevity of the Council on
Library Resources.

Library of Congress
Cataloging-in-Publication Data
Dunn, Joshua M.
Complex justice: the case of Missouri v.
Jenkins / Joshua M. Dunn.
    p. cm.
Includes bibliographical references
and index.
ISBN 978-0-8078-3139-7 (cloth: alk. paper)
1. Segregation in education — Law
and legislation — United States.
2. Segregation in education — Law and
legislation — Missouri — Kansas City.
I. Title.
KF4155.D86   2008
344.73′0798 — dc22   2007039029

cloth   12 11 10 09 08 5 4 3 2 1

for **Charles** and **Carol Dunn**

CONTENTS

Acknowledgments ix

Introduction 1

1 An Even Hollower Hope? 8

2 From Segregation to Litigation
  The Ambiguous Racial History of Missouri and Kansas City 31

3 Courthouse Magic
  Educational Vice Becomes Legal Virtue 57

4 The Field of Dreams 82

5 Waking Up
  Implementing an Educational Disaster 113

6 Ambivalence and Anger
  The Response of Kansas City's African American Community 139

7 The Last Days of Desegregation? 159

Conclusion 181

Notes 191

Bibliography 215

Index 221

Illustrations and Tables

Illustrations
Proposed Kansas City, Missouri, "superdistrict"   84
KCMSD recruitment advertisement   121

Tables
1.1 Constraining Cases and Precedents on Desegregation and Education, 1954–1977   23
2.1 Level of Desegregation in KCMSD Schools, 1955–1957   37
2.2 Kansas City's Black and White Populations, 1920–1990   37
3.1 Outcomes of KCMSD School Levy Elections, 1964–1983   62
3.2 KCMSD Student Racial Composition, 1974–1984   63
4.1 Parent Evaluation of Child's Education, 1986   96
5.1 KCMSD Student Racial Composition, 1984–1995   120

Acknowledgments

In setting out to write this book, it was my good fortune to have the advice and support of several remarkable individuals: Jim Ceaser, Martha Derthick, Sid Milkis, and Brian Balogh. I owe a special thanks to Martha Derthick and Jim Ceaser, who have supported this project in many ways from the very beginning. It was, in fact, Martha who initially suspected that *Missouri v. Jenkins* was hiding something interesting and suggested a closer look. As I've found with everything else, she was correct.

Several other friends, colleagues, and institutions have helped me along the way. In 2000–2001, I was a Fellow in Public Affairs at the University of Virginia's White Burkett Miller Center, which provided significant financial and intellectual support. This fellowship also supplied the pretext for asking Shep Melnick's advice on the project. He has been an invaluable mentor ever since. From 2002 to 2004 the Department of Government at the College of William & Mary was an exceptionally congenial and supportive environment for a visiting professor. In particular, John McGlennon and Ron Rapaport made Morton Hall a delightful place to work. Joel Schwarz and the Roy R. Charles Center provided research support at a critical time as well. Since coming to the University of Colorado–Colorado Springs as an assistant professor, I have been blessed with the support of my department chair, Jim Null, and the Center for the Study of Government and the Individual. Dan Ponder and Paul Sondrol have provided guidance that only senior colleagues can. John Dinan read the entire manuscript and saved me from many errors. Bob Stacey, Rob Martin, Dan DiSalvo, Jim Colvin, and Octavius Pinkard endured my many musings on the case. I was fortunate that the University of North Carolina Press asked Jeremy Rabkin and David Levine to be external reviewers. Both provided exceptionally thorough and helpful comments, criticisms, and suggestions. I am also greatly indebted to Chuck Grench of UNC Press, who supported me at a very early stage and navigated me through the entire process. As well, Katy O'Brien and Mary Caviness at the Press deserve my deepest gratitude for their significant efforts producing and editing this book.

Many individuals from Kansas City, including Arthur Benson, Clinton Adams, Edward Newsome, Mark Bredemeier, Jack Cashill, John Rios, and Eugene Eubanks helped me navigate the history of the case and Kansas City's educational politics. In particular, Arthur Benson and Clinton Adams were extraordinarily generous with their time and answered many questions I know they must have tired of by the time I arrived. The staff at the Western Historical Manuscript Collection at the University of Missouri–Kansas City helped me navigate Arthur Benson's files from the case.

Finally, I owe the greatest debt to my family. Their support and encouragement has meant more than they know. My brother, Charlie, and sisters, Teresa and Maria, have expressed an interest in this project for its entirety, with Teresa providing a sharp editorial eye. My wife, Kelly, has read multiple drafts of this book and has shown me undeserved patience. Without her this book would not exist. My children, Joshua, Benjamin, and Elizabeth, give me more joy than I thought possible. My parents, Charles and Carol, to whom I dedicate this book, have provided lifelong love and support and shown me the educational value of a happy home.

COMPLEX JUSTICE

Introduction

On the corner of Indiana Avenue and Linwood Boulevard in a decaying neighborhood in Kansas City, Missouri, the unsuspecting driver will come across a surprising sight: Central High School, a building that America's wealthiest school districts could only dream of. Walking inside—past armed guards and a bank of metal detectors—is to enter an unparalleled educational facility. A computer for every pupil, a six-lane indoor track, a natatorium with an underwater viewing room, and an Olympic-quality gymnastics center are just some of the amenities. The facilities are so extravagant that the building has been dubbed the "Taj Mahal."

Just a few miles south of Central is another surprising sight: the Paseo Academy of Fine and Performing Arts, a school with every amenity a drama or music teacher could imagine. The surprises continue a few miles away at Southwest High School. There you will find a model United Nations with simultaneous translation capability.[1] In fact, pick almost any public school in Kansas City, whether elementary, junior high, or high school, and you will find that it is housed in a state-of-the-art facility or in a completely renovated building with additions like climate-controlled art galleries, greenhouses, and petting zoos.

How does an urban school district afford such facilities? How does a school district, whose enrollment fell from 70,000 students in 1970 to less than 26,000 in 2006, justify them? The answer: *Missouri v. Jenkins*.

Missouri v. Jenkins, *Brown*'s Grandchild

In 1954, with its decision in *Brown v. Board of Education*,[2] the Supreme Court ruled that *Plessy v. Ferguson*'s[3] doctrine of separate but equal no longer applied to public schools. The decision would be the beginning of a long judicial effort to desegregate America's schools. Even though the issue in *Plessy* was racial segregation in railroad cars, the Court referred to segregated school systems to buttress its claim that separate did not imply unequal: "The most common instance of this [legal segregation] is connected with the establishment of separate schools for white and colored children, which has been held to be a valid exercise of the legislative power even by courts of States where the political rights of the colored race have been longest and most earnestly enforced." With *Brown*, the Court attacked this previous holding and ruled that Topeka's segregated school system violated the Fourteenth Amendment's equal protection clause. The Court, however, based its decision on more than just constitutional grounds. It also struck down segregated education because of its psychological impact on black children: "To separate them from others of similar age and qualifications solely because of their race generates a feeling of inferiority as to their status in the community that may affect their hearts and minds in a way unlikely ever to be undone." Because segregated education led to feelings of inferiority, the Court argued, it was unequal. The Court thus married social science with the Constitution.

It has been an extraordinarily strong marriage, if not an altogether successful one, eventually leading to the most massive and expensive judicial experiment with education. In the case of *Missouri v. Jenkins*, Judge Russell Clark would order over $2 billion in educational improvements in order to desegregate the Kansas City, Missouri, School District (KCMSD). His goal was to bring Kansas City in line with the judicial doctrines pronounced in *Brown* and its progeny. The task proved to be far more difficult than he had imagined.

During the 1950s and 1960s the Supreme Court played a relatively passive role in desegregation. Its proclamation in *Brown II* that desegregation must take place with "all deliberate speed" meant that very little desegregation would in fact occur.[4] All deliberate speed provided just the room needed to defer and delay. Most southern states resisted desegregation, perhaps most famously Virginia, with its policy of "massive resistance."

Outside of the Old South, border states were slightly more receptive to the elimination of dual school systems. Missouri, for instance, eliminated its requirement of segregated education and allowed localities to decide how to respond to *Brown*. The school board in Kansas City chose to eliminate its dual school system and adopt a neighborhood school system. Residential segregation limited the amount of integration that occurred under this new neighborhood system, but the KCMSD was modestly successful. And while southern school systems such as Little Rock's faced violent protest over even a handful of black students attending formerly all-white schools, nothing violent or even newsworthy happened in Kansas City. The *Kansas City Star* did not run a single story about the elimination of legally enforced segregation in the KCMSD. The relative tranquility in Kansas City meant that the courts had no reason to intervene.

Kansas City managed to escape judicial oversight during the 1950s and 1960s, but by the end of the 1960s, the Supreme Court began to sanction more aggressive remedies to combat segregation. In 1968, the Court ruled in *Green v. New Kent County School Board* that desegregation plans had to be judged by their effects in producing substantial integration, not whether legally enforced segregation was technically eliminated.[5] In short, school districts had an "affirmative duty" to desegregate. Therefore, neighborhood school systems with racially isolated schools would no longer pass judicial scrutiny. Then, in 1973, in *Keyes v. Denver School District* the Court blurred the line between de facto segregation and de jure segregation, making school districts, which had never been legally segregated or had immediately desegregated after *Brown*, vulnerable to litigation.[6]

These two cases helped prompt the KCMSD's 1977 lawsuit against the state of Missouri, several suburban school districts, and three federal agencies. The suit accused the defendants of forcing the KCMSD to operate an unconstitutionally segregated school system. Kansas City had undergone massive demographic changes in the years since *Brown*. Middle-class white flight meant that the school system was over 60 percent minority (it was only 18 percent minority in 1954), and housing segregation meant that busing was unattractive to both white and black parents. Additionally, the school system was unable to maintain its facilities because of mismanagement and insufficient financing. A lawsuit leading to a metropolitanwide busing plan seemed the only way to bring middle-class money and children into the failing school system.

In 1984, after a tortuous seven-year discovery process and six-month trial, Judge Russell Clark ruled that the KCMSD, which Clark had realigned as a defendant, and the state of Missouri were operating an unconstitutionally segregated school district. All the other defendants were dismissed. Because the Supreme Court disallowed most metropolitanwide busing plans in *Milliken v. Bradley*, Judge Clark had to produce an alternative remedy for Kansas City.[7] His remedy would be a massive program to renovate the physical plant of the KCMSD and to institute a districtwide magnet-school program. This plan was supposed to draw white suburban children into the KCMSD and improve the academic performance of black children. While Clark required the state of Missouri to pay for 75 percent of the plan, he made the KCMSD responsible for the remaining 25 percent. Without sufficient funds on hand, the KCMSD could not pay its share. This shortfall led Judge Clark to take the unusual step of ordering a tax increase on property in the KCMSD. Clark's magnet plan and his tax increases were sufficiently significant to be reviewed by the Supreme Court in both 1990 and 1995.

The Significance of *Missouri v. Jenkins*

"Why study this particular case?" *Missouri v. Jenkins* deserves scrutiny because the remedy was unprecedented in scope; because it sheds light on the lengths and limits of judicial power; and, perhaps most importantly, because it shows the effects of a major attempt to reform an urban school district. While the Supreme Court's 1990 and 1995 rulings in *Missouri v. Jenkins* generated a great deal of constitutional commentary, what actually occurred in Kansas City received surprisingly little attention.[8] Most treatments of the case, whether favorable or unfavorable toward judicial policymaking, concentrate on the Supreme Court decisions and overlook the effects of the lower court rulings on the community.[9]

The two rulings in *Missouri v. Jenkins* are of interest as well because they are in tension with one another. In 1990, the Court essentially upheld the power of district court judges to raise taxes.[10] This decision indicated the Court's apparent willingness to allow more expansive and costly remedies for achieving desegregation. But five years later, the Court returned to the case and drastically limited the tools available for judges to desegregate school districts. In a short time, a dramatic change took place in the Supreme Court's position, from a posture promoting activism to one requiring restraint. While turnover in the Court's composition was largely responsible for this change, the majority took notice of what happened "on the ground" in Kansas City to justify its decision. To understand these conflicting opinions, we must examine more than the doctrinal issues that were at stake: we must examine the effects of Judge Clark's rulings.

The case is also of great interest for the scope and character of the experiment involved. The desegregation program in Kansas City was the most expansive and expensive of its kind. Over $2 billion was spent. The cost is important because the remedy imposed by the district court (primarily the building of magnet schools to attract suburban white children) was conceived as an alternative to forced busing. This case also allows us to study the response Kansas City's black community had to busing alternatives. The community's response shows that imputing motives and desires to disadvantaged groups is often dangerous. It turned out that black community leaders believed the district court was focusing on an anachronistic problem unrelated to the pressing issues facing children in their city.

A final reason for studying *Missouri v. Jenkins* is that the case exemplifies what many have labeled "judicial activism" at its peak. Alexander Hamilton in "Federalist No. 78" defended the Constitution from the attacks of Anti-Federalists such as Brutus, who argued that federal judges would be able to "mould the government into almost any shape they please."[11] Hamilton famously responded that the judiciary was the "least dangerous" branch because it "has no influence over either the sword or the purse; no direction either of the strength or the wealth of the society, and can take no active resolution whatever."[12] With *Missouri v. Jenkins*, we find a federal judge claiming the power of the purse and mandating tax increases on the citizens of Kansas City. *Missouri v. Jenkins* undeniably represents an act of judicial legislation.

This book does not try to refight the war over whether the courts should have the power to make policy: in fact, they do. Rather, the goal is to understand why the courts have this power and the ramifications of its use. Since, in the language of statistics, this case is a sample of only one, it can provide only a partial answer to questions about the courts' current role. The court's use of judicial power in *Missouri v. Jenkins* was unprecedented. Therefore, this case may allow us to see the nature of that power more clearly than by studying a set of cases where it has been used more modestly.

Some today might argue that desegregation and even extensive judicial policymaking are dead issues. The Court (it is said) seems to be retreating from supervising school districts, and in other areas where it has created policy, such as prison reform, it seems to be more reluctant in exercising power. In fact, the Supreme Court's 1995 decision in *Missouri v. Jenkins* marked the Court's attempt to speed the withdrawal of the federal courts from desegregation cases.

While there may be some merit to this argument, there are nonetheless two reasons why the lessons of *Missouri v. Jenkins* are still important. First, the Supreme Court is closely divided in these controversial areas. The replacement of a single justice could spark a new round of policymaking. Second, many state courts have taken up where the Supreme Court has left off. In particular, state courts are increasingly entertaining so-called adequacy suits intended to increase funding for education. Adequacy proponents claim that states are failing to provide an "adequate" education and that courts should order increased expenditures to remedy this failure. The initial results from these suits indicate that state courts will face problems similar to those that Judge Clark faced in *Missouri v. Jenkins*.

The organization of this book is straightforward. Chapter 1 provides the larger historical and theoretical framework necessary for understanding the case. Primarily it analyzes how the development of desegregation law and the doctrine of standing shaped what occurred in Kansas City. Most importantly, it argues that Supreme Court doctrine limited the options available to the district court. This chapter introduces a distinction between "emergent" and "mature" policy areas. In emergent areas, higher courts have not set down precise policy boundaries, while in mature areas, doctrines are settled, leaving little room for discretion for lower courts. Because desegregation was a mature policy area by the time *Missouri v. Jenkins* developed, many of the most controversial features of the case were in fact largely predetermined.

Chapters 2, 3, and 4 trace the origins and history of the case through the Supreme Court's 1990 decision. They show how prior racism and segregation, conflicting constitutional doctrine, and the limited discretion of a district court judge combined to create *Missouri v. Jenkins*. Prior state-sanctioned segregation invited judicial intervention, and the Supreme Court provided the justification and even obligation to intervene. But the Supreme Court's doctrine limited the remedial power of judges to address only those school districts that were responsible for the current segregation. The shortcomings of *Missouri v. Jenkins* were sown years before Judge Clark ordered magnet schools and tax increases. This case provides a compelling example of how the Supreme Court has difficulty controlling the lives of its own doctrinal children when they enter the real world of social policy.

Chapter 5 explains how the case failed to desegregate the school district or improve student achievement. While the plan was intended to draw thousands of white students from the suburbs and bring student achievement to national averages in five years, the evidence from Judge Clark's own appointed experts documents nothing but year after year of disappointment. Chapter 6 focuses on the reaction of Kansas City's black community to the case. Because black community leaders had little influence over the case and black children were often excluded from the plan's best schools, the black community was often ambivalent and even hostile toward the remedial effort. Judges, of course, are not supposed to draft policy based on public opinion. They are not legislators or executives. But when legal doctrine demands that they make policy on behalf of a particular community, it should not be surprising when that community objects that its interests are being neglected.

Chapter 7 discusses the Supreme Court's withdrawal from desegregation, which culminated in the Court's 1995 decision in *Missouri v. Jenkins*. This chapter also traces the case to its conclusion in 2003, as well as the KCMSD's continued failure to solve its educational problems.

Finally, a word about the title of this book, *Complex Justice*: those familiar with books on desegregation should recognize its debt to Richard Kluger's *Simple Justice*. In no sense can this book compete with Kluger's extraordinary history of *Brown v. Board of Education*. It does attempt, though, to show how what was obvious and "simple" became so complex and difficult. The Court in 1954 could not have envisioned the detailed and complicated measures to which Judge Clark was forced to resort in Kansas City. How the courts arrived at *Missouri v. Jenkins* after starting with *Brown v. Board of Education*, I believe, is a worthy story in its own right.

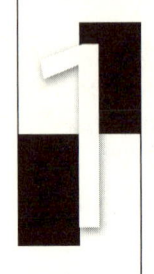

1 An Even Hollower Hope?

It appeared to be a victory. The Supreme Court's 1990 decision in *Missouri v. Jenkins* (*Jenkins II*) upheld the federal court's power to mandate tax increases to pay for a desegregation plan for the Kansas City, Missouri, School District (KCMSD). The plan was pouring hundreds of millions of dollars into the city's largely failing schools. Judge Russell Clark, who presided over the case, had ordered a school improvement plan that turned all the district high schools and middle schools and half the elementary schools into magnet schools. To house the new magnet schools, he ordered a massive rebuilding and renovation program to create an unsurpassed physical plant. The state of Missouri, a defendant in the case, had to pay for most of these improvements. But the KCMSD, which very willingly supported the suit against it, had to pay for part of the remedial plan as well. The KCMSD, however, could not convince voters to approve the tax increases necessary to fund its portion of the cost. As a result, Judge Clark mandated a property tax increase on residents of the district. The Supreme Court, which had declined to review the appropriateness of the remedy—a victory in itself for the school district and plaintiffs—also upheld in principle the power of federal judges to raise taxes. Judge Clark could not set a specific rate, according to the Court, but could enjoin state laws allowing the school district to set its own rate without the public's approval.

To those outside Kansas City, this decision appeared to validate the court's educational experiment. But in Kansas City severe skepticism and harsh criticism of the plan was mounting. The educational gains promised by the court had not materialized. More importantly, black parents were growing disillusioned and even hostile to the court. Within a few years, their opposition grew so intense that a group of parents successfully launched a campaign to take over the school board.

Today, *Missouri v. Jenkins* stands as a $2 billion educational failure that also caused a substantial part of Kansas City's black community to reject the goal of judicially mandated desegregation. Thus, *Missouri v. Jenkins* was a political failure as well as a policymaking one. From one perspective, the power of the courts could not have been greater. The Supreme Court had ruled that federal judges could raise taxes to fund their remedial plans, and opponents had no recourse. But at the same time, the use of this awesome power was quickly discredited in Kansas City.

In this chapter I argue that the existing literature on judicial policymaking cannot explain the outcome of *Missouri v. Jenkins*. Previous studies, such as Gerald Rosenberg's *The Hollow Hope*, explain how courts could succeed in making policy but only under a set of very exacting conditions. In *Missouri v. Jenkins* those conditions were met. However, to understand the policy failure requires one to make a distinction between "mature" and "emergent" judicial policymaking.

The political failure, which was just as significant and was not primarily caused by the ineffectiveness of the court's remedial plan, was driven by the nature of institutional reform litigation. One word explains black opposition: exclusion. The black community did not choose the lawyer who represented their children in court. Black parents then found their children excluded from the district's best schools because of the policies recommended by that lawyer. In lawsuits demanding changes to how public agencies and institutions operate, the resulting policy changes will necessarily affect broad classes of people. The danger in this kind of litigation, which was realized in *Missouri v. Jenkins*, is that the policies proposed by the attorney representing the official plaintiffs will not match the interests of those affected by his proposed policies.

The Policymaking Court:
Power Invested, Promise Unfulfilled?

The furor prompted by *Brown v. Board of Education* almost alone reignited a debate over judicial activism.[1] After Franklin Roosevelt's Court-packing plan induced the "switch in time that saved nine," the judiciary's role seemed settled.[2] Courts were to be deferential to the political branches. But *Brown* revived old conflicts once thought buried with the discredited *Lochner*-era jurisprudence. The states' inferior status, made even more inferior by the New Deal, left them susceptible to increased judicial oversight. The Court, buoyed by the moral authority it earned with its attack on segregation, moved beyond desegregation, entering into such areas as legislative redistricting, police procedure, prison reform, and reproductive rights.

By the 1970s, judges at all federal levels were entertaining a variety of political issues not traditionally considered part of the judicial role. Resolving these new issues required judges to devise political or policy solutions. Previously, judges were limited to legal remedies, but now they had an entire horizon of legislative solutions to choose from. Scholars labeled this new type of litigation "public law" or "institutional reform litigation." Judges operating under the public-law model heard cases involving classes of plaintiffs. Indeed, anyone who could claim to be affected by some policy or action had the right to be included as a plaintiff. In contrast to "public law" litigation, under the "traditional" model, courts were limited to cases involving individual litigants claiming violation of individual rights.[3]

A number of influential critiques have been leveled against the effectiveness of judicial policymaking. Two of the most prominent are *The Courts and Social Policy*[4] by Donald Horowitz and *The Hollow Hope*[5] by Gerald Rosenberg.[6] Both scholars argue, for quite different reasons, that courts are constrained in important ways when trying to make effective public policy. Horowitz contended that courts are poorly equipped for making policy. His concerns centered on the informational problems confronting judges. He argued that judges receive inadequate and biased information from partisan expert witnesses, that the adjudicative process isolates issues that are connected in the real world, that the binary nature of adjudication limits the ability of courts to consider how their decisions affect groups not part of the litigation, and that judges are generalists often lacking any specialized knowledge of the policy issues brought before them.[7] In contrast, Rosenberg focused most of his analysis on highlighting another constraint on judicial policymaking, primarily the inability of judges to compel others to take actions necessary for accomplishing judicial goals. The courts, he argued, could only overcome their constrained position under certain very narrow conditions. There must be

1) ample legal precedent for change[;]
2) support from substantial numbers in Congress and from the executive[;]
3) support from some citizens or at least low levels of opposition from all citizens; and either
   a. positive incentives [must be] offered to induce compliance, or
   b. costs [must be] imposed to induce compliance, or
   c. court decisions [must] allow for market implementation, or
   d. administrators and officials crucial for implementation must be willing to act and see court orders as a tool for leveraging additional resources or for hiding behind.[8]

Studying the courts' attacks on segregation and enforcement of abortion rights on a national level, Rosenberg found that the courts have been unable to bring about social change on their own. In fact, he argued, the courts seem quite powerless without the help of Congress and the executive branch to bring about social change.[9]

At first glance, Rosenberg's thesis appears to reconfirm a constitutional truism: courts need the support of other institutions, which is a testament to separation of powers, federalism, and representative government. His argument, then, provides a powerful verification of "Federalist No. 51," which explains how the Constitution is designed to frustrate and impede the exercise of government power. Thus, there appear to be two main limitations on judicial policymaking. Horowitz's analysis focuses on internal limitations, while Rosenberg concentrates on external constraints.

My purpose in this book is to call attention to a third type of constraint that is aptly illustrated by *Missouri v. Jenkins*: lower court judges, in particular, are often constrained by Supreme Court precedents that hinder their ability to frame effective policies and secure their implementation. The evidence from *Missouri v. Jenkins* supports the general argument that courts are constrained but also shows that they are sometimes constrained for reasons other than ones given by Horowitz and Rosenberg.

Mature versus Emergent Judicial Policymaking

Superficially, *Missouri v. Jenkins* appears to be the archetypal case that critics and skeptics of judicial policymaking envisioned. It involved a judge with little personal knowledge of education policy and whose insulation from politics deprived him of essential information. In addition, the adversarial process gave him poor information from biased expert witnesses. He then ignored constitutional principles of federalism and separation of powers, not to mention American Revolutionary and constitutional principles, such as "taxation without representation is tyranny" and "the power to tax involves the power to destroy," and mandated tax increases on Kansas City's property owners.

Looking more closely, though, we see that doctrinal precedents constrained Judge Clark more than lack of information or external constraints. In fact, he was warned from a variety of sources that his plan would not work. In addition, citizens and political institutions offered little resistance and were easily compelled to follow the court. The court provided positive incentives to induce compliance and imposed costs for not complying. Finally, officials responsible for implementing the court's decisions were willing to act and use the court to leverage additional resources.

By its very nature, the Supreme Court must decide legal controversies. Lower courts are then obliged to follow the Court's decisions. When these controversies involve public policy, the Court's decisions often limit the policy choices available to lower court judges, who then lose flexibility when crafting public policy. In fact, Supreme Court precedent can actually force judges to adopt inappropriate policies. In *Missouri v. Jenkins* Judge Clark had little choice but to adopt an extensive, costly remedy that failed to address the fundamental problems afflicting Kansas City's educational system. This case then points to a difference between "mature" and "emergent" areas of judicial policymaking. Horowitz's and Rosenberg's analyses apply to emerging areas of judicial policymaking in which higher courts have not set down many policy boundaries for district court judges. By the time Judge Clark had to rule in Kansas City, however, desegregation was a mature area of judicial policymaking. By the late 1970s the Supreme Court had issued multiple decisions and the contours of its approach to desegregation were settled. In fact, the Court offered no opinions on desegregation in the 1980s. Judges presiding over late-developing desegregation cases had few remedial options. Thus, if the doctrines laid down by the Supreme Court failed to match the policy problems of a particular community, the likely result was ill-conceived public policy.

This is not to say that the adversarial process did Judge Clark any favors. The expert witnesses routinely exaggerated the effectiveness of their proposed remedial programs and provided unjustified assurances to Judge Clark. One would not describe them as circumspect. However, Judge Clark was compelled largely by doctrinal precedent to adopt an extremely large and costly remedial plan. Even a cursory examination of the KCMSD during the 1980s and 1990s reveals that it was incapable of effectively implementing any large or costly program. Under the Court's precedents, Clark was required, one could say, to accept the offer of the highest bidder, which was naturally the plaintiffs.

Desegregation was the most sustained and detailed effort at policy change undertaken by the courts. It is surely revealing that this process removed nearly all meaningful discretion from Judge Clark. *Missouri v. Jenkins* was, in a sense, foreordained to fail. Precedent required Clark to attack a deep, complicated social problem with meager and impotent weapons.

From Simple Justice to Complex Remedies: The Maturing of Desegregation Law

Institutions both constrain and compel action. Their rules and customs guide the behavior of those under their influence. In considering the judiciary as an institution, its precedents and hierarchical structure hold judicial action within boundaries and channel judicial decisions in a certain direction. Judges in the lower courts are obliged to follow the doctrines set down by superior courts. Flagrantly disregarding precedent is generally not an option. To do so can cause judges to suffer both legal and personal penalties. Perhaps the most reliable restraint on idiosyncratic judicial behavior is the embarrassment that comes from a judge's decision being overturned on appeal. This amounts to a message to the legal community that he misunderstood the law.[10] Thus, knowing Judge Clark's personal motives is less important than understanding the doctrinal constraints under which he operated.

Taken as a whole, the desegregation precedents in place before *Missouri v. Jenkins* appear either contradictory or, at the very least, in tension. While the Supreme Court never explicitly called de facto segregation unconstitutional, its doctrines in practice largely made it unconstitutional. The Court also almost simultaneously limited judges' resources to attack it. Racial isolation was in most cases unconstitutional, the Court held, but judges were unable to force those not responsible for the violation to participate in a remedy. Hence, suburban school districts could not be consolidated with urban school districts to offset the racial isolation of inner-city students. Judges were left with substantial obligations but given limited methods for meeting them.

Because of such doctrinal tensions, there is a temptation to criticize the Supreme Court as myopic. Yet when examining its desegregation decisions individually, each one can be viewed as an attempt to shore up the weaknesses or correct the errors of prior holdings. The Court was simply solving problems as they came along. Charles Lindblom's idea of "muddling through," or incrementalism, as Malcolm Feeley and Edward Rubin have argued, can aptly be applied to how courts behave in crafting public policy.[11] Feeley and Rubin persuasively applied the concept in the area of prison reform. Prisons, though, are obviously different from schools. That prisoners are, in a very real sense, a captive population means that the problems confronting prison reform would be stable over time. In contrast, desegregation was a moving target. Massive demographic shifts forced the Court to adapt its doctrine to these changing social conditions. Thus "muddling through" in desegregation led to a set of opinions that seemed plausible in isolation but were incoherent as a whole.

Such judicial incrementalism led the Court to try to repair prior errors and oversights. In attempting to do so, however, the Court created new problems that it either could not foresee or believed insignificant. This doctrinal development extended or matured through three generations. Examining the generational development of desegregation law reveals an internal and reasonable logic to the Court's decisions that created the potential for chaos when applied as policy by district court judges.

Generation 1: The Demise of Separate but Equal

The first generation began with *Brown v. Board of Education of Topeka Kansas*. It was a hopeful beginning with a unified Court presaging the end of a shameful feature of American society. But the principles pronounced in *Brown* proved insufficient for eliminating the blight of legally enforced segregation.

In *Brown I* the Court asked simply, "Does segregation of children in public schools solely on the basis of race, even though the physical facilities and other 'tangible' factors may be equal, deprive the children of the minority group equal educational opportunities?"[12] It answered, "We believe that it does." The Court argued that segregated education was "inherently unequal" and therefore in violation of the Fourteenth Amendment's guarantee of equal protection.

Lurking in *Brown* was an additional assumption that would later prove controversial. Unwilling to ground its decision solely on "inherent" inequality, the Court ruled that segregation was also unequal because of the psychological damage it inflicted on minority children. "To separate them from others of similar age and qualifications solely because of their race," the Court wrote, "generates a feeling of inferiority as to their status in the community that may affect their hearts and minds in a way unlikely ever to be undone."[13] The Court's logic went in only one direction, though. Racial isolation, the opinion assumed, hurt black children but not white children. In fact, that was the implication of social scientific evidence cited in the decision's famous Footnote 11. Eventually, this part of *Brown I* would be used to argue that to improve black education, black children must be in school with white children.[14]

The Court offered no remedies in *Brown I*, finding that "the consideration of appropriate relief was necessarily subordinated to the primary question—the constitutionality of segregation in public education." Presumably, *Brown II* would provide the appropriate remedies.

In contrast to the august constitutional tone of *Brown I*, *Brown II* addressed the more mundane subject of appropriate relief. "School authorities," the Court held, "have the primary responsibility for elucidating, assessing, and solving these problems; courts will have to consider whether the action of school authorities constitutes good faith implementation of the governing constitutional principles." Additionally, because "of their proximity to local conditions and the possible need for further hearings, the courts which originally heard these cases can best perform this judicial appraisal."[15] Because the problem was broad and often idiosyncratic, judges were by necessity thrust into an area of social policy with great discretion and little expertise.

Perhaps because of the uncertain terrain, the Court gave judges wide latitude, saying that desegregation should occur with "all deliberate speed."[16] This oxymoron turned out to be a standardless standard. The Court gave no precise guidelines for a remedy and then said that whatever the remedy was, there would be no precise timetable for enforcing it. Such vague guidelines would ultimately be untenable since school boards and sympathetic judges could define "deliberate" and "speed" to their advantage.

While the Court was unclear about what desegregation was (the term did not even appear in *Brown II*) and how long it would take, it was quite clear that judges had substantial power to end segregation. The Court said that judges "will be guided by equitable principles," which would allow for "a practical flexibility in shaping" remedies and the ability to accommodate "public and private needs."[17] Basing judicial authority on equity power gave extraordinary and unprecedented discretion to district court judges. The law would be what district court judges thought was in the best interest of the community and was sustainable on appeal.

Even though judges received this staggering power in *Brown II*, very little desegregation occurred in the following ten years. Judges could not act on their own, which meant that public-interest groups or individuals with limited resources had to bring lawsuits. When judges did act, southern school districts and state legislatures showed remarkable and perverse dexterity in resisting the judicial demands. "As long as we can legislate we can segregate" was the southern mantra. In 1954, .001 percent of black students in the South and border South were attending school with whites. In 1964, only 2.3 percent were.[18] Gerald Rosenberg morosely concluded, "The numbers show that the Supreme Court contributed *nothing* to ending segregation of the public schools in the Southern states in the decade following *Brown*."[19] Significant desegregation would not occur until Congress, the president, and the federal bureaucracy joined forces with the Court.

Generation 2: Administrative Assistance, Affirmative Duties, and Presumptions of Guilt

After John F. Kennedy's assassination in 1963, Lyndon Johnson used the moment to reinvigorate his predecessor's stalled civil rights agenda. Drawing on his considerable legislative skill, Johnson guided the 1964 Civil Rights Act through Congress. With the Civil Rights Act, opponents of segregation gained an invaluable weapon, federal money.

While Title IV of the Civil Rights Act of 1964 authorized the Department of Justice to sue states and school districts "for the orderly achievement of desegregation in public education," it was Title VI that would provide the impetus for most of the desegregation in the 1960s. Title IV provided much-needed relief for the exhausted NAACP Legal Defense Fund, which had borne the responsibility for suing belligerent school boards. But Title VI would provide something far more helpful, administrative oversight of state and local education. Section 601 in Title VI of the 1964 Civil Rights Act stated that "no person in the United States shall, on the ground of race, color or national origin, be excluded from participation in, be denied benefits of, or be subjected to discrimination under any program or activity receiving Federal financial assistance." This provision was supposed to "make litigation unnecessary."[20] The Department of Health, Education, and Welfare (HEW) could withhold funds until the offending districts reformed their behavior. The courts would be less important if not vestigial. Alexander Bickel predicted that Title VI would "become the main instrument for accelerating and completing the desegregation of southern public schools."[21] Bureaucratic oversight would supplant judicial oversight. Ponderous adversarial court battles would be replaced by the simpler, cleaner use of administrative coercion. The U.S. Commission on Civil Rights proclaimed that Title VI "heralded a new era in school desegregation" that "promised speedier and more substantial desegregation" than "district by district litigation" could produce.[22]

But the courts were not displaced from their role because Title VI contained no guidelines for determining when a school district was segregated.[23] That responsibility was left to HEW. Had there been precise guidelines, HEW could have compared them with a school district's policies and determined if the district was in compliance. Instead, when devising its first guidelines in

1965, HEW linked some of them with judicially determined standards for desegregation. Thus the courts were still necessary for determining when those standards had been met.

The partnership between the courts and HEW allowed each to overcome weaknesses that inhibited its ability to attack segregation in isolation. While the idea of allowing HEW to cut off funds sounded "marvelously simple," it suffered from several flaws, which HEW could overcome only by working with the courts.[24] Most importantly, the loss of federal funds worked better as a threat than as an actual punishment. Removing funds would harm all students, black and white, hardly the desired result. In addition, the funds could be cut off only after a hearing, which in turn could be used to create delays. And finally, some school districts could afford to forfeit the money since federal funds, on average, accounted for only 8 percent of a district's budget. Only the poorest districts would find this money impossible to recoup. The threat of a funding cutoff convinced some districts to comply with HEW, but it was insufficient to convince all of them.

The courts' requiring school districts to meet HEW's guidelines or face judicial sanctions became the primary way to overcome this obstacle. Southern school officials' failing to follow HEW's guidelines could lead to a contempt of court citation and a stint in jail, generally an unacceptable risk to even the most obstinate of them.[25] Additionally, the courts could exercise more direct oversight of the school districts' operations. School officials could either comply voluntarily or face more judicial interference. This partnership contributed to a substantial increase of black students attending schools with whites. From 1965 to 1968, the percentage of black students in the South and border South attending school with whites jumped from 6.1 percent to 32 percent. Until the Supreme Court reasserted itself in 1968, HEW and the courts operated almost as coequal partners with each one reinforcing the other.

The Reascension of the Supreme Court
Throughout much of the 1960s the Supreme Court remained conspicuously silent on desegregation. Its efforts in *Brown* had led to very little desegregation, creating the impression that its rulings could be indefinitely flouted. Instead, its most prominent decisions in the 1960s dealt with legislative redistricting, criminal rights, school prayer, and contraception. But reinforcement from Congress, the presidency, and bureaucracy gave the Court additional political capital. It just needed an appropriate case to renew its attack.

The Court found such a case in *Green v. New Kent County School Board*.[26] New Kent County, Virginia, had two schools for the entire county—one K-12 school on the west side of the county for black students and another on the east side for white students. After the 1964 Civil Rights Act, the school board adopted a freedom-of-choice plan to keep HEW from withholding federal funds. Black parents filed suit, arguing that the plan had not desegregated the school district. After two years under the plan, no white students had enrolled in the black school and just 15 percent of black students had enrolled in the formerly all-white school.

The Supreme Court's ruling in the suit, handed down in 1968, accomplished two objectives: it created an affirmative duty for school districts to desegregate, and it detailed what constituted a desegregated or "unitary district." The first objective meant that ending compulsory segregation was not enough. From *Green* on, desegregation plans would be judged by their results—how effectively they eliminated racially identifiable schools. Justice Brennan wrote for the Court: "School boards such as the respondent then operating state-compelled dual systems were nevertheless clearly charged [in *Brown II*] with the affirmative duty to take whatever steps might be necessary to convert to a unitary system in which racial discrimination would be eliminated root and branch. . . . The obligation of the district courts . . . is to assess the effectiveness of a proposed plan in achieving desegregation."[27] The second objective, unitary status, meant that all aspects of a school district's operations had to be considered when determining whether judicial relief was warranted. School systems had to be nondiscriminatory in student assignment, faculty assignment, staff assignment, facilities, transportation, and extracurricular activities. A school system needed to conform to these six "*Green* factors," as they came to be known, to achieve unitary status.

After *Green*, the South was forced to acknowledge that segregation would not be tolerated. *Green* prompted a flood of lawsuits that dramatically reduced segregation. Between 1968 and 1970 the percentage of black students attending school with white students went from 32 percent to 85.9 percent in the South and border South.[28] The legal and political assault on segregation overwhelmed remaining opposition.

Because much southern segregation only existed through legal means, desegregation was relatively simple in many school districts. The advent of neighborhood schools eliminated segregation in many communities, but larger cities remained a problem. The residential segregation that existed in many southern cities was less pronounced in smaller towns. But cities such as Charlotte, which had resisted desegregation after *Brown*, found it difficult to show statistical evidence of desegregation. Neighborhood schools in metropolitan areas left many black children in overwhelmingly black schools. Cities' prior resistance, combined with residential segregation, made neighborhood schools look like yet another attempt to elude desegregation. Thus, such plans would fail any test that gauged success by numerical measures. The Supreme Court still needed to resolve what was to be expected of more populous communities.

In 1971, the Court confronted urban segregation in *Swann v. Charlotte-Mecklenburg School Board*.[29] The primary question before the Court was whether judges could require busing to force desegregation. The Court unanimously affirmed the power of district court judges to require busing. After this decision, busing became virtually synonymous with desegregation. Just as important, though, was the Court's justification for its decision. The legal rationale for busing dramatically expanded both the powers and the duties of federal judges. The Court held that there were no precise limits to desegregation remedies and that the judicial equity power was virtually unlimited in combating segregation. But most important, the Court held that a prior history of segregation "warrants a presumption against schools that are substantially disproportionate in their racial composition."[30] Thus, any school system in the South or border South with racial disparity in any of its schools was presumptively unconstitutionally segregated. Judges had to act in such cases. In making racial imbalance a prima facie case for unlawful segregation, the Court moved even closer to saying that de facto segregation was unconstitutional and to attacking "northern" segregation.

Considering the South's history of resistance after *Brown*, the *Swann* and *Green* decisions were necessary to eliminate de jure segregation. Requiring districts to show evidence of racial balance in their schools provided the impetus for southern school districts to stop evading desegregation. Additionally, the Court made it clear in *Green* that a school district could satisfy the demands of the Court. Judicial oversight need not continue in perpetuity. School districts had an incentive to comply in order to limit the duration of judicial supervision. The results following *Green* and *Swann* show that the judicial effort to desegregate after 1968 was remarkably successful. By 1972, 91.3 percent of black children in formerly segregated states attended school with white children.

"Northern" Segregation

After such a stunning success, it is not surprising that the Court decided to entertain cases challenging de facto segregation outside the South. Civil rights advocates had targeted "northern" segregation, which the Supreme Court did not consider until *Keyes v. Denver School District No. 1*. In *Keyes* the Court addressed "northern" segregation and whether de facto, in addition to de jure, segregation was unconstitutional. According to David Armor, the Court's decision in *Keyes* "left the de facto–de jure distinction alive in theory," but "it had much less practical significance because few school districts at that time could meet a burden of proving that they had not contributed to housing segregation or had not intentionally adopted a neighborhood school policy."[31] School boards had to prove that their school attendance zones did not contribute to segregated housing patterns. Since no school district could actually prove that its school system had no effect on housing patterns, virtually every case of de facto segregation became a case of de jure segregation — in practice, no meaningful distinction remained. The Court held that

> the Board's burden is to show that its policies and practices with respect to schoolsite location, school size, school renovations and additions, student-attendance zones, student assignment and transfer options, mobile classroom units, transportation of students, assignment of faculty and staff, etc., considered together and premised on the Board's so-called "neighborhood school" concept, either were not taken in effectuation of a policy to create or maintain segregation in the core city schools, or, if unsuccessful in that effort, were not factors in causing the existing condition of segregation in these schools.[32]

While the Court did not officially say that the Constitution requires integration, the obvious implication of *Keyes* is that it does. This point was not lost on Justice Powell, who in his concurring opinion chided the Court for not officially abandoning the de jure/de facto distinction. "The Court's decision today," he said, "while adhering to the de jure/de facto distinction, will require the application of the Green/Swann doctrine of 'affirmative duty' to the Denver School Board despite the absence of any history of state-mandated school segregation." In practice, school districts would have an affirmative duty to desegregate even when they had not committed "segregative acts" with "segregative intent."

Because the Court did not officially eliminate the de facto/de jure distinction, civil rights attorneys still had to do the lengthy, laborious, and costly work of deposing witnesses, poring over school district records, and hiring expert witnesses to make claims about the causes of housing patterns. But the results after *Keyes* were a testament to the new standard the Court established and the difficulty school boards had in meeting it. According to Gary Orfield, after *Keyes*, "courts almost always found school districts guilty of unconstitutional segregation whenever litigation was seriously pursued." Occasionally, there were "contrary decisions," but "usually, when appeals were finished, the guilt of local authorities was established."[33]

Generation 3: Judicial Restrictions

After the *Keyes* decision in 1973, the movement for desegregation and integration appeared to be in full force. But, in fact, the Supreme Court was only a year away from placing severe limits on how far judges could extend desegregation remedies. The Supreme Court's ruling in *Milliken v. Bradley I*, for example, would severely limit the power of judges who remained obligated to eliminate urban racial isolation.[34] In limiting judicial discretion, the Court created a new species of desegregation remedies. These new remedies relied on voluntary rather than compulsory means to try to ameliorate racial isolation.

In *Milliken I*, the Court ruled that interdistrict remedies were unconstitutional if there had only been an intradistrict violation. Judges, therefore, could not conscript suburban school districts into metropolitan busing plans. In this case, Judge Robert Merideth had ordered Detroit's school system to be combined with the surrounding suburban school districts. White flight, he realized, made busing just within Detroit ineffective. To meet the Court's requirements he had no choice but to issue a metropolitanwide remedy. The Court, although divided 5-4, decided that such massive programs were not constitutionally required.

This decision to limit judicial power made constitutional, educational, and political sense. Constitutionally it made sense because it would be difficult to compel individuals who have not lawfully required segregation in their school district to eliminate it in another. Why should school districts that never practiced legally enforced segregation be punished? Educationally the decision was plausible because at some point busing must become counterproductive. The time and money spent on busing could be used in more educationally effective ways. Even in *Swann*, the Court had acknowledged that an "objection to transportation of students may have validity when the time or distance of travel is so great as to either risk the health of the children or significantly impinge on the educational process." Certainly the prospect of ever-expanding busing to combat ever-expanding white flight made busing impractical. As white flight continued, the distances required to bus students would increase. Finally, politically the decision was sensible because of the intense political backlash against busing,[35] symbolized by the specter of George Wallace's 1972 bid for the Democratic presidential nomination. Wallace, the segregationist former governor of Alabama, won Michigan's Democratic presidential primary by overtly appealing to racial animus. Michigan proved a receptive audience in part because of Detroit's judicially mandated metropolitanwide busing program. Allowing unlimited busing would have created further racial hostility.

While *Milliken I* made sense on its own, when combined with other decisions, it placed impossible demands on judges. *Milliken I* left intact the principles of *Green*, *Swann*, and *Keyes*, so as white flight created dense concentrations of minorities in urban school districts, judges were left with the order to do something when nothing could be done.

Although technically unrelated to desegregation, another decision handed down by the Supreme Court in the early 1970s would also limit judges' ability to devise desegregation remedies. In *San Antonio v. Rodriguez* the Court ruled that there is no right to equal educational funding since the Constitution does not guarantee any right to an education. "Education," the Court held, "of course, is not among the rights afforded explicit protection under our Federal Constitution. Nor do we find any basis for saying it is implicitly so protected."[36] This decision was significant because during the 1970s it was clear that the educational problems of urban black children stemmed not only from racial isolation but also from the inferior quality of urban schools, along with crime, school violence, and family breakdown. While many black parents would have preferred to bring suits asking for more money for their schools, they would instead have to rely on desegregation as a means for school improvement. Using desegregation for this purpose further distorted the problems of urban education by attributing the problem of educational quality solely to racial isolation. In reality, the problem was far more complex.

Table 1.1 shows the constraints facing judges following *Milliken* and *Rodriguez*. Navigating through these rulings would lead many judges to establish voluntary programs to desegregate school districts—a solution suffering from its own set of problems.

Table 1.1 Constraining Cases and Precedents on Desegregation and Education, 1954–1977

Cases	Year	Precedents
GENERATION 1		
Brown v. Board I	1954	1. Separate is inherently unequal. 2. Segregation causes psychological harm.
Brown v. Board II	1955	1. Judges have equitable discretion in fashioning desegregation remedies. 2. Local school boards are responsible for fashioning and implementing desegregation remedies.
GENERATION 2		
Green v. New Kent County School Board	1968	1. School districts have an affirmative duty to desegregate. 2. School districts must be "unitary" before judicial supervision can end.
Swann v. Charlotte-Mecklenburg	1971	1. Southern school districts with racially imbalanced schools are presumptively unconstitutionally segregated. 2. Judicial equitable power to remedy segregation is broad and undefined. 3. Judges can require busing to create racial balance in school districts.
Keyes v. Denver School District	1973	1. School districts must prove that they did not intentionally adopt policies that perpetuated de facto segregation.
GENERATION 3		
Milliken v. Bradley I	1974	1. Judges cannot require interdistrict remedies for intradistrict violations, i.e., suburban school districts cannot be included in remedial orders unless they intentionally contributed to urban racial imbalance.
San Antonio v. Rodriguez	1973	1. There is no constitutional right to education. 2. Unequal funding for education is not unconstitutional.
Milliken v. Bradley II	1977	1. Compensatory educational programs are appropriate remedies for desegregation.

Voluntary Means for Required Ends

Following *Milliken*, judges increasingly looked for less coercive means to desegregate school districts. The Court even sanctioned compensatory educational improvements in *Milliken v. Bradley II*.[37] Generally this led to the establishment of magnet schools with themes attractive to middle-class white parents. In many instances, magnet schools were a sincere but rearguard effort to eliminate segregation. Also, because *San Antonio v. Rodriguez* eliminated lawsuits calling for school improvements, many advocates for improving urban education saw magnet schools as a means for circumventing the Court's ruling.[38] Because desegregation by voluntary means created less controversy, cases involving magnet schools received little public attention. Additionally, magnet schools married the laudable goals of desegregation and educational improvement. Blacks and whites both criticized busing for sacrificing education on the altar of desegregation. Magnet schools apparently overcame this problem. Unlike the violence surrounding Judge Garrity's forced busing in Boston, magnet schools prompted little if any protest.

Magnet schools, though, suffered from one fundamental problem. They often created a two-tier school district with academically gifted white and black students attending a few magnet schools while the majority of students remained in racially isolated and poorly performing traditional schools. Magnet schools were often symbolic gestures that helped the few who needed help least while neither achieving integration nor improving education for the majority. To prevent a two-tier situation, the whole system required conversion into a magnet program—a costly proposition.

Institutional Reform Litigation and Political Failure

While contradictory Supreme Court precedents complicated the ability of courts to craft successful policy, an additional political difficulty confronted Judge Clark in Kansas City. As I discuss in Chapter 6, a substantial portion of Kansas City's black community deeply opposed the remedial plan, which spent billions of dollars to improve education for black children. Certainly the community welcomed money for its children, but it resented and opposed the way the program was created and implemented. The hostility grew so intense that opponents led a takeover of the school board. This new board grew so disillusioned with the remedial plan and the restraints it placed on them that it actively sought the end of judicial supervision and the case's judicially generated financial largesse. The court could not even sustain political support from the very group it claimed to be assisting. The reason for this can be traced to two related but distinct legal issues in cases such as *Missouri v. Jenkins*: the doctrine of standing and the nature of class actions.

Political versus Legal Representation

In the move from the "traditional" to "public law" model of adjudication, the courts had to change what gave one standing, or the right to have one's complaint heard. The doctrine of standing was really a twentieth-century invention. Traditionally, someone had to show that he or she had a legally protected right that was being harmed. But the Supreme Court, with some congressional assistance, gradually modified this standard and in the process created a more relaxed doctrine. This change largely arose out of administrative law as business concerns financially harmed by the decisions of regulatory agencies sought relief in court. The Court held that no one had a right to be financially unharmed by government decisions; after all, almost everything the government does creates economic winners and losers. However, it did say that, when making their decisions, agencies should consider the financial harm done to such firms. The result was to give the private interests of individual firms privileged control over public policy. Thus, to prevent this perversion of public policy, the courts have to determine who is a proper or representative plaintiff.[39] But making this determination is difficult. Often there likely is no such thing as a proper plaintiff, just a cauldron of competing private interests.[40]

Louis Jaffe, one of the first scholars to closely analyze, and defend, the emerging expansion of standing, said he supported it because it "compelled" the administrative process "to respond to forces and values which previously were underrepresented."[41] Noticeably absent from his defense is any precise method for determining who is underrepresented. Thus, while expanding standing was justified under the democratic-sounding rhetoric of representation, lurking behind it was the possibility that plaintiffs might not be representative at all. Even more ominously, there was no guarantee that the attorneys representing classes of plaintiffs would actually represent the interests of the plaintiffs.

These "public law" cases are not guided by the interests of individual plaintiffs but instead are designed to plead the interests of broad groups, or "classes," of people, and thus called "class action" suits. Hence, in institutional reform cases, the problems associated with standing and class action are closely related. Class action cases will have official "nominal" plaintiffs, but the very nature of the litigation demands that the attorney speak on behalf of a group of "similarly situated people." However, determining the policy interests of a group is often impossible.[42] Even the most ardent defenders of judicial policymaking and institutional reform litigation, such as Owen Fiss, have recognized this difficulty and have devoted substantial attention to how judges might avoid this problem. Fiss forthrightly noted that "the presence of an improper representative on either side of the lawsuit may have consequences that far transcend the interests of the participants. The court may be led into error. The named plaintiff may also wittingly or unwittingly compromise the interests of the victim group in a way that cannot be easily rectified in subsequent proceedings."[43] Thus, courts need tools for sorting out the competing interests of a victim group.

But sorting out these interests is a role traditionally reserved for representative institutions. Courts have no effective mechanisms for gauging what a group wants in the way that legislatures do. Judges are not supposed to take opinion polls when determining remedies for violations of constitutional rights. This problem is even more severe when we recognize that a class of plaintiffs often does not choose its representation but, as happened in *Missouri v. Jenkins*, an attorney appoints himself. According to Robert Kagan, our highly litigious policymaking process is directly related to the ease with which attorneys can bring legal claims: "Because of the unusually broad American rules concerning 'standing to sue,' virtually any interested party—including the world's widest array of public interest lawyers, acting as self-appointed 'private attorneys general'—can bring lawsuits against alleged violations of public law."[44] In describing this phenomenon in administrative law, Jeremy Rabkin starkly, but accurately, said that the process

> allows legal advocates to exercise the claims (or, in the rhetoric of the advocates, "the rights") of other people without the consent of those other people and, most of the time, even without their knowledge. Legal advocates therefore obtain something akin to the authority of medieval lords, speaking for their vassals and serfs as their natural representatives.... By allowing advocates to speak for others without their consent, administrative law makes it easy to exaggerate the number of people who share the advocates' particular preferences—thus attributing preferences to people who do not share them.[45]

Other scholars have also recognized this problem. In *Democracy by Decree*, Ross Sandler and David Schoenbrod concluded that in institutional reform litigation the plaintiffs' attorneys often "advance their own interest of society, often at the expense of their clients" and that parties "harmed by decrees often find they are denied a real voice in the litigation."[46] Rabkin and Sandler and Schoenbrod could have been describing what happened in Kansas City. There, the black community, whose leaders had in fact opposed the eventual remedial plan, found this relationship intolerable and decided to oppose the attorney representing their children. One group of parents unsuccessfully petitioned the court to remove "their" attorney as class counsel because they were being harmed by the decree.

This discussion points to an underlying tension between rights and remedies in institutional reform litigation. If someone has a right that has been violated, the law assumes that there is a remedy. If the remedy is financial compensation, there is a direct connection between the right and the remedy, making enforcement of the remedy relatively straightforward. The remedy in most institutional reform litigation, however, is often an injunction, an order prohibiting some action or compelling a certain course of action. Sometimes a remedial injunction is obvious and easy to enforce, for instance, ordering the removal of the Ten Commandments from a courthouse. The plaintiff's interest might be remote—he could be an infrequent visitor to the courthouse—but the remedy is still the same as if the alleged harm were immediate and regular. In these cases, a direct connection between the right and the remedy is not necessary for devising and implementing a remedial policy.

When the appropriate remedy is not clear-cut, however, the relaxed rules of standing become problematic. If someone can claim to represent the interests or rights of a group of people when the remedy is not obvious, the probability increases that members of that group will disagree with the court's injunction. The court gave little thought to this problem in *Missouri v. Jenkins*. Desegregation case law was extensive and settled, or mature, leading the court to assume that once fault was determined the remedy would be relatively straightforward. In other words, regardless of who brought the complaint, the remedy would be the same. But, of course, the black community in Kansas City had its own preferences about what the remedial plan should be, preferences that were at odds with those of the attorney claiming to represent them. Who was granted standing and who was allowed to represent that group turned out to be extremely important.

The issues of standing and representation, in fact, have a lengthy history in the area of desegregation. As Christine Rossell has pointed out, "the civil rights leadership's almost single-minded pursuit of mandatory reassignment plans in school desegregation litigation from the late 1960s through the early 1990s has either ignored or disregarded the attitudes of ordinary parents."[47] This phenomenon was best illustrated by the *Adams* litigation brought against HEW. After Richard Nixon won the presidency in 1968, it was obvious that HEW would be less than vigorous in overseeing desegregation. The change in administration led to a change in policy. Leon Panetta, for instance, was fired as director of the Office of Civil Rights in March of 1970 because of his opposition to the Nixon administration's policies. From 1965 to 1970 HEW had started funding-cutoff procedures against over 600 school districts. In the year following Panetta's firing it brought none.

The administration's change in policy prompted civil rights groups, led by the NAACP's Legal Defense Fund (LDF) and longtime civil rights attorney and activist Joseph Rauh, to file suit in federal court claiming that HEW had neglected to enforce Title VI of the Civil Rights Act. The nominal plaintiff was Kenneth Adams, a black student from Mississippi, but Rauh also claimed to represent a class of plaintiffs, the "students, citizens, and taxpayers" of seventeen states. The suit initially faced one fundamental obstacle — it was not clear that the plaintiffs had standing to sue a federal agency. Kenneth Adams could have sued his school district directly. The remaining plaintiffs, "students, citizens, and taxpayers," according to Supreme Court precedent, had to show that they were in immediate danger of "sustaining some direct injury" and were not just suffering "in some indefinite way in common with people generally."[48] The very nature of the case, though, indicated that the plaintiffs were simply dissatisfied with HEW. They were really acting as "private attorneys general" claiming to represent the public interest.

The court solved this problem by ignoring it. In the trial phase of *Adams v. Richardson*,[49] Judge John Pratt of the D.C. District Court found it so unremarkable that Rauh would represent the "students, citizens, and taxpayers" of seventeen states that he neglected to even mention the issue of standing.[50] He ruled that HEW not only had failed to enforce Title VI but also had ignored the Supreme Court's ruling in *Swann* requiring a presumption of unconstitutionality against school systems with racially disproportionate schools. Such school districts, he ordered, should be subject to a cutoff of federal funds unless they could demonstrate that the school district's policies had not contributed to the racial imbalance. The standard was so high that virtually every school system with any racial imbalance would be subject to a cutoff of funds. In his first remedial ruling on the case, Pratt ordered HEW to begin cutoff procedures against 127 school districts, including Kansas City's, that were operating in violation of *Swann's* proportionality principle.[51] The result was that HEW, at the request of the LDF, began demanding busing plans that local black parents often opposed.

Ironically, it was Judge Pratt's first remedial order that would eventually lead to *Missouri v. Jenkins*. Unfortunately, the issue of standing that was left unaddressed in *Adams* would also come to haunt Judge Clark, who also found it unremarkable that a single, unelected attorney could represent the interests of all the students in Kansas City. The structure of class action lawsuits demanded it, and the doctrine of standing allowed it.

Conclusion

As the Supreme Court's approach to desegregation matured, its decisions satisfied no one completely. Critics from the right condemned the Court's "activism" in *Swann* and *Keyes*, while critics on the left condemned the Court for its "restraint" in *Milliken* and *Rodriguez*. In trying to do neither too much nor too little, the Court lost sight of potential conflicts in its ad hoc decisions. Eventually those conflicts would reveal themselves in *Missouri v. Jenkins*. A confluence of factors was at work to influence this case. As the following chapters discuss, Missouri's and Kansas City's racial and educational history, along with the decisions of the school board and plaintiff's attorney, were quite important. But these factors mattered only because of the Supreme Court's desegregation decisions. These decisions simultaneously strengthened and weakened Judge Clark's power. At times he seemed to be granted both too much power and too little. By the time Judge Clark had to decide the case, he was operating under severe constraints but was still required to do something. Racial isolation created a presumption of unconstitutionality. There must be a remedy, but it could not include suburban school districts. Voluntary means were the only ones available. However, by then, everyone knew that small-scale magnet school programs did little to help the majority of urban students. Any plan, then, had to be comprehensive and therefore costly. To pay for such a plan Clark had to assume the power to tax. All of this, though, could not satisfy the object of his judicial generosity, the black community.

Because of these policy and political shortcomings, *Missouri v. Jenkins* raises important questions about the power of the courts. Most importantly the case illustrates a difference between the judiciary's power to command and its power to change. In contrast to the early years of desegregation, when the courts exhibited very little power to order anything and have it obeyed, in *Missouri v. Jenkins* Judge Clark showed an extraordinary capacity to command others and have those commands followed. He ordered the KCMSD and the state of Missouri to build multimillion-dollar school buildings, and they were built; he ordered tax increases on the citizens of Kansas City, and they were imposed. In short, compliance was not a constraint on Judge Clark. However, he was remarkably unsuccessful in achieving his social goals. The black community opposed much of the remedial plan, which failed to either desegregate Kansas City's schools or improve educational achievement.

2

From Segregation to Litigation
The Ambiguous Racial History of Missouri and Kansas City

Knowledge of Missouri's and Kansas City's educational history is an important component to understanding *Missouri v. Jenkins*. Critics and defenders of Judge Clark tend to ignore this history when labeling him as either a robed tyrant or a courageous reformer. This history had a decisive influence on the case's development, conspiring with the Supreme Court's contradictory desegregation precedents to further limit the remedies available to Judge Clark.

Missouri shared the political and social characteristics of both the South and the Midwest, which meant that, in general, blacks faced less discrimination there than in the Deep South. Shortly after *Brown v. Board of Education*, an article in the *Journal of Negro Education* noted: "A Southern state in many of its allegiances, Missouri, nevertheless, is so closely allied in its interests with the Midwest that the Negro has not fared as poorly as he has in some Southern states."[1] While other cities were torn apart over racial strife in the 1960s, for example, Kansas City was calm by comparison. Reflecting on Kansas City's history, the *Kansas City Star* said that "race relations," in light of events in "Newark, N.J., Cleveland, Detroit, and Los Angeles," appeared "to be going well in Kansas City."[2] Kansas City would eventually experience its share of racial unrest, but its share would never reach the magnitude it did in other cities.

Kansas City's comparative tranquility in the 1960s was in many ways traceable to what happened in the 1950s. Because Missouri was relatively progressive on racial matters, it did not resist *Brown v. Board of Education*.[3] So local school boards such as Kansas City's officially eliminated segregated schools after *Brown*. For a while Kansas City appeared to avoid the controversy desegregation caused in other cities such as Boston and Detroit. Boston presented the sad spectacle of white families rioting over busing, and Detroit created the political climate for George Wallace's success in Michigan's 1972 Democratic presidential primary. In the end, Kansas City's compliance merely delayed rather than obviated judicial oversight and led to *Missouri v. Jenkins*, one of the third generation of desegregation cases that relied on voluntary but costlier means of integration.

Missouri, Race, and Education

Missouri joined the United States as a slave state under the Missouri Compromise of 1820. Like other slave states, Missouri forbid educating blacks. In 1847, the state enacted a law declaring that "no person shall keep or teach any school for the instruction of negroes or mulattoes, in reading or writing, in this state."[4] Before the Civil War, Kansas City, then called the City of Kansas, was part of the "Border War," where free-state Kansas Jayhawkers fought Missouri Bushwackers, who were trying to force slavery on Kansas. The Border Wars of Bleeding Kansas began in 1856, when proslavery Missourians raided and burned Lawrence, Kansas. John Brown retaliated by burning plantations and freeing slaves in the City of Kansas.

Although slavery was a fully entrenched institution in Missouri, the state never officially seceded from the Union during the Civil War. Unlike in the seceding states, slavery was not a dominant social, economic, or political issue. Slaves constituted only 10 percent of Missouri's population, and only 1–2 percent of the population owned slaves. Even before the Civil War ended, Missouri had amended its constitution to forbid slavery.

Following the Civil War, Missouri required by constitutional mandate separate schools for blacks and whites. The Missouri Constitution of 1865 said that "separate schools may be established for children of African descent" in localities with twenty or more school-age black children.[5] In other words, educating black children was optional. In a small step forward, the following year the Missouri General Assembly "authorized and required" townships to establish separate schools for blacks.[6] In 1875 Missouri made it a constitutional requirement to establish "separate free schools . . . for the education of children of African descent." Until the Supreme Court's ruling in *Brown*, Missouri remained committed to the notion that separate could be equal. In 1945 Missouri reaffirmed this position in its rewritten constitution, stating that "separate schools shall be provided for white and colored children, except in cases otherwise provided by law."[7] The qualifying phrase "otherwise provided by law" led supporters of desegregation to attempt, unsuccessfully, to eliminate segregated schools through legislation in 1951 and 1953. While the 1945 constitution kept segregation intact, it also required localities to fund black and white schools equally. The state board of education tried to enforce this provision and threatened to withdraw state funds to school systems that allocated less money to black schools than to their white counterparts.

Overall, though, this progress was largely symbolic. In reality, black schools statewide were substantially inferior to white schools. Only in Kansas City and St. Louis did the quality of black education approach that of white education. One reason for this was that most Missouri school districts consisted of one school building with one or two rooms, one or two teachers, and a few dozen all-white students. Since the state constitution required separate facilities for black students, these school districts could not offer an education to the few black children in the district, assuming that they even wanted to. In much of the state, no education was available at all for black children. In 1928 over 4,000 black children had no access to public education, and statewide there were only eight black high schools.[8] Black students in small communities either were unable to attend school or had to travel long distances every day. These difficulties encouraged black families to migrate to communities like Kansas City that could accommodate black students.

Meanwhile, Missouri did show some progress in eliminating other forms of segregation. In 1966, for instance, the *Journal of Negro Education* noted that while "Jim Crow practices were common in the state, ... public transportation was legally nonsegregated, voting was unrestricted, and sports events, parks, auditoriums, libraries, and civil service jobs were generally open to all races."[9] The elimination of Jim Crow laws in these areas indicated that ending school segregation might be easier in Missouri than elsewhere. Missouri's response to *Brown*, therefore, was not surprising.

Shortly after the *Brown* ruling, Attorney General John M. Dalton issued a statement saying that the state constitution and any statutes requiring segregation were "superceded by the decision of the Supreme Court of the United States and are, therefore unenforceable."[10] The state board of education adopted a resolution in support of *Brown* and stated its intent to implement the ruling. Governor Phil M. Donnelly announced that Missouri would not resist *Brown*'s requirements.

Missouri's efforts to desegregate education generated effusive praise from the U.S. Commission on Civil Rights. In 1959, the commission reported that "Missouri experienced desegregation in more school districts in the first year than any other State."[11] In 1963, it noted that the "segregated school systems in Missouri are concentrated in the part of the State which abuts the Arkansas and Kentucky borders, principally in the 'bootheel.' The area is a rural, cotton-growing section, of southern ways and mores. . . . In the remainder of the State, the schools are for the most part desegregated. Indeed the problems of Negro education in St. Louis are northern style; all vestiges of segregation by policy are gone."[12] Even *Time* noted Missouri's efforts and gave Missouri an A in its 1955 "Report Card" on desegregation, reporting that "state education authorities estimate that 55,000 (80%) of Missouri's Negro children are now studying alongside 550,000 whites; there has been no friction."[13] An article in the *Nation* joined the chorus, calling Missouri's actions "encouraging" because of their voluntary nature and even myopically predicted that because of its example — along with that of a few other states — "harmonious integration of the entire American public-school system may be attained within the next year or two."[14] Because most of Missouri's black schoolchildren lived in St. Louis and Kansas City, those cities' efforts were primarily responsible for such approbation.

Kansas City: Desegregation, White Flight, and Financial Collapse

While black education statewide was quite poor, Kansas City's was somewhat better and perhaps comparable to white education. In fact, the history of Kansas City's school system in the years before and after *Brown* indicated that it would be a poor choice for a desegregation suit. The Kansas City Missouri School District (KCMSD) opened in 1867, with four white schools and one black school. Until *Brown*, the system remained segregated, but, unlike many school districts, it did try to fund the two parts equally. Teachers received equal pay in both school systems and funding per child was generally the same. At the elementary level, the district tended to spend more for each white pupil, but at the junior high and high school levels it spent more for each black pupil. Black parents' greatest complaint before *Brown* was overcrowding and poor facilities. Many black schools lacked gymnasiums, cafeterias, and indoor plumbing. Several black parents filed suit to remedy the situation, but the Missouri Supreme Court dismissed the suit, pointing out that many white schools were similarly ill equipped. Some black schools even exceeded the white schools in the district in their overall quality of education. For example, according to one district employee, the all-black Lincoln Academy "had a faculty that compared with the faculty of many small colleges" and had excellent facilities.[15]

Immediately following *Brown*, the KCMSD was one of only fifteen segregated school districts nationwide that voluntarily complied with *Brown* in the year following the ruling.[16] The school board followed a three-phase, one-year plan. Phase one involved desegregating the high school and junior college summer school classes for 1954. According to Mark W. Bills, the school superintendent, the summer session "went off perfectly."[17] Phase two was the desegregation of the junior college and vocational high school in the fall of 1954, and phase three was the integration of the entire system the following school year. By the 1955–56 school year, the district had established a neighborhood system in which each child attended the school closest to his or her residence (see table 2.1).

The integration of the Kansas City public schools went smoothly in spite of expected conflicts. When the formerly all-white Central High School was integrated in 1955, police cars patrolled the school grounds, apparently unnecessarily.[18] The *Journal of Negro Education* reported in 1956 that "desegregation in both the elementary and secondary schools was achieved with little incident."[19] The *Call*, a black weekly paper in Kansas City, reported that there was not a "ripple of difficulty" in desegregated student bodies and summarized the district's performance: "The Kansas City school board has done well as far as the integration of students is concerned. Desegregation in the classrooms has meant just that. School boundary lines were set last spring according to the number of pupils living in districts and the capacities of the school buildings. No attention was paid to the race and color of the children as the survey was made."[20]

While the initial desegregation effort led to little racial conflict after a few years of integration, many schools reported "gangland" behavior with "bullies" of both races extorting money from younger students both white and black. To prevent the violence from escalating, teachers patrolled hallways and bathrooms, frisking students for switchblades, razor blades, and can openers with honed edges. The tension caused one student to transfer from Central Junior High because, according to his teacher, "the extortion racket and fear were just about to produce a nervous breakdown."[21] Black and white teachers blamed the violence "on a small core of Negro bullies," white "chronic malcontents" forced to stay in school by Missouri law, and "nonpupils" invading school grounds to "stir up trouble."[22] A police sergeant predicted "a lot worse situation here than they had in Little Rock."[23] The violence did worsen in 1958 when a group of black students "beat up two white teachers" at Central High School.[24] However, compared to other recently integrated school districts, Kansas City's problems were isolated in a few schools and never approached the level of violence in Little Rock. The racial problems in

Kansas City resembled those of northern urban school districts rather than southern ones. Racial violence plagued many urban schools, not just those that were recently integrated.

Integration created less tension than elsewhere partly because the school board had attempted to run two equal school systems. More importantly, however, white flight, residential segregation, and a long-standing transfer policy simply limited the interaction between black and white students. A steady stream of white middle-class families had been moving out of Kansas City even before *Brown*, while a stream of poor black, and to a lesser extent white, families had been moving in. In 1994 the *Kansas City Star* commented that the continuing white flight was part of demographic "trends that have gone on for seventy years."[25] As table 2.2 shows, Kansas City's black population steadily increased after 1920 and the white population began declining in 1950. Additionally, the white population was becoming older and beyond childbearing years, while the incoming black population was younger with children. This disparity in the population became more pronounced during the 1960s and 1970s when Kansas City experienced a large influx of younger blacks from southern and border states.[26] Because of middle-class white flight in the 1940s and early 1950s, many majority-white schools were not at full capacity. For example, one white elementary school could fill only eleven of its twenty classrooms because white families were relocating to the suburbs.[27] Many black children were thus able to enroll in previously all-white schools. The fact that few white students had to enroll in majority-black schools undoubtedly helped mute any potential complaints, which, in turn, kept the issue out of the news. While many black children enrolled in majority-white schools, very few of the white children assigned to majority-black schools matriculated. The school district expected that 921 white children would attend majority-black schools in the 1955–56 school year, but only 117 white children actually enrolled.[28]

The school district was also residentially segregated.[29] With the establishment of race-neutral neighborhood attendance zones, only those schools close to both black and white neighborhoods became integrated. As table 2.1 shows, a majority of elementary schools and secondary schools remained overwhelmingly of one race. Contributing to this situation was the school district's transfer policy, which had been in effect before *Brown* and allowed any student to request a transfer to any school not at full capacity, thus making it easier for white students to avoid attending largely black schools.[30]

Showing the limits of its relatively tolerant attitude toward integration,

Table 2.1 Level of Desegregation in KCMSD Schools, 1955–1957

	Total Number of Elementary Schools	Number of Officially Desegregated Elementary Schools	Number of Elementary Schools at Least 90 Percent Black or White	Total Number of Secondary Schools	Number of Officially Desegregated Secondary Schools	Number of Secondary Schools at Least 90 Percent Black or White
1955	80	32	71	19	10	14
1956	80	35	66	19	13	14
1957	84	39	67	19	12	14

Source: "Report on Progress of Desegregation," Kansas City, Missouri, Public Schools, Department of Pupil Services, September 18, 1957.
Note: Even schools in which up to 99 percent of the students were of the same race were considered officially desegregated.

Table 2.2 Kansas City's Black and White Populations, 1920–1990

Year	Total Population	Black Population	White Population
1920	324,410	30,719	293,517
1930	399,746	38,574	357,741
1940	399,178	41,574	357,346
1950	456,710	55,655	400,695
1960	475,539	83,146	391,348
1970	507,087	112,005	391,496
1980	448,159	122,699	312,836
1990	435,146	128,768	290,572

Source: United States Census.

the KCMSD in the years after *Brown* did adopt one policy that would later be used to argue that it had been running a segregated district. During the early 1960s, facing overcrowding in two overwhelmingly black schools, the district decided to bus children and faculty who would normally be at these schools to underused majority-white schools. But they also decided to keep the bused children in separate classrooms from the white children and to have separate lunchtimes and recess. The district called the policy "intact busing."[31] According to James Hazlett, a longtime superintendent of the school system who strongly supported integration, the idea behind the policy was to maintain the neighborhood school system. At least some of the black teachers preferred the policy of intact busing. Cortez Bradley, a black elementary school teacher, believed the policy was beneficial since it helped limit conflicts between the black and white children.[32] The practice's damage to the students outweighed such meager benefits, so the school district quickly abandoned the policy. When, in *Jenkins v. State of Missouri*, the KCMSD was later charged with operating a segregated school system, Judge Clark found that implementing this one policy was the only action taken by the KCMSD that fostered segregation after *Brown*.[33]

In retrospect, the KCMSD's efforts may appear as merely "token" integration.[34] But this charge ignores the significance of the KCMSD's actions. At the time, its policies more than complied with the Supreme Court's demands. Significantly, no one at the time called it "token" integration. Strangely, the KCMSD has also been criticized for desegregating but not integrating.[35] In *Brown* the Court never said that "integration" was required or that a certain racial mix was needed to comply with *Brown*. In fact, the NAACP supported geographic assignment of students regardless of race. It was not until after 1960 that the NAACP moved toward more aggressive attempts to force school integration.[36] While, following *Green v. New Kent County School Board*, the Court's standards required statistical evidence of desegregation, it is simply erroneous to condemn the KCMSD for not following a standard no one could have imagined at the time. Even expert witnesses supporting *Missouri v. Jenkins* would later grudgingly admit that Kansas City's actions appeared "constructive" compared to how other segregated school systems responded to *Brown*.

Accurately evaluating KCMSD's policies requires remembering that *Brown v. Board of Education* was precipitated by the fact that Linda Brown was forbidden to attend the school closest to her home. Instead, she had to travel an hour and twenty minutes each morning and afternoon across town. The absurdity of that commute is part of what made *Brown* a case of "simple" justice. The obvious solution to the problem was to have students attend schools closest to their homes. One would hardly have expected to see school districts impose what was seen as injustice in *Brown* as remedy for the injustice *Brown* was supposed to end.

Overall, there were few complaints in Kansas City following *Brown*. Black civic groups and community leaders generally endorsed the neighborhood system. Not until 1963 did a concerted effort develop to change the school board's policies. The Kansas City Congress of Racial Equality (CORE) organized a march on the Board of Education building calling for total integration. The march attracted around 200 protesters. Included in their demands was greater sensitivity to racial issues in "the selection of new school sites, in granting transfers, and in faculty assignments." The school board responded by announcing a policy favoring maximum racial integration "without destroying the fundamental principle of the school as a major service unit to the neighborhood of which it is a part."[37] CORE called the policy "another milestone in the history of educational progress in this city."[38] After announcing this new policy, Superintendent Hazlett regularly met with black civic leaders to discuss their concerns. But hovering in the background, and making Hazlett even more sensitive to the black community, was the possibility of a lawsuit.

As in other urban areas, racial tensions began to mount in Kansas City during the 1960s, and Martin Luther King Jr.'s assassination in April of 1968 exposed those tensions. The race riots, which erupted in more than 100 cities, finally came to Kansas City five days after King's death. There had been some hope that Kansas City would be spared. During the summers of 1965 and 1967, when dozens of riots erupted in cities across the country, Kansas City remained calm. In fact, some in Kansas City had grown overconfident. One black resident even said the racial unrest occurring elsewhere in the 1960s "could never happen here."[39]

But in 1968, rioting broke out and continued over three nights after a protest at Kansas City's Central High School against the school board's decision not to close the schools for a march in memory of Dr. King turned violent. Looters ransacked hundreds of stores, arsonists set fire to hundreds of buildings, and snipers shot at police and firefighters. Ironically, the decision not to close schools was made with the support of Herman Johnson, head of the Kansas City branch of the NAACP, who later said, "We thought that letting the children out . . . may cause trouble."[40] But after the Kansas City, Kansas, school district closed classes for the march, black students at several high schools in the KCMSD planned a walkout for the morning of Tuesday, April 9. The students planned to conclude with a demonstration at Central High School. The demonstration eventually led to a march on city hall. As the march progressed, it grew disorderly, leading to the violence. After an unsuccessful attempt to hold classes on Wednesday, the district closed schools a day early, on Thursday, for a long Easter break. When students returned after the break, the tensions had subsided and no further disturbances were reported. The only good news in the riot's aftermath was that Kansas City experienced less death and destruction than other cities.[41]

In what could not be called fortuitous timing, just one month before the riots, James Hazlett had proposed an integration plan called "Concepts for Changing Times." While he had always supported eliminating de jure segregation, he saw that legal doctrine was moving toward requiring school districts to eliminate de facto segregation as well. Inactivity, Hazlett accurately saw, would soon be enough to show racial animus. Hazlett's plan recommended integrating students by drawing them from across the district into magnet schools.[42] The school board, however, rejected the plan.[43] Henry Poindexter, who voted against the plan, later acknowledged that Hazlett's prediction was correct: "I think that Hazlett, who was a professional, saw more clearly than some of the board members that the laws were going to cause change."[44] Poindexter still maintains that Kansas City would not have accepted or supported the plan and that adopting it would have only divided the community. Since the board considered the plan in the months following the riot of 1968, Poindexter's claim has some plausibility.

The school board itself was a source of dissatisfaction in the black community. The board had six seats, and elections were a mere formality. The Democratic Party and the Republican Party each nominated three candidates, who were then unopposed in the general election. Those candidates overwhelmingly came from the white and wealthy southwestern part of the city. Only one board member before 1970 was black. The board's exclusive composition earned it the label the "silk stocking board."[45]

In 1970, however, a new method for electing board members went into effect. The new board consisted of nine members elected to two-year terms. Six of the members were elected from subdistricts with the remaining three being elected for districtwide at-large seats. While this plan increased the representativeness of the school board, the trade-off was stability. After 1970, the board was plagued with constant turnover. With new members routinely joining the board, the board suffered from a lack of institutional memory. The advantage of the "silk stocking" board was that it knew how the district operated because the board members served for lengthy terms. But under the subdistrict plan, representatives served shorter terms and were often off the board before they had mastered the minutia of district operations.

While black parents consistently voiced their complaints about the deteriorating quality of schools in the late 1960s, apparently no one seriously considered a desegregation lawsuit. In 1967, the Department of Health, Education, and Welfare (HEW) investigated the KCMSD because of allegations that the district was not in compliance with Title VI of the Civil Rights Act. HEW's investigative team held a meeting to provide parents an opportunity to air their concerns. The overriding complaint was overcrowded schools. The parents were particularly angry over the use of trailers as "mobile classrooms," which they referred to as "Hazlett Huts." They complained about black principals not being hired for majority-black schools, not enough black teachers, schools not teaching black history, and not being informed of their children's truancy. Integration was rarely mentioned.

In regard to the truancy issue, Hazlett did have one defender, Robert Roe, a representative from the NAACP, who said, "I'm quite well aware of most of the problems that exist, but I think many of us are putting more on Hazlett and the school board than they deserve. . . . We're asking the school system to be disciplinarians for us. Those schools are educational institutions. They are not penal institutions. If your child goes to school or is supposed to go to school and doesn't stay there, that isn't their fault. Don't blame them. Blame yourself." Roe seemed particularly concerned that going to the school board with "trivialities" would undermine the black community's ability to rectify its more serious grievances.[46] After concluding its investigation, HEW never cited any violations in the KCMSD, nor did the Justice Department after its investigation in 1968.

In 1973, four years after Hazlett retired, Emmanuel Cleaver, a local pastor and the executive director of the Kansas City chapter of the Southern Christian Leadership Conference (SCLC), filed suit in federal court requesting a metropolitanwide busing plan and $50,000 for each black child in the KCMSD.[47] Cleaver, who would eventually be elected mayor of Kansas City, abandoned the suit because of limited funding and lack of community support. A series of community meetings he held revealed very little support for busing but substantial support for increasing black influence in the district. He concluded that "the problem" for the community was not "the lack of integration and money (for the district)" but "lack of black influence."[48] Increasing black voter registration, Cleaver thought, would be more effective for promoting black interests in the school district.

While Hazlett was sponsoring programs to end de facto segregation in Kansas City, white flight and black inmigration were quickly eliminating any opportunity for meaningful integration. Two years after Hazlett's plan was rejected, white students became a minority in the school district. After 1969, the last year white students constituted a majority, any attempt to integrate the district would have been symbolic at best, as well as short-lived. Few options were available once black students became a majority. Reducing racial isolation was impossible when the district was itself racially isolated. A study of Kansas City's schools from 1956 to 1974 showed that white enrollment declined dramatically once schools reached 30 percent black enrollment.[49] The few remaining majority-white schools would quickly become majority-black schools under any plan to create more integration.

Two prominent examples of this white flight were Paseo High School and Central High School. In 1959, out of 1,859 total students at Paseo, 6.6 percent were black. In 1964, the school had 1,648 students, of which 50.2 percent were black. In 1969, there were 1,534 students, of which 97.8 percent were black.[50] The transformation of Central High was even more dramatic. In 1955, Central had 1,533 white students and 195 black students. By 1965, there were only 16 white students and 2,648 black students.[51] Central High School, located in the geographic center of the KCMSD, was in many ways a metaphor for the entire district. As black families moved from the north of the district to the south, white families moved either south or out of the district entirely.

The growing minority percentage also paralleled the financial decline of the KCMSD. Kansas City did not pass a bond initiative or a tax levy to support the schools after 1969. The plaintiff's attorney in *Missouri v. Jenkins* would later attribute this lack of financial support to racism. However, several other factors also explain Kansas City's reluctance to approve tax increases. First, the city's majority-white population was becoming increasingly elderly. Young, middle-class whites were leaving the city. Elderly persons, for obvious reasons, would have little personal interest in supporting the school district. Second, Kansas City had always had a large number of private schools. Parents of these students would be unlikely to vote to increase their taxes for a system offering them no direct benefit. Third, during the 1970s the administration of the KCMSD gained a reputation for being incompetent and bloated. The perception of incompetence only hurt the district's attempts to raise money. Fourth, Missouri law required that any local tax initiative receive approval by at least two-thirds of the voters. This was an extraordinarily high threshold for a school district with dwindling numbers of voters with children in the public schools. Fifth, Superintendent Hazlett retired in 1969, only to be succeeded by a series of less successful and short-tenured superintendents. Hazlett, who was well-respected by both the black and white communities, had led the district for fifteen years, guiding it through desegregation following *Brown* and during its demographic upheaval during the 1960s. No one who followed him commanded the kind of respect he inspired among school board members, the district administration, or Kansas City's parents. Over the thirty years after he retired, the school district was led by nine different full-time superintendents and twelve interim or acting superintendents. From 1867—when the KCMSD was founded—to 1970 the school district had only ten full-time superintendents and three acting superintendents.

But the most important reason tax levies and bond initiatives failed was teachers' strikes. Teachers' strikes in 1974 and 1977 prompted an exodus of students and greatly undermined the community's faith in the school district. The 1974 strike lasted six weeks, from mid-March to late April. During the strike, schools were widely vandalized, causing over $30,000 worth of damage in broken windows alone.[52] When a state judge ordered an end to the strike and the teachers' union refused, he levied a $30,000 fine against the union and sent the union president, Norman B. Hudson, to jail for ten days.

While the strike continued, the *Kansas City Star* reported that hundreds of parents had already transferred their children to private schools or made arrangements to move out of the district.[53] The strike finally ended with the union and district agreeing to an 8 percent pay increase for teachers with an additional 2 percent to follow if a tax levy passed during the summer. The tax levy was voted down. Meanwhile, student enrollment declined by nearly 10 percent, with the district losing 5,985 students. The number of white students declined by 4,050, and the number of black students declined by 1,919.

Less than two months after ending its strike, the teachers' union began hinting that it might call for another strike in the fall.[54] In 1975, the union threatened another strike but opted against it.[55] In the spring of 1977 the union finally did strike again. This strike was even more destructive than 1974's. Lasting seven weeks, it destroyed trust not only between parents and the school district but also between teachers. Some teachers who voted for the strike decided it had gone on too long, so they reported to work anyway, opening "freedom schools." Other teachers, however, were sent to jail for disorderly conduct while picketing.[56] The *Kansas City Star* quoted one teacher who said that once the strike was over, he wanted to return to work so he could "spit in the faces" of teachers who voted for the strike but then broke picket lines to return to work.[57] District historian John Duncan, who was a principal during both strikes and whose wife was a district teacher, believes the second strike "destroyed" the school district by ruining the "camaraderie of the staffs." Friendships, he says, "that existed for years were over . . . and I see it to this day."[58] Another exodus of students followed this strike. Student enrollment fell by 5,321 students, 3,182 white and 1,975 black.

With crisis upon crisis plaguing the school district during the 1970s, its facilities rapidly deteriorated. At times the district was up to a year behind in paying its bills. Rats ate any food left in the cafeterias. The phone system was so poor that a local construction company donated its old system. The district could barely keep the grass cut outside its buildings, and principals had to use duct tape to secure carpets to keep students from tripping.[59]

While struggling to remain financially solvent, the KCMSD was about to suffer another economic blow from the Supreme Court's decision in *Swann v. Charlotte-Mecklenburg Board of Education* in 1971.[60] As white flight and black inmigration made the district's schools increasingly racially imbalanced, majority-black schools became the norm. In Title IV of the Civil Rights Act of 1964, Congress had defined "desegregation" as "the assignment of students to public schools and within such schools without regard to their race, color, religion, or national origin." Desegregation "shall not mean the assignment of students to public schools in order to overcome racial imbalance." Accordingly, the KCMSD was in compliance with the Civil Rights Act. However, in *Swann*, Chief Justice Burger swept aside congressional intent and used the "judiciary's historic equitable remedial powers" to justify the use of busing in order to achieve more racial balance. The Court invoked the power of equity "in the quest for attaining the full compliance with the spirit as well as the letter of the equal protection of laws clause of the Fourteenth Amendment."[61] By making simple statistical racial imbalance the standard for determining whether a school district was practicing illegal segregation, the Supreme Court made Kansas City a target for federal investigation.

Swann, as discussed in Chapter 1, provided the justification for the *Adams* litigation. In 1972, the Department of Health, Education and Welfare was sued for not enforcing the Civil Rights Act of 1964. Citing racial imbalances the suit alleged that HEW had allowed several hundred school districts, including Kansas City's, to operate illegally segregated systems. The judge in the case, John H. Pratt, ruled against HEW and ordered the agency to notify the racially imbalanced school districts that they would be required to "explain or rebut" any racial imbalances within the districts' schools. If a district could not satisfactorily explain its racial imbalances, then HEW had to cut off its federal funding. In his decision, Pratt explicitly relied on the Supreme Court's ruling in *Swann*, stating, "HEW's continuation of financial assistance [to racially disproportionate systems] thereto violates the rights of plaintiffs and others similarly situated protected by Title VI of the Civil Rights Act of 1964. Defendants, before advancing or continuing to advance Federal funds in violation of Title VI, have a duty to require districts presumptively in violation of *Swann* or other controlling Supreme Court decisions to explain or rebut such presumptions."[62]

Judge Pratt handed down his order on February 16, 1973. Sixty days later the KCMSD received a letter from HEW asking the district to "explain or rebut" its racially imbalanced schools. Unable to rebut the charge, the district tried to explain it by referring to the demographic evidence. HEW considered the response unsatisfactory, and in November of 1973 its Office for Civil Rights announced that it would launch an investigation of the school system.[63] This announcement marked the beginning of a seven-year legal battle between the KCMSD and HEW.

After HEW began its investigation, the KCMSD realized that its financial status was becoming increasingly precarious. HEW potentially had the power to cut off over $10 million in federal funds to the district. Even though its decaying physical plant made the financial expense of a large busing program a low priority, the school board decided to investigate how to design a desegregation plan that would satisfy HEW. In October of 1974, the school board commissioned a comprehensive study of school attendance boundaries with the goal of desegregation listed as one criterion. Six months later, in April of 1975, the KCMSD received a letter from HEW charging the district with operating an illegally segregated system and demanding that the district produce a comprehensive desegregation plan within a month. Unable to meet HEW's demanding schedule, over the next month and a half the school board debated four possible desegregation plans. The board finally approved a proposal called Plan E, which tried to avoid a large busing plan by manipulating attendance boundaries. The plan also called for exploring the creation of a few magnet schools open to students throughout the metropolitan area as a way of drawing suburban students into the district. The board forwarded the plan to HEW, and ordered its administration to begin implementing the plan. HEW, however, rejected the plan in mid-July and gave the district thirty days to construct a new plan. Upon receiving HEW's rejection, the school board decided to keep the same attendance boundaries from the year before and to fight HEW in court. Dr. Robert Medcalf, the district superintendent, told HEW that the district was unwilling to force a "crash program" of "numerical balancing" on the parents and children of Kansas City.[64]

The district began making preparations for a court battle, but it also established another task force to study possible desegregation plans in the event that it lost in court.[65] Over the next two years the school board was pushed in two different directions by HEW and Kansas City's parents. HEW insisted that the board adopt a massive busing program, and Kansas City's parents pressured the board to retain its neighborhood school system. Overall, the Kansas City community opposed busing for integration. A 1977 *Kansas City Times* poll of 202 families — 117 white and 84 black — showed that 81 percent of parents supported integration but that 75 percent opposed busing. While more white parents, 87 percent, opposed busing than black parents, a significant majority of black parents, 61 percent, also opposed it.[66] The message from the community was clear: integration was fine if it did not fragment communities or neighborhood schools. One black parent said, "It's ridiculous to have our kids used as guinea pigs.... Every time the white people move, are we going to have to follow them?"[67] The widespread sentiment reported among black parents was that any money used for busing would be better used upgrading their neighborhood schools.

But eventually and inevitably HEW won. After an administrative court hearing, Judge Rollie D. Thedford ruled in favor of HEW and ordered the KCMSD to adopt a busing plan. During the trial, the KCMSD claimed that the current racial imbalance in the school system was the result of demographic trends that were beyond the school district's control. The KCMSD also pointed out that it had been investigated by HEW in 1967 and by the Justice Department in 1969 and had been found in compliance with the law on both occasions.[68] But judicial precedent had changed since then, so the school board found itself having to adopt a desegregation plan called Plan 6C, version C of the sixth plan proposed. The school board adopted the plan in 1977 without HEW's approval, prompting immediate protests in the community and accusations that the school board was out of touch with the interests of both parents and children. The school board, however, was trying to satisfy its constituents, HEW, and Judge Thedford. HEW rejected the plan.

Luckily for the board, HEW had to capitulate on Plan 6C after two more years of fighting because Congress had recently restricted the agency's ability to mandate busing. Plan 6C did not eliminate the neighborhood school system; it only modified it. The major feature of the plan was that it would require all schools in the district to have a minimum of 30 percent minority students.[69] But even with the adoption of the most moderate desegregation plan available, white flight immediately increased. In the first year of the desegregation plan, 1977–78, the district lost 21 percent of its white students.[70] And four years after the plan began, more black children attended racially isolated schools than in 1977. One district official summed up the situation: "There are not hordes of white kids sitting in ivory white towers that can be brought in to desegregate the schools."[71] Neither the white nor the black community was happy with the plan, but black parents remained some of its most vocal critics, arguing that it placed a greater busing burden on black students than whites and weakened the sense of community blacks formerly had under the neighborhood system.[72] The primary difference between the two groups was that white parents more often than black parents had the resources to either enroll their children in private schools or move to the suburbs.

Filing Suit

At the same time that it was battling with HEW, the school board was also planning a possible retaliatory lawsuit. Because the district was over 60 percent minority, the school board realized that it would never be able to achieve the level of integration that HEW wanted. The only way to integrate the Kansas City schools would be to allow two-way transfers between the KCMSD and suburban school districts. The suburban school districts would never voluntarily cooperate, so judicial decree would be necessary to force such transfers. Just as important to the school board, though, was retaliation against HEW. The school board, still angry over HEW's investigation, felt, with some justification, that many of HEW's policies had aggravated the racial isolation plaguing Kansas City.

The school board hired two University of Missouri–Kansas City professors to study a possible lawsuit against both HEW and the suburban districts. The professors, Daniel Levine of the School of Education and Robert Freilich of the School of Law, determined in their two years of research that Kansas City had excellent prospects for a lawsuit.[73] They based their conclusion on *Green v. New Kent County School Board*[74] and *Keyes v. Denver School District*.[75] While *Green* was significant for creating an affirmative duty to desegregate, it was *Keyes* that gave the professors the most hope. The *Keyes* decision was instrumental in Freilich's recommendation to file suit because, as he put it, "if you can prove there is segregation in one part of the district, there is a presumption of segregation in the rest of the district." He even interpreted *Keyes* to mean that "if area school districts fostered segregation in the 1950s there could be a 'presumption' that they continued to do so in later years."[76]

Of course, the Court had already ruled in *Milliken v. Bradley*[77] that suburban districts could not be forced to participate in a remedy for a violation they were not responsible for. To overcome *Milliken*, Freilich argued that the racial isolation of the KCMSD created the presumption that the suburban school districts and the state had helped foster this segregation.

Based on the professors' advice, the school board filed suit on May 26, 1977. Previously, desegregation cases had been filed by citizens or civil rights organizations. This was the first time a school board had filed a desegregation suit.

The school board's initial complaint contained the core arguments that would shape the course of the litigation. Running throughout the complaint was the assumption that if a governmental action does not have a segregative intent but does have a segregative effect, the government has violated the Constitution. Hence, since the states of Missouri and Kansas "intentionally caused public education to be provided on a piecemeal basis by separate governmental units with arbitrarily determined boundaries," they were responsible for having "provided public education in a manner which has caused and increased racial segregation between defendant school districts [suburban districts] and plaintiff district [KCMSD]."[78] The most important word in this argument is "intentionally." Missouri and Kansas did not intentionally cause segregation, but they did intentionally give local school boards control over their school districts. Moreover, the district argued, Missouri and Kansas were responsible for "the concentration of minority race persons within the boundaries of plaintiff school district. In fact, the defendants, their agencies, subdivisions and officials have by various acts and refusals to act in the field of housing, and by refusing to act in such areas as school reorganization, encouraged the racial isolation of plaintiff school district."[79] The district argued that these demographic shifts were directly attributable to state actions: "The racially discriminatory actions of defendants have resulted in a movement of middle class families away from the plaintiff district, impacting said district with a progressively higher percentage enrollment of economically and socially disadvantaged minority race students."[80] According to the district, a large demographic movement that results in racial isolation obligates the state to resist or stop that movement. By the district's reasoning, no action or inaction of government, whether local, state, or national, should affect where a person decides to live or move. Or if they do, they should affect all races equally.

The district did not limit its complaints to Missouri and Kansas. In a rather clever retaliatory claim against HEW, the district argued that HEW "violated" its affirmative duty to "prevent and encourage elimination of racial segregation in public schools" by "intentionally caus[ing] greater segregation by seeking racial balancing of the schools within the plaintiff district only."[81] HEW, therefore, by carrying out the order of a federal judge, actually violated its duty to eliminate segregation. The agency, the district argued, should have "required school authorities in the metropolitan area to desegregate on a metropolitan basis as a condition of receiving federal funds." The district asserted that HEW should force school districts that were not unlawfully segregated to help a district that allegedly was unlawfully segregated.

The district also filed claims against the Departments of Transportation (DOT) and Housing and Urban Development (HUD). The DOT had, according to the district, "in the course of constructing highways, relocated, or permitted recipients of federal aid to relocate, population in a manner which has promoted residential housing segregation by such actions as relocating minority race persons from integrated neighborhoods to predominately minority neighborhoods."[82] Housing segregation, in turn, caused school segregation. The suit did not charge that the agency intentionally caused segregation, only that segregation was an unintentional by-product of its policies. The same was true of the district's allegation against HUD. In fact, HUD's alleged wrongdoing was its policy of considering only income and not race in its housing policies. HUD had "administered and promoted policies" toward low- or moderate-income families that promoted "residential segregation which in turn increased racial isolation and identifiability of school districts" in the metropolitan Kansas City area "and thereby racially discriminated against the public school children in plaintiff district [KCMSD]."[83]

Shortly after filing this brief, the district suffered two setbacks that threatened the entire lawsuit. The initial setback came when the judge originally assigned to the case, John W. Oliver, recused himself after the defendants questioned his impartiality. Oliver had been an attorney for the school district before his appointment to the bench in 1962 by President Kennedy. Missouri, Kansas, and the suburban school districts believed that his prior association with the KCMSD made him sympathetic to its complaint.[84] More importantly, though, Oliver was thought to be one of the most activist judges in the country. He had also recently gained notoriety as the judge who ruled against major league baseball on free agency, breaking the stranglehold clubs held over their players. After removing himself from the case, Oliver transferred it to Russell G. Clark. Oliver said that he made the assignment because Clark was the "least likely to have any possible apparent connection with the pending litigation."[85]

The KCMSD viewed Clark's appointment as a depressing development. His background discouraged any hope that he would order a metropolitan-wide remedy or even any remedy at all. Born in 1925 in rural and southern Oregon County, Missouri, Clark was the youngest of ten siblings on a 450-acre farm. His older brother taught him to read in the local one-room schoolhouse. After graduating from high school he served as an officer in Europe during the closing months of World War II. Upon returning from Europe, he enrolled in the University of Missouri, finishing his undergraduate and law degrees in five years. He then moved to Springfield, Missouri, where he joined the law firm of Allen and Woolsey. Practicing privately for twenty-five years, Clark specialized in representing insurance companies against the claims of other insurance companies. Though a successful lawyer, he retained his "homespun" ways. His son Vincent reported that his father taught him to repair fences and castrate cattle, and described him as "very plain-spoken, sometimes a little too plain-spoken."[86]

Based on the recommendation of Senator Thomas Eagleton, in 1977 Jimmy Carter appointed Clark to the District Court for the Western District of Missouri. A longtime Democrat, Clark had worked on Eagleton's senatorial campaigns. His association with Eagleton encouraged opponents of the desegregation lawsuit because, although he was a longtime supporter of desegregation, he was critical of HEW's efforts to force busing in urban school districts. Efforts to desegregate cities would be counterproductive, he thought, and might cause further white flight. In fact, the same year that Judge Clark assumed control of the case, Eagleton sponsored the Senate bill that restricted HEW's ability to force busing in cities with racially isolated schools.[87] Clark's background and associations marked him as a moderate-to-conservative judge who would cast a skeptical eye on any requests for a judicially mandated desegregation plan.

True to expectations, Clark had a quick and almost devastating impact on the school district's litigation. One year after assuming control of the case, he issued a surprising and somewhat confusing order. Clark ruled that the KCMSD lacked standing to sue the state of Missouri since it was an entity of the state and existed at the state's discretion. But instead of dismissing the case, what normally occurs when a plaintiff is denied standing, Clark, in a truly extraordinary move, decided that the KCMSD should be "realigned" as a defendant. In addition to KCMSD's lack of standing, Clark cited "other factors" that required him to realign the district:

> Among these are the possibility that the economic injury to the KCMSD may be relieved by alternative financing methods for school districts. Thus, if the economic difficulties of the KCMSD are alleviated, will the KCMSD continue to zealously argue for the rights of the aggrieved student? Will the litigation be abandoned in midstream due to disgruntled taxpayers bringing pressure upon the elected school officials? Will future board members possess the same views as the present members in this litigation which will be measured in years due to the almost certainty of frequent appeals?[88]

The KCMSD, Clark saw, filed the case for financial reasons, not because of any real sense of duty to desegregate the district.

Comparing the KCMSD's case to a traditional "private" law case illustrates the order's bizarre nature. If someone brings a suit claiming that Ford made a defective product causing him to have an accident, a judge could not reassign that person as a defendant and claim that he made the defective product. Judges are not entitled to select who will be plaintiffs and who will be defendants. But in a very real sense this is what Judge Clark did, since he also ruled that the remaining plaintiffs had a conflict of interest because they were children of school board members. To survive as plaintiffs, their parents had to resign from the board and terminate any official affiliation with the district. If they did not, new plaintiffs would have to come forward. The parents opted not to resign and withdrew their children from the lawsuit.

In a much more defensible part of the order, Clark ruled that the Kansas defendants had insufficient contact with the KCMSD to warrant his jurisdiction, although he held open the possibility of bringing them back in at a later time. The remaining defendants were the state of Missouri, the KCMSD, the eleven suburban Missouri school districts, and the three government agencies, HUD, DOT, and HEW.

While the KCMSD initially considered Clark's ruling a lethal setback for the case, the realignment actually put the district in a rather perverse and possibly advantageous position; it could only lose by winning and win by losing. After the ruling, the KCMSD, which had previously argued that it was running a unitary school district, consistently argued that it was running an unconstitutionally segregated system.[89]

The scope of the case meant that it would be lengthy, costly, and possibly unsuccessful. Finding someone willing and able to pursue it proved difficult. The American Civil Liberties Union (ACLU) and SCLC both stated that the cost of funding the suit would likely prohibit them from becoming plaintiffs. The NAACP had opposed the initial suit because of disagreements with the school board and remained leery even after the district's realignment as a defendant.[90]

St. Louis: Voluntary Mandatory Plans

As the suit in Kansas City languished after Clark's ruling, an ongoing case in St. Louis, *Liddell v. Caldwell*, provided hope for anyone willing to take the KCMSD's place as plaintiff. In 1972, a group of black parents filed suit against the St. Louis School District for operating a segregated school system. The parents were asking for minimal relief and in fact opposed any substantial attempt to desegregate the school district through coercive means. The relief they sought was to have the school district stabilize current black-to-white ratios to prevent further segregation. However, the local branch of the NAACP, with the support of the national organization, inserted itself as an additional plaintiff and called for a major desegregation plan with substantial busing. The district court judge sided with the initial plaintiffs and approved a few modest measures to try to stabilize district enrollment.

In making this decision, Judge James Meredith dealt with issues raised in Kansas City. He noted several factors mitigating the claim that St. Louis was illegally segregated. Before *Brown*, the St. Louis Board of Education had prepared "plans for the desegregation of the school system." Immediately following *Brown*, the board implemented a districtwide desegregation plan—which Kansas City imitated—that was widely praised as a model for recalcitrant states and school districts. Much of the plan was designed by a black administrator and was approved by the NAACP and the National Urban League. The U.S. Commission on Civil Rights said that St. Louis's "1954–56 transitions, then, were solidly conceived and brilliantly carried off. They represented a signal breakthrough in human relations, and everywhere those who prize man's dignity were properly impressed." Judge Meredith held that the current segregation was largely the result of enormous demographic changes that had nothing to do with pre-*Brown* segregation. The black population of St. Louis, he noted, represented 17.9 percent of the total population in 1950 but by 1970 it represented 40.9 percent.[91]

While St. Louis was not responsible for the current segregation, Judge Meredith did decide that *Keyes* obligated the school board to try to ameliorate it. The district had to consider race when building new schools and drawing attendance boundaries. Additionally, the school district had to establish a few magnet schools to help retain some of the white population.

The NAACP appealed Judge Meredith's ruling to the Eighth Circuit Court of Appeals. The result for Judge Meredith was humiliating. The court held that he "was clearly in error as to the constitutional requirements imposed on defendants who have formerly discriminated pursuant to state law" and he also "erred" in his "evaluation of the extent to which the defendants have met those requirements."[92] According to the appellate court, racial imbalance was unlawful in spite of St. Louis's history of supporting desegregation. A monumental effort was required to integrate the district.

The court remanded the case to Judge Meredith and ordered him to consider the plan of Gary Orfield, a well-known professor and author of *Must We Bus*, for desegregating the district.[93] Orfield's plan included a much larger magnet-school system, large-scale busing across the district, and a misnamed "voluntary" transfer plan. Without any sense of irony, the court approvingly cited Orfield's testimony that voluntary transfer plans can help desegregate a district "because parents know that if they don't transfer voluntarily they'll be reassigned."[94]

The ruling in St. Louis made it obvious that the Eighth Circuit Court of Appeals would demand extensive remedies in Kansas City. The demographic changes in Kansas City were virtually identical to those in St. Louis. Also, Kansas City's record on desegregation after *Brown*, while praised at the time, was less impressive than St. Louis's. If St. Louis could not escape massive judicial intervention, then Kansas City was an inviting target.

The Plaintiff's Attorney

Several months after Judge Clark realigned the KCMSD as a defendant, a local attorney, Arthur Benson, assumed responsibility for litigating the case. Initially, Benson thought that he could not pursue the case because of the cost. But the allure of the case made him willing to use his own money and incur substantial debt pursuing it. Recalling when he was asked to represent the students, he said, "I was so excited I couldn't sleep."[95]

Benson, who came from a privileged Kansas City family, graduated from the city's most exclusive private school, Pembroke Country Day. He told the

Call that he "became a liberal in high school when John Kennedy became president.... Kennedy and Martin Luther King inspired a lot of us who believed in those non-violent principles, tolerance and equality. That's when I decided to become a lawyer."[96] He then attended Williams College and graduated with honors and a degree in economics. After attending Northwestern Law School, he returned to Kansas City in 1969 and worked for the Legal Aid Society until 1971, when he went into private practice. Upon returning to Kansas City, he immediately took up liberal social causes and Democratic Party politics. His first wife, Karen, was a state legislator and later became a member of Congress representing Kansas City. He established a reputation for suing "sleazy inner-city car dealers, unscrupulous landlords," and anyone else who "preyed on the poor." His activities were not without costs. He was assaulted while issuing a summons to a car dealer, and a firebomb exploded suspiciously close to his office. He defended a man charged with desecrating the American flag by sewing it onto the back of his jeans. While defending a prostitute, he was able to overturn a city anti-loitering ordinance. He also served as counsel for opponents of the construction of the Truman Dam.[97] Suing to reconstruct education in metropolitan Kansas City was ideally suited for such a bright, energetic, and politically liberal attorney. Throughout the case, even those who completely disagreed with him acknowledged that he was a deeply principled man who was willing to endure much criticism in defending those principles.

Benson officially represented eleven students. The first of these students was Craig Jenkins, who would lend his name to the case. Craig's father, Carroll L. Jenkins, who later changed his name to Kamau Agyei, volunteered him to be the lead plaintiff. After Craig graduated from high school, other Jenkins family members would take his place. Carroll Jenkins assisted Benson in locating black residents of Kansas City from before 1954 to testify at trial. Their testimony, Benson believed, proved to be crucial to his case.[98] Long after Craig Jenkins left the KCMSD, Benson remained the plaintiff's attorney and eventually represented all current and future students of the KCMSD, whom Judge Clark certified as a class in 1985.

The parts Clark and Benson played in *Missouri v. Jenkins* would be the defining roles of their careers. At times it appeared as if Clark and Benson were working in unison. In the coming years Benson rarely failed in any legal appeal he made to Clark. This superficially cozy relationship eventually led black community leaders to accuse Clark and Benson of ignoring the true interests of black children. Judicial scholars often remind us that judges are essentially passive—they cannot act until someone else brings a suit—but in this case, Clark never had to wait. Clark, in a way, defined the structure of the suit by picking the plaintiffs and defendants. Realigning the KCMSD as a defendant allowed Arthur Benson to speak on behalf of the children. With the two of them in place, those who opposed the lawsuit or desired a less comprehensive remedial plan, such as black civic organizations, had little influence. Benson spoke for the students, and Clark spoke for the law. It would be a powerful combination.

However, to charge that they had a close working relationship or that Clark rubber-stamped every motion Benson put before him would be a mistake. Even after twenty years of working with Clark, Benson told Jack Cashill, a Kansas City writer and advertising executive, that Clark was "a small man, about 5'3"." Cashill points out, "In fact, Clark is actually about 5'7" [and] that Benson could so underestimate Clark after a 20 year relation says a good deal about the ambiguous nature of their relationship and the distance that the reclusive Clark has kept between them."[99] As discussed in Chapter 4, because of Supreme Court precedent, Clark refused to give Benson what he wanted most—a metropolitanwide busing plan. Benson had to settle for a more costly plan that he considered less effective. Since *Missouri v. Jenkins* developed late in the history of desegregation, Clark had to work under the doctrinal restraints of *Milliken v. Bradley*. But Missouri's and Kansas City's educational history also compelled him to do something to offset the racial imbalance in Kansas City's schools. Thus, Clark would be free to approve almost anything Benson proposed to ameliorate racial isolation that did not compel surrounding school districts to participate.

Conclusion

A review of Kansas City's educational and racial history shows that time was an important variable in the development of *Missouri v. Jenkins*. Because the KCMSD was led by a superintendent sensitive to the concerns of the black community and had complied with *Brown v. Board of Education*, the onset of the suit was delayed, pushing it into the third generation of desegregation cases. Had the suit been brought earlier, a busing remedy like the one the school board eventually adopted would have satisfied the Supreme Court's precedents. But by the late 1970s, busing within the KCMSD proved to be a futile and counterproductive rearguard action against racial isolation.

In addition, by the time the case developed, the interests of the black community had moved beyond what the courts had claimed were their interests. Community leaders had many opportunities to pursue a case but decided not to. Certainly they supported desegregation, but they did not want its pursuit to make the quality of education suffer. Only a majority-white school board and a white attorney were willing to pursue a lawsuit. Benson did eventually receive assistance from the NAACP Legal Defense Fund (LDF), which joined the suit in 1982, but local civil rights organizations and black community leaders had no role in the suit. But as *Missouri v. Jenkins* would come to illustrate, the interests of local black communities and national civil rights organizations such as the LDF often differed. These differences were also evident among black elites such as Derrick Bell, who after supervising more than 300 desegregation cases as an LDF attorney decided that the goal of integration was misplaced. He believed that civil rights advocates should instead focus on improving education for black children, a position held by many black parents and community leaders in Kansas City.

Because the black community did not determine for itself whether to file suit, bitter disagreements developed between the community and Benson, undermining the legitimacy of his efforts. No one could doubt Benson's sincere desire to improve the lot of black children in Kansas City. However, many in the black community deeply disliked the paternalistic implications of a self-appointed white attorney telling black parents what was best for their children, and they would openly, and effectively, oppose Benson's proposed remedies.

3

Courthouse Magic
Educational Vice Becomes Legal Virtue

When *Missouri v. Jenkins* finally came to trial in 1983, Judge Clark found himself in an unenviable position. The KCMSD's schools were obviously in a state of physical and educational disrepair. In some buildings, decayed asbestos fell from pipes, windows fell out of rotted panes, ceiling tiles hung precariously, and hallways "reeked of urine."[1] And each year the results of standardized tests prompted a fresh dose of vitriol directed at the KCMSD. The children of Kansas City were clearly suffering an injustice.

Many of the KCMSD's problems were the fault of the district school board and administration. But Clark was presiding over a lawsuit in which the plaintiffs and the KCMSD claimed that the school district's problems flowed only from racial isolation. Complicating matters was that Arthur Benson, as plaintiff's attorney, was the only one who believed, or was at least willing to argue, that race was the root cause of Kansas City's educational afflictions. The KCMSD, as Judge Clark recognized in 1978, was arguing this point for financial reasons. No one doubted that race was a factor that led many parents to leave the school district or to vote against increased tax levies. But race was only one factor, and, as election data reveal, it could not have been the most important one. Nevertheless, Supreme Court precedent demanded Clark rule for the plaintiffs. In addition, a verdict for the defendants had the unattractive effect of leaving the students of the KCMSD in the same unjust position.

Clark had to find someone responsible. Who this would be — the state, the KCMSD, or the federal agencies — and how the finding would influence the remedy was still unknown. The continued decline of the KCMSD and the evidence presented at trial gave Judge Clark few options for framing the verdict in a way that would also make it possible to fashion an educationally beneficial remedy. These difficulties led to an unusual ruling. Clark strongly and unequivocally held that the state and the KCMSD were operating an unconstitutionally segregated school system, but he based this finding on the weakest possible rationale.

"An Educational Titanic"

The early 1980s offered more grim news about the KCMSD. In 1983, the *Kansas City Star* reported of Kansas City's schools, "The generally known and, unfortunately, accepted problems now have faces and names. The city has seen textbook shortages in real classrooms. It has seen young people turned away from the job of their hope, the college of their dream because they were cheated for 13 years. It has listened to principals trying to be nurses and fundraisers and counselors, too busy to be educators. It can see children bouncing up the grade ladder, promoted for any number of reasons — except that they've mastered appropriate skills." In short, everyone knew that the district was failing and that it was a systemwide failure. A columnist for the *Call*, a local black news weekly, ridiculed the legal effort to improve the KCMSD, calling the district an "educational titanic."[2]

The district's problems were more than evident several years before. In 1979, the school board, along with the superintendent, decided to adopt a five-year plan to improve the quality of education in Kansas City. A problem with this plan quickly emerged. The plan did not exist. The school board hired the Midwest Research Institute at a cost of $166,000 to study the school district and provide suggestions about what the district's five-year plan should include. In "an atmosphere filled with self-congratulation," the *Kansas City Star* reported, "members of the Board of Education were euphoric on Halloween 1979 about developing the plan." One board member said, "I feel, as it were, kind of on a high."[3]

The euphoria quickly ended. The consultants completed their study and reported their findings, which included a list of problems with the district, such as too much central administration, too little parental involvement, too much social promotion (passing students on to the next grade when they should be held back based on academic performance), and too many unruly students. The school district was supposed to take these findings and develop a plan. But after two years into the five-year plan, and long after the consultants reported their findings, no one still had any idea what was in the plan. When asked about it, Carl Struby, a member of the school board, said, "It's a lot of things. Sometimes its difficult to explain." When asked, teachers professed ignorance. One said, "It sounds like it will be a great idea, but aside from working to improve student achievement, I don't know much about it." Another said, "It's sort of a nebulous thing."[4] Generally, the school district decided to exhort teachers and principals to improve the quality of education and called these exhortations a "plan."

Even when the district followed its consultants' recommendations and took concrete steps to improve its schools, it executed them in educationally thoughtless and unsound ways. One example was the district's decision to cut 192 positions from central administration to help combat its bloated image. However, many of the positions it eliminated were part of the district's teacher-training program. These administrators were some of the few who regularly worked with the schools to improve teaching and who provided one of the few bridges across the chasm between the schools and the central administration. Additionally, other "eliminated" senior administrators were reassigned to classroom teaching; to make room for them, schools had to release younger teachers who lacked seniority or tenure. Many of these reassigned administrators had not taught for years. One district employee said that the "nuts and guts of it is that [the decision to cut administrative positions] was not a decision that any responsible administrator in education would have made. . . . It was a decision that was forced on us. People across the country are awed at what we have done to our system."[5]

Since the previous study led to no beneficial results, in 1984 the district decided to commission another study. This time, the public received the news with justifiable skepticism. The *Call* asked in an editorial: "Why Another Study?" The "Board of Education has voted to have another study made, at a cost of over $300,000, of its administrative structure," it reported. "To the average layman and taxpayer, this seems like a waste of money . . . . The average parent and patron of the schools does not understand why it takes an outsider to tell educational professionals how to staff a school district."[6]

The *Call* echoed what had become the overwhelming theme of reporting on the school district. One article in the *Kansas City Town Squire*, a local weekly, argued that the school board was "more preoccupied with stimulating minority employment; with encouraging minority suppliers and contractors, and with placating diverse ethnic elements within the community than with the more mundane task of providing sound, basic education[;] the board talks of cake when the students have no bread."[7] Walter Burks, the author of the article, scoffed at the idea that the school district was failing because the public was unconcerned. After a recent tax levy had been voted down by a 3-1 margin, Sue Fulson, a school board member, said, "I'm pretty shocked. I think it says that our city has abandoned our children." Burks responded,

"Oh, come now! The outpouring of negative votes indicates no such abandonment. It was a simple cry of protest against a school district that has already abandoned the children; a school district that cannot, with more than 90 million dollars a year at its disposal, teach 37,000 students how to read and write." Even school district employees and past supporters of the district, he pointed out, failed to support the tax levy. The charge that people voted against the levy for racist reasons also left Burks unpersuaded. "In the February [1983] levy election in Kansas City," he said, "less than fifteen percent of the voters in the heavily black wards bothered to vote, and even these wards failed to carry a simple majority for the levy."[8] The KCMSD also liked to point out that its operating levy of $3.75 per $100 of assessed property value had not changed since 1970. But property valuation, Burks noted, had increased, so property taxed at the same rate produced far more revenue in 1983 than it did in 1970, even after taking inflation into account. The KCMSD, therefore, had the same revenue in real dollars that it did in 1970, when it had nearly twice as many students and apparently provided a better education.

Prominent civil rights leaders in the community also criticized the school district. For example, Jeremiah Cameron, a professor at a local community college, former teacher in the school district, and former president of the local branch of the NAACP, wrote a weekly column in the *Call* in which he often condemned the KCMSD school board and its administrators. In early 1984 he wrote:

> The education of children in Kansas City has been a disgrace . . . . Past boards of education were no more interested in the quality of instruction in the schools than they were in dusts of a distant planet. The plain and simple fact is that a goodly number of the past boards — this one too — have simply lacked qualifications for seeing that a school system delivers quality learning. [And] none of the superintendents in the past 14 years could really be called educators. The boards did not look for an educator; they wanted someone who could rack in federal funds, which were largely misused to prop up a system that was not worth a tinker's damn. What they got was technicians — second rate ones at that — not educators who really had any substantive learning themselves or knew or cared what learning is all about.[9]

Cameron made sure that the black community was well aware that the school district was guilty of creating many of its own problems.

The voters' unwillingness to approve tax levies was an important expression of this opinion. Arthur Benson would argue at trial that the tax levies failed because white residents of the KCMSD who sent their children to private schools were unwilling to fund a majority-black school district and that other white parents who would normally vote for school taxes had left for the suburbs because of racial animus. "A significant number of voters," he later said, "who were most likely to support measures to support the schools financially were young white families with school-age children and as a result of the violations a lot of those were getting out of the school district so they were no longer there to counterbalance the elderly vote; [and] the white voters who remained were polarized by the racial divisions. . . . So you drive out your base and those who remain get polarized by race."[10] While some people undoubtedly voted against the levies because of racial animus, this theory cannot explain the data. A commonly overlooked reason the levies failed was the change in Missouri law about raising property taxes. As table 3.1 shows, several levies after 1969 gained similar levels of support as those passed before 1969. Even after the two-month-long teachers' strike of 1974, 54 percent of the voters supported a property tax increase. Only ten years later, support for the school district had almost completely vanished among both blacks and whites.

The 1983 levy election was especially revealing for two reasons. First, it was the first levy election in ten years. For a school district claiming to be in deep financial trouble, ten years was a long time between levy elections. A. H. Kilpatrick, a board member during the late 1970s and early 1980s, testified that he did not think the school district was really in financial trouble, just that it was poorly managed. "The school district," he said, "had a peculiar way of coming up with hundreds of thousands of dollars whenever the chips were down at one time or another. We would be crying that we were broke, and that we had no money, and all at once we found we had half a million dollars, or even as much as $6,000,000."[11] Second, the measure received only 8,078 votes. If race determined one's vote, as Benson argued, there should have been more support since the school district had more than 25,000 black students at the time.

The most telling sign of the public's dissatisfaction with the KCMSD was the consistently declining student enrollment during the 1970s and early 1980s. District enrollment data show that from 1974 to 1984 the school district lost nearly half of its students (see table 3.2). The school district lost 10,117, or 29 percent, of its black students and 15,433, or 61 percent, of its white students. The district was becoming increasingly black but

Table 3.1 Outcomes of KCMSD School Levy Elections, 1964–1983

Date	Vote For	Vote Against	Percentage For	Percentage Required	Result
Nov. 3, 1964	42,077	34,123	56	50	Passed
Jan. 8, 1966	20,392	24,160	46	50	Failed
Jan. 24, 1967	23,364	15,310	60	50	Passed
Apr. 1, 1969	17,582	21,619	45	66⅔	Failed
May 20, 1969	29,371	25,664	53	66⅔	Failed
July 1, 1969	28,359	16,608	63	50	Passed
June 23, 1970	12,965	11,628	53	66⅔	Failed
May 18, 1971	18,467	15,863	54	66⅔	Failed
Aug. 10, 1971	17,611	16,161	52	66⅔	Failed
Dec. 7, 1971	17,774	20,475	46	66⅔	Failed
June 11, 1974	29,342	24,733	54	66⅔	Failed
Feb. 8, 1983	8,078	23,073	26	66⅔	Failed

Source: "Summary-School Levy Election from 11/3/64 to 3/31/87," Benson Papers, Box D506.

only because whites were leaving at a faster rate than black students were moving in.

The bad publicity the KCMSD received in the late 1970s and early 1980s, one supposes, would be distressing for anyone preparing to go to trial in a desegregation case. The KCMSD's continuing decline was at least partly the result of mismanagement. However, Arthur Benson wisely used that decline to strengthen his argument. Whites, he said, left the school district because of racial animus, which led to racial isolation, which led to failed tax levies, which led to financial collapse. While negative portrayals of the KCMSD in the press and overwhelming evidence of mismanagement would seem to weaken this case, Benson labeled them as further proof of underlying racism and as the remaining effects of Missouri's former system of segregated education. Simply put, the poorer the education, the stronger his case.

The Trial: Convincing a Hostile Judge

Deposing hundreds of unfriendly witnesses from eleven suburban school districts, two federal agencies (the Department of Transportation had been dropped from the case), and the state government took Benson several years.

Table 3.2 KCMSD Student Racial Composition, 1974–1984

Year	Black	White	Other	Total	Percentage Black
1973–74	34,920	25,455	2,310	62,685	54.3
1974–75	33,001	21,405	2,294	56,700	55.7
1975–76	32,454	19,090	2,181	53,725	58.2
1976–77	31,208	17,560	2,279	51,047	60.4
1977–78	29,233	14,378	2,115	45,726	61.1
1978–79	28,721	12,771	1,860	43,352	63.9
1979–80	27,686	11,507	1,830	41,023	66.3
1980–81	26,368	10,923	1,787	39,078	67.5
1981–82	25,496	10,312	1,802	37,610	67.5
1982–83	25,227	10,184	1,853	37,264	67.8
1983–84	24,803	10,022	1,825	36,650	67.7

Source: "Total Student Membership: School Years 1955–56 through 1999–2000," Kansas City, Missouri, School District, Research Office (2000).

The defendants found no need to expedite a process they considered illegitimate. With the help of LDF lawyers and student volunteers, Benson was finally ready to go to trial after four years of preparation.

Heading into the trial in October 1983, Benson was confident, and with good reason. He knew that the Eighth Circuit would be watching Clark closely and that Clark knew he was being watched. Benson later recalled, "As we started out there were a couple of opinions out of St. Louis that helped with the legal roadmap . . . and we knew we had a court of appeals down there that had already spoken, that had already sent the *Liddell* case back to the district court and had outlined the history of segregation there and we knew our history was very similar. So we felt quite strongly that if we could marshal the same kind of evidence—and we knew we could—that we had a very strong case."[12] He thought that obtaining a verdict against the state and the KCMSD would not be difficult. In fact, Benson said, ruling for the state was never "a viable option for him [Clark]."[13] But a verdict against the suburban districts was not guaranteed.

Benson's strategy for the trial had five main parts. First, convince Judge Clark, through the testimony of blacks who lived in Kansas City prior to *Brown v. Board of Education*, that the dual system of education had been so invidious that its effects must still be lingering. If this general argument persuaded

Judge Clark, rulings against the state and the KCMSD would follow and possibly ones against the suburban school districts and federal defendants as well. Second, argue that because Kansas City had racially isolated schools prior to 1954 and in 1983, the dual system had never been eliminated. Third, prove that the suburban school districts had been complicit in perpetuating a dual school system after *Brown*. Fourth, argue that the federal agencies also perpetuated the racial isolation in Kansas City. And finally, show that the state of Missouri failed to take active steps after *Brown* to dismantle its dual school system.

With his first argument, Benson faced opposition not only from the state of Missouri but also, to his disappointment, from a very disagreeable judge. The state had asked Clark to forbid anecdotal testimony about pre-*Brown* segregation, saying it had no value for determining present segregation. Benson responded that the "plaintiffs fail to see how the testimony of former *victims* of the very racial discrimination at issue could *not* be relevant." Benson argued that personal recollections of blacks who lived in Kansas City were as valuable as expert testimony. "While we agree that expert testimony will be of value in resolving this factual issue, and do not intend to oppose efforts by the defendants to introduce it," he argued in his briefs, "surely that testimony is not of greater probative value than the testimony of blacks who lived in the Kansas City area during the years in question."[14]

Clark allowed Benson to present anecdotal testimony, but he quickly grew hostile to the dozens of witnesses Benson brought to testify. According to Benson, Clark was saying "things from the bench on the record that were very hostile to our case and he was telling us to stop calling witnesses," referring to them as "repetitive."[15] Even at the risk of further angering Judge Clark, Benson continued to call witnesses who described life in Kansas City before 1954. The typical witnesses testified about the long distances they were forced to travel to attend school when a white school was nearby or how their family moved to Kansas City because there were no black schools in their rural county. Clark's antagonistic attitude toward these witnesses and Benson's expert witnesses was so dispiriting that Benson's co-counsel from the LDF, Theodore Shaw, wrote him after leaving Kansas City confessing, "My feelings about the experience are mixed. As you know, being away from home for such extended periods of time takes its toll on many fronts. Add to that the unpleasant experience of trying a case before a hostile judge and one cannot help but hope that the experience will never be repeated again."[16]

Clark's testy response to one of Benson's more far-fetched arguments is illustrative of his hostility. Benson argued that segregation had entrenched racist practices, which were reflected in Kansas City's segregated housing. Prior state-sponsored segregation, according to Benson, caused real estate agents to harbor racial animus and push blacks toward black neighborhoods and whites toward white neighborhoods. Since real estate agents were licensed by the state, he argued that the state was thus responsible for this behavior. Of course, doctors and lawyers are licensed by the state, but no one would argue the state is responsible for their actions. This argument was not likely to succeed.

In an effort to buttress these strained claims with expert testimony, Benson called Gary Orfield, who designed the St. Louis desegregation plan, to testify about how patterns of segregation prior to 1954 were still evident. While Shaw questioned Orfield, Clark interrupted, saying that he was "tired" of listening to "repetitive evidence" and instructed Shaw to finish his questioning within thirty minutes. After a recess, Clark scolded Shaw: "You had twice as much time with this witness as you needed. We have been over the same areas over and over and over."[17] The attorneys were having such difficulty with Judge Clark on the vestiges of prior segregation that Benson worried about what kind of opinion Clark would deliver. He never thought that Clark would rule for the state or the KCMSD, but he said, "There was a lot of concern about how strongly he would rule or how strong his opinion would be."[18]

With the second part of his strategy, proving that Kansas City schools were racially isolated in 1954 and 1983, Benson only had to present readily available numerical data. Arguably, based on total numbers, Kansas City schools were more racially isolated thirty years after *Brown* than they were in 1954. Benson argued that a prima facie case against the state, the KCMSD, and suburban school districts could be based on this situation alone. In his briefs Benson consistently said that "no substantial desegregation occurred in 1955 or thereafter," and he pointed out that the KCMSD still operated all-black schools and the suburban school districts were mostly white.[19]

Benson also made several additional arguments against the KCMSD to bolster the claim that Kansas City schools were racially isolated. According to Benson, the KCMSD's neighborhood school attendance policy after *Brown* was evidence of discriminatory intent. In addition, Benson charged that the open transfer policy in effect until the late 1960s in the KCMSD, which allowed any student to transfer to any school not at full capacity, had a segregative effect. Whites could afford transportation for their children to schools out of their neighborhoods, but blacks could not. According to Benson the

KCMSD also failed to adopt "stabilizing policies" in schools undergoing racial change.[20]

These charges would have been difficult to justify but for the fact that the KCMSD was supporting the plaintiffs and that none of the other defendants, including the state of Missouri, cared if Judge Clark held the KCMSD liable. Highlighting the obvious collusion between Benson and the KCMSD, Judge Clark said the two had a "friendly adversarial" relationship. The open attendance policy, for instance, had been in effect before 1954, and its entire rationale was to stabilize neighborhoods and to prevent middle-income families from leaving the school district. Henry Poindexter, president of the school board during the 1960s, testified that once the board tightened its transfer policy, white flight to the suburbs accelerated. Poindexter said, "I voted against the Board change to a more restrictive transfer policy because I felt that, if you imposed rigid restrictions on people and did not allow them to move within the District under certain modified guidelines, the end result would be that people would simply sell their homes and move, and it would destabilize a neighborhood served by a school we were trying to integrate. Ultimately this phenomenon occurred."[21] Also, the neighborhood attendance policy adopted after *Brown* was praised for having brought the school district into compliance with the Court's directives. The school board refused to end its neighborhood attendance policy because it complied with the Supreme Court's rulings and doing away with the policy would prompt middle-income families to move to the suburbs.[22]

The third part of Benson's strategy, proving that the suburban school districts were complicit in perpetuating segregation, also relied primarily on undisputed statistical evidence. Because the suburbs remained majority white, Benson implied, something unconstitutional must be going on. Benson's evidence beyond this assertion was weak. The suburban districts had opposed state legislation that would have forced them to consolidate with the KCMSD. Because the suburban districts had opposed their own elimination, according to Benson, they had unconstitutionally obstructed efforts to create integration.[23] Additionally, the suburban districts refused to cooperate with the KCMSD in special education programs, which also had a segregative effect, if not intent.[24] Seeming to acknowledge the weakness of his evidence, Benson argued that "even if these suburban districts are innocent of any constitutional violations . . . they are, nonetheless, appropriate parties to the litigation" because if actions by one district caused segregation in another district, that district can be included in a judicial remedy.[25] Benson also argued that because the suburban districts offered no high school education to blacks before 1954, black students were forced to move into the KCMSD. Therefore, the current racial isolation in the KCMSD resulted from prior de jure segregation.

As with the testimony about pre-1954 segregation in the KCMSD, Clark was unreceptive to Benson's arguments against the suburbs. Clark threw out much testimony and even refused to admit evidence comparing suburban housing patterns to those in the KCMSD. Before Benson had even concluded his case, he said he was expecting to have to appeal.[26]

The evidence against the federal agencies, HUD and HEW — now just the Department of Education after President Carter split HEW in 1979 — also relied on effects rather than intent. Benson argued that HUD's policies had the effect of concentrating blacks in the urban core of Kansas City. HEW, he said, should have brought funding cutoff procedures sooner against the KCMSD.

Benson's remaining and most important arguments were directed at the state of Missouri. If the state was not included in a desegregation remedy, he reasoned, it was hard to imagine how one could be funded. Fortunately for Benson, he knew that the Eighth Circuit was receptive to claims against the state. With that in mind, his primary argument against the state was a straightforward recitation of Missouri's constitutional and statutory requirements to operate segregated schools prior to 1954. As if to remind Clark of the Eighth Circuit's ruling in St. Louis, Benson repeatedly referred to appellate rulings in the *Liddell* case that documented Missouri's history of segregation. Benson also charged that the state took insufficient action to desegregate the KCMSD.

The charges centered on two pieces of proposed legislation. The first one was known as House Bill (H.B.) 171. Until 1957, Missouri law required that a school district become coterminous with city boundaries once a city reached a population of 500,000. But this bill, which was passed in 1957, raised the population requirement to 700,000.[27] Kansas City's population would briefly and barely exceed 500,000 in the late 1960s and early 1970s but never came close to 700,000. Because of the changed requirement, the KCMSD did not automatically merge in the late 1960s with parts of the suburban school districts whose boundaries overlapped with the city of Kansas City. Hence, this bill, according to Benson, had the effect of concentrating blacks in the KCMSD and therefore implied racial animus on the state's part.[28]

The second piece of legislation, known as the Spainhower proposal and introduced in 1969 as H.B. 437, would have consolidated school districts throughout the state. The Spainhower Commission had been formed to study ways to improve education in Missouri. Creating racial balance was never mentioned as one of its objectives. Rather, the commission proposed consolidating school districts as a way to improve school financing. After meeting with vehement protest from all sections of the state, the measure failed. Its opponents argued that consolidation would lead to excessive centralization and a loss of local control and influence. Benson argued that the real reason behind its failure was race: "Proof of the conformity of legislative and administrative action to the racially motivated desire of constituents as well as the invidious motivation of individual legislators from areas of the state where proposed legislation would have a racially integrative effect is, of course, compelling evidence that the legislative inaction was itself invidiously motivated."[29] He added that the state board and commissioner of education did not endorse the proposal even though the commissioner said that the proposal was "educationally defensible."

Finally, Benson argued that Missouri's decision to change the requirements for school districts to expand "made it progressively more difficult for KCMSD to annex or consolidate with surrounding school districts, first by raising the signature requirement for annexation petitions from ten persons to ten percent of the voters, then by requiring affirmative votes in both districts, not just one." These added burdens "were thus impermissible racial classifications in violation of the Fourteenth Amendment." Even if adopted without "unlawful intent" they still violated the Constitution because "their effect is adverse to the interests of minorities where there is no compelling justification for the legislation."[30]

Benson began presenting his case on October 31, 1983. After offering more than 2,100 exhibits, calling over 140 witnesses, and designating 10,000 pages of depositions, he would conclude on March 6, 1984, the sixty-fourth day of trial.

The KCMSD could be counted on to voice a hearty second to all of Benson's arguments. Benson and his colleagues could have just as easily written the district's briefs. They contained the same allegations and were likewise larded with less than subtle references to the Eighth Circuit's *Liddell* opinions. Mark Bredemeier, an attorney who later opposed parts of Benson's case, described the school district's attitude at trial as "please don't throw me in the briar patch."[31] The KCMSD summed up its position to Clark:

Although the KCMSD has taken major desegregation steps, and although its current student, teacher, and staff assignments are in compliance with the law, KCMSD has not yet achieved a unitary status. Its students remain in racial isolation. A majority of the black students in the KCMSD are enrolled in schools which are more than 90% black. Many of the educational problems resulting from the past history of segregation and the continuing racial isolation of the entire KCMSD are still to be addressed. KCMSD is engaged in an ongoing task of desegregation; the State should begin shouldering its share of that burden.[32]

The Defendants' Response

The responses of the state, suburban districts, and federal agencies to Benson's charges were dismissive and bordered on derisive. Of all the defendants the federal agencies, HUD and HEW, appeared to be in the strongest position. Even though judges had shown themselves more willing since the 1960s to second-guess the choices of federal administrators, courts were still likely to presume that agencies had justifiable reasons for their decisions. Both agencies argued that they had such reasons.

HEW argued that it had to make choices based on its resources and that, considering its limited budget, its choices were rational and more than responsible. Benson had argued that HEW should have investigated the KCMSD sooner and devoted more resources to making it a "unitary" school district in the 1960s. HEW countered that there was no reason for it to devote resources to Kansas City when there were more pressing problems elsewhere. "There is," it argued, "no requirement that the Secretary distribute the same amount of resources to Missouri school districts as he does to South Carolina school districts."[33]

HUD argued that Benson did not show any evidence of intentional discrimination by HUD and that, contrary to his claim, it had tried to alleviate housing segregation. HUD had established low-income housing throughout the metropolitan area and most of it was built outside the KCMSD. Additionally, HUD contended, race did not influence where it directed people for housing or how it appraised houses or approved loans. In fact, it argued, Benson's own evidence contradicted his accusation. Benson had argued that HUD had channeled blacks into the KCMSD and not given them the opportunity to look at low-income housing in the suburban school districts.

However, one of Benson's own witnesses, Ruth Schechter, a director of a low-income housing project in suburban North Kansas City, testified that she had engaged in "extensive" marketing to attract minorities but was only able to attract a small percentage.[34] As with HEW, HUD said that it did what it could with the resources at its disposal and that racial isolation in Kansas City was not from a lack of the agency's efforts to eliminate it.

The suburban school districts also seemed to sense that they were in a strong position, and justifiably so; *Milliken v. Bradley* was in their corner. In their briefs, the suburban districts offered four main arguments. The first was that school districts were largely autonomous under Missouri law, which made them inappropriate targets by Benson. Education, they argued, had always been under the control of local school districts dating back to the state's original constitution of 1820. Even when Missouri law expanded state control over education, local school districts retained "full authority and autonomy" in the election of school boards and in their day-to-day affairs, including acquiring property, making boundary changes and annexations, regulating schools, employing personnel, selecting textbooks, establishing curriculums, tracking pupil attendance, overseeing transportation, and determining taxation and managing other financial matters.[35] The suburban districts argued that under *Milliken* Judge Clark had no power to find them liable or include them in any possible remedy. A "comparison of the Missouri statutes to those Michigan statutes relied on in *Milliken* to show local control," they maintained, "demonstrates that Missouri school districts are more autonomous than Michigan school districts." This was especially true, they argued, in the power of local citizens to establish school district boundaries.[36] Where Benson saw a narrow opening in *Milliken*, they saw a brick wall.

Their second argument was that they in no way tried to concentrate black children in the KCMSD or keep them out of their school districts. As proof, they showed steady increases in their black student population since 1953 while Kansas City's peaked in the early 1970s and had steadily declined since. The KCMSD lost most of its black students during the 1970s at the same time it was losing many white students. What these facts showed, they argued, was that anyone with the means, black or white, was leaving the KCMSD. The numbers proved that there was no racial animus.[37]

Their third argument was that the KCMSD alone was responsible for its current educational and fiscal morass: "[The] KCMSD has not been without difficulties[,] including administrative problems [and] an excessive administrative staff, and it has been plagued with personnel problems including two major teacher strikes. Indeed, its major loss of students in the 1970s is attributable directly to two prolonged teacher strikes. KCMSD's difficulties, however, have been of its own making rather than the result of acts or omissions attributable to these districts."[38]

Finally, the suburban districts argued that the lawsuit was little more than "an effort to end-run *San Antonio School District v. Rodriguez*." Benson's idea for a metropolitanwide district was a ploy to gain access to suburban money. This, they believed, was illegitimate not only because of the Court's decision in *Rodriguez* but also because the KCMSD already had enough money.[39] The KCMSD did not need suburban money; it needed to make more efficient use of the money it had. The corporate and industrial development in Kansas City made property in its school district more valuable than that in the suburban districts, which had more residential property. Hence, with a lower tax rate, Kansas City produced more revenue per pupil than the majority of the suburban districts. In fact, they pointed out, the per-pupil spending in the KCMSD was almost twice that in the average suburban district.

The state of Missouri was, of course, the most vulnerable defendant next to the self-accusing KCMSD. Having already lost in St. Louis, the attorney general's office knew that the odds were unfavorable in Kansas City. Since Benson argued that suburban school districts were controlled by the state, the state found itself in the position of having to defend them.

The state's first line of defense was Benson's own evidence. His own witnesses, the state argued, could not show any intentional discrimination since 1954: "Witness after witness, including witnesses who had been actively involved in the promotion of civil rights, testified that they knew of *no* acts by the suburban school districts or State Defendants that were done with discriminatory intent."[40] These witnesses included Lucille Bluford, the longtime editor of the *Call*; Dr. Edwin Fields, a longtime black administrator and former interim superintendent; Dr. Robert Wheeler, a former black superintendent; and Joyce Stark, the current president of the school board and an initial supporter of the desegregation suit. The state also pointed out that Gary Orfield "acknowledged that in comparison to states of the Deep South engaged in massive resistance[,] the policies of Missouri looked constructive after *Brown*."[41] Moreover, many of Benson's witnesses had testified in 1975 in the school district's fight with HEW that the KCMSD was a unitary district in full compliance with the law. For instance, Dr. Phillip Olson, a sociologist at the University of Missouri "found himself in the unique position of having to completely reverse himself from the testimony he had given in the 1975 HEW hearing," as did Dr. Daniel Levine, a professor of education at the University of Missouri.[42]

The state's second line of defense was that the current racial isolation in Kansas City could not be attributed to the prior dual school system. Benson and the KCMSD argued that the racial isolation was the result of blacks moving from the three-county area (Clay, Jackson, and Platte) surrounding the KCMSD before 1954 to take advantage of Kansas City's black schools. The state countered that from 1930 to 1960 "blacks in the three county area decreased by 550 while KCMSD blacks increased by 45,000,"[43] so most of the black population moving to Kansas City could not have been from these three counties. In fact, they argued, the largest inmigration of blacks before 1954 occurred during World War I, the Great Depression, and World War II because of those periods' peculiar economic conditions. Education was not the dominant factor drawing blacks to Kansas City. The state also pointed to the mass migration of blacks from the Deep South and to the Midwest during the 1950s and 1960s as the primary reason for the KCMSD's current racial composition.

Missouri also had to defend the state legislature's passing H.B. 171 and rejecting H.B. 437. Regarding H.B. 171, the purpose of which was to prevent complications from reorganizing entire metropolitan school districts, the state pointed out that no black or white legislator opposed it. In fact, Representative J. McKinley Neal, a black civil rights activist who represented a district in the KCMSD, supported the bill. Moreover, the state argued, since the KCMSD supported the measure and was majority white at the time, it was silly for Benson to argue that the KCMSD was trying to discriminate by concentrating blacks within its own district.[44]

On the rejection of the Spainhower proposal, which would have combined school districts, Spainhower himself testified that there was enough opposition from rural areas with few blacks to defeat the bill. Hence, race could not have been the fundamental reason for its defeat. And the debate in the legislature was about local control, so it was impossible to prove that its rejection was motivated by race.[45]

Finally, the state, as did the suburban districts, argued that the KCMSD's problems were of its own making, calling special attention to the testimony of Gary Orfield and Joyce Stark. Orfield had acknowledged that teachers' strikes can erode parental confidence in a school district and lead to enrollment declines, and Stark had admitted that the teachers' strikes and high salaries, which contributed to the financial strain and physical deterioration of the school district, caused a loss of students and that poor management might have caused the proposed tax levies to fail.[46]

The state, though, was unable to present evidence to counter the moving testimonies of blacks who had lived in Kansas City prior to *Brown*. No one could doubt that their lives had been affected by segregation in deep and painful ways. This testimony left unexplained, though, how a desegregation plan would redress the harm to those who had experienced the full force of segregation. The state thus argued that since 1954 it had done nothing to perpetuate segregation and could not be held responsible for behavior that was constitutionally permissible before 1954.

Releasing the Suburbs

Before the suburbs were allowed to present their case, Clark delivered a devastating blow to Benson and released the suburban districts. On June 5, 1984, Clark delivered a memorandum opinion that said, "There is no credible or substantial evidence of a constitutional violation by these suburban school districts." Making it clear that he would not consider a metropolitanwide busing plan, he said that a "study of plaintiff's witnesses' testimony both at trial and by deposition reveals that none identified any acts of the suburban school districts done with the intent to discriminate on the basis of race, to contain blacks in the Kansas City, Mo., school district or to keep blacks out of the suburban districts." Clark even pointed out that Benson's own witnesses corroborated the suburbs' contention that they had done nothing discriminatory.[47] Twelve years later, when his desegregation plan had clearly failed to accomplish its objectives, Clark somewhat crudely explained, "The very minute I let those suburban school districts out, I created a very severe problem for the court and for myself, really, in trying to come up with a remedial plan to integrate the Kansas City, Missouri, School District. . . . The more salt you have, the more white you can turn the pepper. And without any salt, or with a limited amount of salt, you're going to end up with basically a black mixture."[48] Of course, the facts and precedents drove this decision and neither supported a ruling against the suburban districts.

For Benson, this ruling was a crushing loss. His primary goal was to create a metropolitanwide busing plan. He would now have to convince the Eighth Circuit that the trial judge, who was responsible for determining the facts of the case, was mistaken when he found that the suburban districts did nothing to create the racial isolation in Kansas City. Benson still thought that Clark might consider including the suburbs if he found against the state since the school districts were part of the state, but he acknowledged that this outcome was unlikely. To the many people observing the proceedings, Clark's ruling put Benson's entire case in jeopardy. Clark's memorandum, the *Call* reported, "probably foretells that his final decision in the case will go against the plaintiffs."[49]

The discouraging news continued for Benson. While not as significant as his dismissal of the suburban districts, on July 16 Clark dismissed HEW because Benson did not show that the agency acted with racial animus or abused its discretion. This decision also signaled that Clark would more than likely rule in favor of HUD as well. Benson could only hope that Clark would be mindful of the Eighth Circuit when ruling on the state and the KCMSD.

An Unusual Verdict

Benson would have to wait two months after Clark's ruling on HEW to hear his final opinion. On September 17, 1984, Judge Clark ruled against the state and the KCMSD in the strongest possible way but on the weakest possible grounds. Clark, at times, seemed contemptuous of Benson's claims. One by one, he refuted Benson's arguments but in the end found a rationale for the verdict.

Clark started the opinion by explaining why he dismissed the eleven suburban school districts. Relying on *Milliken v. Bradley*,[50] Clark stated that the "plaintiffs simply failed to show that those defendants had acted in a racially discriminatory manner that substantially caused racial segregation."[51] The specific charge against HEW was "also dismissed for plaintiffs' failure to prove the agency acted with racial animus or abused its discretion in the enforcement of Title VI."[52]

After this brief explanation, Clark then dismissed the case against HUD on similar grounds. The plaintiffs had made "numerous claims" against HUD, but Clark reached the same conclusion in each one: that HUD acted with no "racially discriminatory intent or purpose." These would be Benson's only losses. Clark's decision to dismiss these defendants is interesting because he essentially reached the same conclusion about the remaining defendants, the state and the KCMSD. Clark found that since 1954, except for the case of intact busing, which he said did not contribute to the current segregation, neither had acted with discriminatory intent.

In the claims against the state and the KCMSD, Clark found that the evidence showed no illegal discrimination. Most importantly, Clark discounted all of the specific evidence Benson relied on to prove his case. The plaintiffs had argued that the state, suburban school districts, and HUD had orchestrated the movement and concentration of blacks within the KCMSD. Clark specifically rejected the arguments of the plaintiffs' key witnesses on this point. "Dr. James Anderson, plaintiffs' expert historian," Clark said, "opined the black migration into Kansas City was from a depopulation of blacks in the surrounding three-county area moving to the city primarily for schools." Dismissing this argument, he said that the "Court finds the greatest influx of blacks came from southern and border states and that they migrated because of a host of factors." Clark also rejected the testimony of Dr. John Kain, a Harvard professor and the plaintiffs' expert on the "determinants of residential location." Kain testified that blacks would have been "dispersed throughout the metropolitan area" had it not been for housing discrimination. Kain denied that factors such as "job location, ethnic clustering and personal preference" had any influence on where people chose to live. "The Court," Clark said, "disagrees to the extent Dr. Kain rejected the possible influence of other factors in his analysis."[53]

Clark then dismissed Benson's arguments that the state was responsible for private acts of discrimination by local real estate agents. Benson had argued that several real estate agencies had engaged in practices that isolated blacks in Kansas City. Because the state was responsible for licensing the agents, according to Benson, it followed that it was also responsible for ensuring that they did not engage in discriminatory behavior. Clark found, as he had to, that the "mere fact that activities of these private individuals or entities were either licensed by or subject to regulation by a state agency does not convert the private action into a state action." Moreover, the "only complaint involving illegal activities of realtors which was filed with the Missouri Real Estate Commission led to the permanent revocation of the real estate license of the agent involved."[54]

To Benson's final charge that the KCMSD's intact busing had a segregative intent and effect, Clark noted that the school board did choose "to bus entire classrooms of black students to predominantly white schools [and] keep them as an insular group, not allowing them to be mixed with the receiving population," but "because the practice was stopped in the 1960s . . . no continuing violation exists."[55] Clark found that the only action by the KCMSD with segregative intent and effect, intact busing, was inconsequential. Clark concluded that no specific action by the state or the KCMSD after *Brown* warranted judicial intervention.

At this point in the opinion, Benson appeared to have disregarded Judge Clark's admonition five years earlier. In 1979, Clark told Benson that he needed "to concentrate on segregative action since the 1950s."[56] This admonition not only demonstrated that Clark was highly involved in structuring the case but also showed what Clark expected Benson to do to prove his claims. Based on Clark's analysis, Benson had failed. An exoneration of the state and the KCMSD, one would have expected, would be forthcoming. Clark, however, was undeterred by the lack of specific, post-1954 evidence that implicated either of them. Instead he found that the KCMSD was still an unlawfully segregated school district solely because there was racial isolation both in 1954 and 1984. This, of course, forced Clark to confront the fact that the KCMSD had complied with the Supreme Court's demands in *Brown v. Board of Education I* and *II* and had seen many majority-white schools integrate and then resegregate because of the demographic changes he cited.

Clark dealt with this troublesome point by denying that there was any such thing as resegregation. Many witnesses in the case testified that the KCMSD had become resegregated during the 1960s and 1970s because of demographic trends, but Clark held that those changes were irrelevant: "The Court notes that several witnesses used the term 'resegregated' when describing racial change in the schools and housing patterns, usually changing from predominantly white to predominantly black. That may be correct terminology in the context of their testimony but the Court finds it has no legal significance. A segregated District cannot become resegregated until it is first integrated. The KCMSD has not yet become integrated on a system-wide basis."[57] Clark accepted the evidence that showed that Kansas City had experienced massive demographic changes, which had nothing to do with intentional state action, but then dismissed that evidence as irrelevant. According to Clark, it did not matter that residential segregation was the result of private choice. All school districts should be integrated.

To prove this point, Clark offered a deluge of statistics showing that many Kansas City schools were still racially isolated:

> As of 1977, 25 one-race schools under the pre-1954 system remained 90% or more of the same race. In addition, there were four black schools from the dual system that were still predominately black when they closed in 1968. In summary, as of 1974, 20 years after *Brown I*, 39 schools were more

than 90% black; another 38 had 10 to 90% black enrollment. Eighty percent of all blacks in the District attended schools that were 90% black; only 19% of the blacks attended a school that was 10 to 90% black. With the adoption of Plan 6C in 1977, the District eliminated the 16 entirely white schools and reduced the number of 90 + % black schools to 28. During the 1983–84 year, no school had less than 30% black enrollment; 24 schools however are racially isolated with 90 + % black enrollment. The Court finds the district did not and has not entirely dismantled the dual school system. Vestiges of that dual system still remain.[58]

Relying on *Keyes*, Clark held that this racial disparity constituted evidence of illegal segregation.

In a rather strange piece of legal reasoning, Clark also relied on the Supreme Court's "psychological harm" thesis from *Brown I* to support his decision. "Several witnesses," Clark said, "confirmed the conclusion reached by the Supreme Court in *Brown* I that forced segregation ruins attitudes and is inherently unequal. [Segregation] may affect their hearts and minds in a way unlikely ever to be undone."[59] The Court, of course, was referring to legally enforced school segregation, which the KCMSD had abolished shortly after *Brown*. Clark, however, was referring to segregation, which, according to his own analysis, the Court would have found constitutional.

Clark offered one final argument in support of his ruling: Even though the state of Missouri had ended forced segregation after *Brown I*, it was still responsible for private acts of racism. Missouri, Clark noted, enforced segregation before 1954. Therefore, he reasoned,

> these actions had the effect of placing the State's imprimatur on racial discrimination. It created an atmosphere in which the private white individuals could justify their bias and prejudice against blacks. A large percentage of whites do not want blacks to live in their neighborhood and a large percentage of blacks do not want to reside within a neighborhood in which they are not wanted. This has and continues to have a significant effect on the dual housing market in the Kansas City area. Thus, the Court finds that the State has encouraged racial discrimination by private individuals in real estate, banking and insurance industries.[60]

This rationale was extremely weak for several reasons. Primarily, Clark assumed that the state action caused the private racism, when it was more likely that private racism caused the state action. If the people of Missouri did not want a dual school system, why would their representatives have established one? Clark argued that the people of Missouri were victims of their government when the people were responsible for its action. However, Clark could not hold the people of Missouri responsible, but he could hold their government responsible.

Additionally, according to Clark's rationale, the Supreme Court should also have been sued and held liable for its decision in *Plessy v. Ferguson*.[61] Undoubtedly, *Plessy* placed the Supreme Court's "imprimatur" of approval on segregation and allowed private individuals to justify their acts of discrimination. Congress should also be liable since it had established a dual school system within the District of Columbia.

Finally, and most importantly, Clark offered no evidence of how this prior state action was currently causing racial discrimination. According to Clark, housing segregation in Kansas City during the 1980s was unnatural and, therefore, must be the result of previous state action. Without the state's imprimatur, Kansas City would have been filled with integrated neighborhoods. With this argument, Clark ignored his own ruling, which held that a variety of factors influenced where people lived. These other factors were all much more definite and concrete than this vague idea of a hovering state imprimatur.

Because Clark dismissed all of the specific charges against the state and the KCMSD, only the vague charges remained. Since the offenses, or the effects of the offenses, were unclear, the solution to them could not be precise. Any solution would have to combat this "imprimatur" from forty years before.

Why?

The extraordinarily weak and contradictory rationale for Clark's opinion, along with his dismissive tone toward the plaintiff's evidence, would seem to imply that he did not really believe that the problems of the KCMSD resulted from previous racial segregation. So why did a "hostile" judge rule in Benson's favor and against the state? Why did he base his decision on the weakest possible grounds?

The simplest explanation is that he had to. Clark clearly believed that the Supreme Court's doctrines from *Green*, *Swann*, and particularly *Keyes* required his verdict. And the Eighth Circuit would obviously have overturned him if he had ruled differently. Pete Hutchison, a lawyer for the Landmark

Legal Foundation, which would eventually appeal many of Clark's rulings to the Eighth Circuit, said that exonerating the state and the KCMSD was impossible. "The Eighth Circuit wasn't going to put up with that [exoneration]. The Eighth Circuit was very keen on aggressive desegregation in its cities and it made that clear in the St. Louis case."[62] This could be called the "it's the system" explanation. While generally an unhelpful abstraction, in this case the system was quite real. Clark had to confront institutional realities. He was a district court judge underneath an appellate court that would tolerate nothing less than a finding of unconstitutional segregation.

Two other theories to explain Judge Clark's ruling have been offered by the case's participants but are possibly more helpful in explaining Clark's generosity when he crafted a remedial plan. Benson theorized that his strategy of bringing dozens of witnesses to testify about their personal experiences both before and after 1954 wore Clark down. "So over the months," Benson said, "[Judge Clark] had to listen to all of these people testify about how segregation of schools had adversely affected their lives. And he just heard that over and over and over again and I think it changed him so that by the spring [of 1984] when the state started putting on their expert witnesses and their case, all of those opinions about how this doesn't affect anybody and there are other causes for this rang hollow after he had heard these very human stories about how segregation had completely stunted their lives."[63] The state, based on this theory, correctly feared personal testimonials because of their emotional power.

The second theory, offered by both Benson and others, was that Clark harbored latent feelings of guilt about his upbringing in southern Missouri, which undoubtedly was not the most progressive, and he felt compelled to make up for this past. According to Pete Hutchison, "There was some thinking that part of his motivation in this was an overreaction to his personal background and the prejudices he was exposed to as a kid. . . . I think that he was a Depression-era kid, that World War II generation, and I suspect that he might have harbored some shame or personal reason for thinking, you know I've got to make this right."[64]

The Remedy?

A *Kansas City Times* headline the day after Clark announced his decision read: "Judge's Desegregation Ruling Leaves Solution Unclear."[65] No one knew what kind of remedy Clark could order. How, for instance, could one relieve racial isolation in an overwhelmingly minority school district without including the suburbs?

Clark ordered no specific remedies, but he did provide some idea of what he expected. He ordered the state and the KCMSD to present separate short-term plans to begin eliminating the vestiges of prior segregation in the district. Several factors, according to Clark, had to be taken into consideration. The plans should "to the extent possible, see that students are permitted to attend a school nearest the student's home so long as by so doing it does not deter from properly integrating the students in the KCMSD. They should also bear in mind cost factors as well as the purpose of the public schools in this state, that is to furnish quality education to its students." These instructions were sufficiently imprecise to give both the state and the KCMSD the freedom to submit any plan that they wished. Also, because they had so much latitude, predicting that the state and the KCMSD would present entirely different plans would not have been difficult. Clark essentially told the KCMSD that money would be no object: "It is also the Court's opinion that much of the cost for preparing and implementing a plan to dismantle the vestiges of a dual school system should be borne by the State."[66]

While Clark had previously said to keep cost in mind, the implication that the state would have to pay for most of any remedial plan was an invitation to the KCMSD to submit a plan that ignored cost. After the ruling, the *Kansas City Star* reported that several KCMSD administrators believed that a possible way to integrate the district would be to "design a plan to pour state money into the schools to provide specialized 'magnet' programs, more teachers and better academic opportunity, hoping white students will be attracted back to the public schools."[67] This speculation would turn out to be prophetic, but immediately after Clark's ruling this kind of plan seemed unlikely. Clark's hostile attitude at trial indicated that he might order a remedy that required a token amount of busing along with opening a few magnet schools.

Conclusion

In a few short years the KCMSD went from complete disrepair to being on the verge of receiving a massive infusion of judicially mandated cash. Arthur Benson's efforts, the KCMSD's own mistakes, public contempt, and failed tax levies all helped justify judicial intervention. It was an impressive legal accomplishment for Benson.

Benson, however, was dissatisfied with the outcome. He knew that without suburban participation, reducing racial isolation in the KCMSD would be difficult, but he did not think it was impossible. Clark recognized these difficulties as well but was unwilling to involve the suburban school districts in his remedy for both political and legal reasons. He would later confess that besides not having any evidence against the suburban districts, he wanted to avoid inflaming racial passions, as happened in Boston.[68] And while the Eighth Circuit might have upheld a verdict against the suburbs, such a decision would certainly have invited Supreme Court review since the evidence against Kansas City's suburbs was no stronger than it had been against Detroit's in *Milliken v. Bradley*.

But Benson was unwilling to give up on his dream quite yet. Immediately after Clark's ruling, he began crafting a metropolitanwide busing plan and an appeal to the Eighth Circuit. He would never succeed and would quickly have to accommodate himself to the KCMSD's wish of using desegregation as a front for school improvements. He would prove to be as adept at procuring money for the KCMSD as he was at securing a verdict against the state.

4 The Field of Dreams

In 1984 Judge Russell Clark ruled that the state of Missouri and the Kansas City, Missouri, School District were running an unconstitutionally segregated school system. After the decision, *Missouri v. Jenkins* appeared to be a rather ordinary desegregation case. The KCMSD had racially isolated schools, so Supreme Court precedent required a finding of liability. However, correcting racial imbalance in a racially isolated school district limited the range of judicial remedies. By the mid-1980s, most cases resembling *Missouri v. Jenkins* resulted in remedies requiring modest amounts of busing, along with establishing a few magnet schools.

But Judge Clark's remedies were far from ordinary. From 1985 to 1990, he would double the property taxes on residents and businesses within the KCMSD, raise the income taxes of individuals who worked within the KCMSD, order hundreds of millions of dollars in capital improvements for the KCMSD, and convert over three-quarters of the KCMSD's schools into magnet schools. An idiosyncratic judge can always hand down unusual rulings, but that is partly why we have appellate courts—to reign in wayward judges. So next to Judge Clark's remedies, the most surprising thing about *Missouri v. Jenkins* is that the Eighth Circuit Court of Appeals and the Supreme Court overturned none of his remedies, except for the income tax surcharge.

Knowing only the dramatic remedies Judge Clark ordered, one would be tempted to ascribe Clark's actions to a liberal political ideology and activist judicial philosophy. But that judgment is inaccurate. Clark's biography reveals that this conservative "law and order" Democrat was hardly a social crusader. His actions were shaped by a complex set of influences, including the need to follow Supreme Court precedent, appease the Eighth Circuit, keep political protest to a minimum, help the students of the KCMSD, and—ironically—follow principles of judicial restraint. Although he miscalculated the public's response to his actions and the educational efficacy of his remedial plans, his behavior nevertheless had an understandable logic. This chapter will examine the legal battle between 1985 and 1990 to see how Clark made his extraordinary remedial decisions and how the Eighth Circuit and the Supreme Court framed their responses.

The Superdistrict

After Judge Clark's ruling against the state and the KCMSD, the plaintiff's attorney, Arthur Benson, attempted to persuade him to include the suburban school districts in his remedial order. The case, Benson said, "became an effort to do an end run around *Rodriguez* but that didn't happen until January of '85. Before that time we were still trying to get in through that very narrow opening that *Milliken* left about interdistrict remedies if you can either prove intent by the state or effect in the suburban districts."[1] When Clark ruled against the state, Benson assumed that the verdict implied discriminatory intent. Benson also believed that a metropolitan plan could create integration, which would be educationally beneficial for black children and socially beneficial for white ones. A properly designed metropolitan plan could also overcome the major problem of forced busing, white flight. The plan would just have to extend far enough into the Missouri farmland north, east, and south of Kansas City so that families would have nowhere to go but Kansas.

From October of 1984 to January of 1985, Benson and the KCMSD's attorneys crafted a metropolitanwide desegregation plan. The plan was officially the KCMSD's but Benson was its primary architect. It was a massive piece of social planning. Twelve school districts would be combined into one "superdistrict." The proposed superdistrict would be divided into three subdistricts. The new district would cover more than 700 square miles and have 118,000 students — 35,000 students from the KCMSD and 83,000 from the eleven suburban school districts. In the 157-page plan, Benson outlined a system of electing the new school board, financing the new district, desegregating staff, and busing students across the metropolitan area.

The plan was not designed with educational quality as a fundamental goal, although Benson did speculate about how it would improve educational achievement. Its purpose was putting black and white students in the same school buildings. Benson would later say, "We [the lawyers] sat down and pretty much just carved up the surrounding districts and paired schools and developed that plan without a lot of input from educators or experts." The plan apparently suffered from the likelihood that it would prompt white

84 THE FIELD OF DREAMS

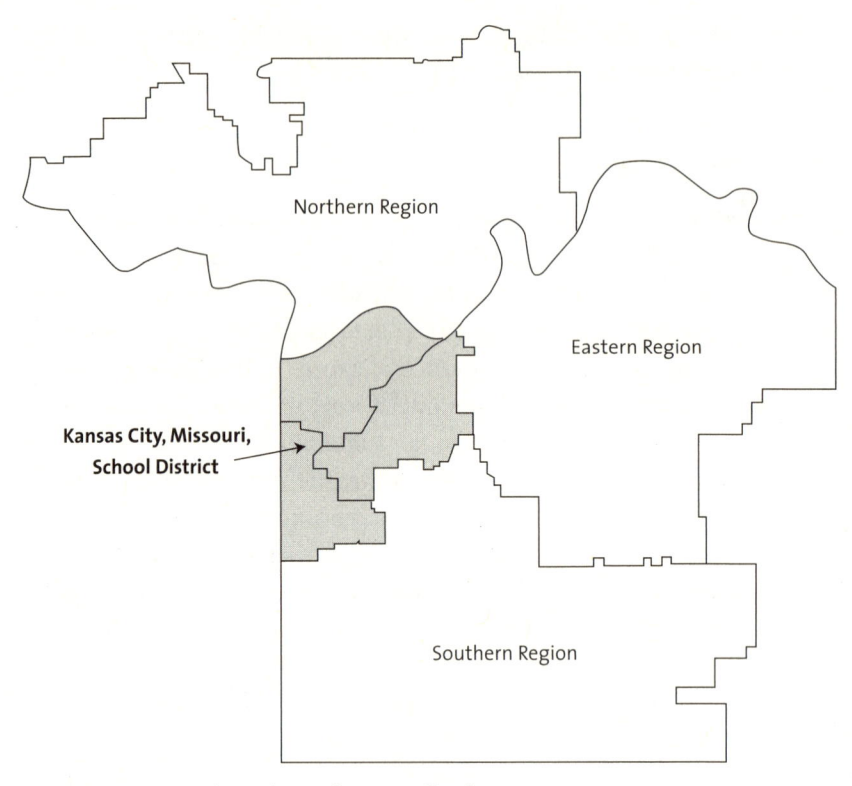

Proposed Kansas City, Missouri, "superdistrict"

flight. At trial Benson had argued that whites left the KCMSD because of racial animus, so it would seem that this plan would just create further flight. But this would not have been a problem, Benson later said, because "there wouldn't have been anywhere to flee to.... They [white families] would have had to go out into the farmland and we would have picked them up out there anyway."[2]

The KCMSD filed Benson's plan on Friday, January 18, 1985. One week later, Clark dismissed it. Judge Clark commended the KCMSD for being "thoughtful and thorough."[3] But, he said, he had no authority to "restructure or coerce local governments or their subdivisions." Given his later rulings, Clark's dismissal seems ironically guided by principles of judicial restraint. He said that "because of restrictions on this court's remedial powers in restructuring the operations of local and state government entities, that portion of the Kansas City school district plan which would require the consolidation of eleven suburban school districts with the Kansas City district goes far beyond the nature and extent of the constitutional violation this court found existed."[4]

An "End Run" on *San Antonio v. Rodriguez*

Judge Clark's rejection of Benson's busing plan brought the remedial strategy more in line with what the adjudicated victims, the black community, wanted. While some black leaders still advocated a metropolitanwide busing plan—for instance, Kansas City's leading black newsweekly, the *Call*, regularly ran editorials lamenting Clark's dismissal of the suburban districts—this opinion apparently was not shared by the black community. While Benson was "carving up" the surrounding school districts, a common complaint according to one black community leader was that "the money being spent on desegregation ought to be spent on upgrading the quality of education."[5]

Because of Clark's refusal to consider a metropolitanwide plan, Benson and the educational experts responsible for devising a new remedial plan were forced to concentrate on educational improvements. Any plan that was devised to reduce the racial isolation of the Kansas City schools would have to draw white students from private and suburban schools by improving the quality of education in the KCMSD. The new plan would have this as a fundamental goal. After Clark dismissed the first plan, Benson had only a few weeks to submit a plan concentrating on educational improvements. Admittedly lacking any knowledge of educational programs, he turned to Daniel Levine and Eugene Eubanks, both professors at the University of Missouri–Kansas City's School of Education. Emerging from their planning was an assortment of educational programs and capital improvements loosely arranged around what was called "effective schools."

The plan called for reduced class sizes, early childhood education programs, early language development programs, additional counselors, a precollegiate curriculum, and effective schools projects. Levine was the principal architect of the educational components and was at the time, according to Benson, steeped in the "effective schools" movement.[6] The effective schools movement developed in the 1970s as perhaps the dominant model of school improvement. According to its advocates, effective schools research had identified "correlates" of school success, such as strong instructional leadership, a clear sense of mission, demonstrated effective instructional behaviors, high expectations for all students, frequent monitoring of student achievement, and a safe and orderly environment.[7] While being vaguely tautological—effective schools appear unsurprisingly to have effective practices—the effective schools movement mistakenly believed that mimicking the attributes of effective schools would transform failing schools into successful ones. In other words, knowing the rather obvious point that strong instructional leadership helps make a school effective does not mean that one will know how to make good teachers out of the same people who had manifestly failed as teachers before. But Levine and other expert witnesses testified that the chronically failing teachers and principals of the KCMSD could be transformed into effective ones if their recommendations were adopted. The plan's projected cost, $68,917,000, was almost three-quarters of the KCMSD's yearly budget.

The state, as Clark required, also submitted a plan. Considering the KCMSD's ineffective management, the state's plan made some educational and fiscal sense, but considering Clark's precarious position with the Eighth Circuit, it was strategic suicide. The state made it clear from the beginning that its plan was not just a litany of programs to be thrown at the district. As it liked to point out, in contrast to the KCMSD, the state actually had a set of "guiding principles" and a "rationale" for its plan. The state said that its guiding principles would "aid in selecting the most productive components—those which efficiently accomplish the purposes set forth by the Court, while also avoiding the faddish, unproven, unrelated, and needlessly expensive components that are unlikely or unnecessary to accomplish the fundamental purposes." The state argued that the court's plan should not "be directed at general improvements in education" but only at "racially isolated black children." The plan should also "not be directed for the benefit of educational professionals, the general community, black children in integrated schools or white children."[8] The state contended that Kansas City's educational problems had more to do with mismanagement, dysfunctional families, parental apathy, and crime than racial isolation. To emphasize the importance of parental involvement, the state's plan devoted 30 pages out of 115 to outlining programs for promoting more parental involvement. These programs were designed to encourage parents to "alter the 'curriculum of the home.'" The state hoped to help parents monitor their children's leisure activities, promote more out-of-school reading, reduce television watching, and ensure that children did their homework. The total cost of the state's plan, $40,662,726, while costly, was significantly less than the cost of the KCMSD's plan.

Because of the Eighth Circuit's aggressive approach to desegregation,

Judge Clark could not seriously consider the state's plan. The Eighth Circuit had made it clear in the St. Louis *Liddell* case that narrowly tailored desegregation programs were unacceptable. Hence, a plan concentrating on students in racial isolation without trying to fundamentally transform education in Kansas City would have little chance of legal success. The state's vigorous opposition to the desegregation plan in St. Louis would undoubtedly make Judge Clark and the Eighth Circuit suspicious of the sincerity and the helpfulness of any of the state's proposals in Kansas City.

The state's legal strategy often seemed distorted by the political motivations of Missouri's attorneys general. The attorney general's office, which was responsible for devising the plan with the help of the state Department of Education, never offered competitive remedial plans for political reasons. An attorney general perceived to be funneling state revenues to Kansas City at the expense of school districts throughout the rest of the state would be in politically dangerous territory. Hence, each attorney general would present less-expensive plans, which were bound to be rejected, and then tell the state's voters that he was bravely but unsuccessfully defending the state's treasury from a rapacious federal judge. This was a pattern started by Attorney General John Ashcroft in the St. Louis desegregation case and continued by his successors in Kansas City.

Ashcroft, in fact, oversaw *Missouri v. Jenkins* until he was elected governor in 1984. He was succeeded as attorney general by Republican William Webster. Webster made no secret of his political ambitions and desire to follow the example of his predecessors. In the previous twenty years, Thomas Eagleton, John Danforth, Kit Bond, and John Ashcroft had successfully used the attorney general's office as a springboard to higher office. Part of Webster's strategy was to maintain a high public profile by shepherding controversial cases to the Supreme Court. Webster even admitted asking his staff to troll for potential Supreme Court cases, especially ones disputing the power of the federal government over the states. In his first six years as attorney general, the Supreme Court heard ten cases Webster oversaw, including *Cruzan v. Harmon*,[9] in which the right to die was at issue, and *Webster v. Reproductive Health Services*, in which abortion was at issue.[10] *Missouri v. Jenkins* was an ideal case for the ambitious Webster.[11] He could not only defend principles of federalism but also curry favor with Missourians for opposing "raids" on the state treasury. Webster was ultimately unsuccessful in his bid for higher office, losing the race for governor in 1992 to Mel Carnahan.

Webster's replacement, Jay Nixon, a Democrat, came into office with the same political ambitions as Webster and followed the same strategy on desegregation. He vehemently opposed the desegregation efforts in St. Louis and Kansas City and consistently appealed to the Supreme Court for relief. Nixon, however, was not ideologically wedded to federalism and opposed the desegregation plans on more prudential grounds, such as not wanting to waste resources. He would also be the only attorney general to have any success before the Supreme Court, which sided with him in its 1995 decision in *Missouri v. Jenkins*. But, like Webster, Nixon failed to win a higher elective office, losing to Kit Bond in a particularly contentious 1998 Senate campaign. His stance on desegregation, particularly in St. Louis, clearly hurt him. Bond received one-third of the black vote in the election. Considering their stalled political careers, Webster and Nixon's strategy of offering significantly less expensive remedial plans appears to be a miscalculation that possibly cost the state of Missouri hundreds of millions of dollars. This mistake became evident in the debate over the initial remedial plan.

In hearings before Judge Clark, both Benson and the state called witnesses to discuss the merits of their plans. Levine, the main architect of the district's plan and Benson's primary expert witness, testified regarding the KCMSD's plan that "basically, the goal in mind in putting together the components was and is in terms of academic achievement the goal expressed in the district's strategic plan." Levine told Clark that the "goal is in four or five years' time average achievement will be raised to the national average."[12] Levine's confidence was only partly justified. The literature on effective schools seemed to indicate that substantial improvements could be made in individual schools, but there had never been an attempt to implement an effective schools program throughout an entire district. Benson said that Levine "believed that if we could take the effective schools model and effectively and fully implement it in Kansas City classrooms that it would indeed bring achievement scores up to national norms in five years." But, Benson said, "there were two things wrong with that. One was that neither Dan Levine nor anybody else [involved with the case] had ever had any experience in doing that even in a single school. Not only they had no experience doing it in a single school, nobody at that time understood the problems of scaling something up to a districtwide remedy."[13]

In direct response to Levine's testimony, the state called Dr. Herbert Wahlberg, a professor of educational psychology at the University of Illinois at Chicago. In a piece of analysis that now reads like prophecy, Wahlberg testified that increased spending does not correlate with higher educational achievement and that the programs proposed by the KCMSD could actually hurt the quality of education in Kansas City. Wahlberg explained that such programs were harmful for three reasons. First, they are often adopted because they are new "rather than based on the fact that research has indicated or objective evaluation has indicated that they actually affect learning." Second, these programs create more bureaucracy in a school district. "Adding all of these extra programs and administrators," Wahlberg said, "causes administrative complexity, that is to say so many people in charge of so many programs they don't allow the teachers to do their jobs." Finally, such programs often interfere with students' learning basic skills. Wahlberg believed "that many of these programs don't add directly to direct services to the student; that is, teachers and programs that are actually delivered, but they are rather in the nature of a supplementary kind of thing that tends to pull children out of their regular classes for a special program here and a special program there rather than concentrating on the basic achievement levels which we would like to have for our students."[14] The contrasting views of the state's witnesses and the KCMSD's witnesses provided the backdrop for Judge Clark's opinion. He had to choose between a less expensive approach, which focused on traditional educational skills and making parents more active in their children's education, and a more expensive approach, which featured a myriad of special programs that could only be established and carried out by a cadre of expert administrators.

Much to the state's disappointment, Judge Clark took the path of expense and expertise. In his decision, Clark approved virtually every recommendation Professors Eubanks and Levine made in their remedial plan for the KCMSD. Clark offered no justification for these programs other than that they were necessary, according to his expert witnesses, to offset the detrimental effects of segregation. Clark at this point was clearly more interested in improving the quality of education in the KCMSD than in relieving racial isolation.

Clark's goal of improving education rather than desegregating was evident in his funding plan for implementing Levine's effective schools project. Clark specified that thousands of dollars would be dispersed to each school in the KCMSD according to the following guidelines:

1. For each of the 25 schools with enrollments of 90% or more black;
    a. 1985/86 school year $75,000 each school
    b. 1986/87 school year $100,000 each school
    c. 1987/88 school year $125,000 each school

2. For each of the remaining 43 schools;
   a. 1985/86 school year $50,000 each school
   b. 1986/87 school year $75,000 each school
   c. 1987/88 school year $100,000 each school.[15]

Clark did not specify how the money should be spent. Rather, "local parents, patrons, teachers, and principals would be involved in determining how these resources may be spent in order to increase the student achievement level in that school."[16]

Clark appeared to approve Benson's plan for two reasons. First, it had a better chance than the state's plan of keeping the Eighth Circuit from overruling his dismissal of the suburban school districts. Second, he seemed to accept Levine's prediction that test scores could be raised to national averages within four to five years. These two factors provided powerful practical, if not legal, justification for approving Benson's plan. The state challenged the evidence, but, according to Benson, Levine merely repeated that "the effective schools literature predicts these kinds of outcomes."[17] Levine's assurances and those of Benson's other experts gave Clark the cover of expertise. There was probably some naïveté on Clark's part. According to Benson, Clark's personal training and background had not prepared him to make critical judgments about what the expert witnesses said. "Here was a judge from a small town in south Missouri," Benson said, "who doesn't know anything about education except that his brother was a superintendent of schools and you've got warring experts here. How does a federal judge make sense of it?"[18] Considering the aggressive Eighth Circuit, the confident testimonials from Benson's experts, his own lack of educational expertise, and the state's possible disingenuousness, it is not surprising that Clark approved the costlier plan.

In the final plan, Clark actually granted $20 million more than the KCMSD requested. To pay for this plan, Clark decided that the state was obligated to pay $67,592,072 and the KCMSD was obligated to pay $20,140,472. He argued that "since the minority students in the KCMSD are the victims of racial discrimination which was mandated by the Constitution and statutes of the State of Missouri, it is only equitable to place the greatest burden of removing the vestiges of such discrimination and the continuing effects of same on the State rather than on those who are the victims."[19]

Besides approving Eubanks's and Levine's programs, Judge Clark also made several other important decisions in this opinion. First, he instructed the KCMSD to begin making plans for a districtwide magnet-school program. He ordered the KCMSD "to conduct extensive surveys within the KCMSD and throughout the Kansas City, Missouri, metropolitan area in order to determine what magnet themes appear to be most likely to attract non-minority enrollment."[20] The magnet plan that the district eventually presented to Judge Clark would become the most expensive desegregation plan in history.

Judge Clark also established a Desegregation Monitoring Committee (DMC) to oversee the implementation of his programs and to track their results. The committee had twelve members, but most of the power was vested in its chairman, Eugene Eubanks. Next to Clark and Benson, Eubanks would have the most influence on the case. For nearly a dozen years, he exercised more authority over the KCMSD than many of its superintendents.

Eubanks, who is black, grew up in Meadville, Pennsylvania, in the northwest corner of the state. After graduating from Edinboro State College in Pennsylvania (now Edinboro State University), he taught math in the Cleveland public schools for five years. He went on to earn a doctorate in educational administration from Michigan State. After a brief stint at the University of Delaware, he went to the University of Missouri at Kansas City in 1972. Almost as soon as he arrived he became involved with the KCMSD and has had, as he puts it, "an extensive and hopefully meaningful involvement with the district" ever since.[21] During the 1970s he helped the school district in devising and implementing the modest busing program, Plan 6C. In 1984 he served as interim superintendent of the KCMSD. When the school board asked him to be the full-time superintendent, he declined. To some, Eubanks's declining this office was the surest sign of his good judgment and intelligence. His term as interim superintendent made him well aware of the KCMSD's problems. An example he likes to mention was his attempt to implement a professional development program for the teachers of the district. Each Wednesday from 1 to 4 P.M. principals were supposed to provide programs to help teachers improve their instruction. One Wednesday afternoon he received a call from an irate teacher who complained that the school's principal was going to show them a film for professional development but the projector broke. Instead of letting the teachers leave, he made them sit in the classroom for the next three hours. "He [the principal]," Eubanks said, "never understood. It wasn't that I was trying to make people sit around a room for three hours." He concluded that he was "not going to win this one . . . with that kind of support out there."[22]

As chair of the DMC he had the support he needed—the power of the

United States Federal Court. He answered directly to Judge Clark and advised him on the programs. A ruling by the committee, which invariably followed Eubanks's lead, had the same authority as a ruling by Judge Clark if no one appealed within fifteen days. Since Clark almost always upheld Eubanks, few rulings of the DMC were ever appealed. The fact that Eubanks was named as chairman of the committee did raise questions about a conflict of interest. Eubanks, who helped design many of the remedial programs and was a friend and colleague of the other expert witnesses, was often accused of partiality. Once people started questioning the efficacy of the programs, Eubanks consistently defended them and blamed any failures on the KCMSD school board or administration.

Clark's final ruling was a mandated tax increase. The Missouri legislature had recently approved a property tax rollback, which reduced the funds available to the KCMSD. To make sure that the KCMSD could pay its share of the funding his plan required, Clark forbid the tax cut for anyone living in the KCMSD. Since the people of Kansas City did not receive their tax reduction, Clark's action amounted to a tax increase. Since 1969 the voters had rejected educational tax levy increases nineteen times, so Clark believed that Kansas City would never approve a tax increase to pay for school improvements. His defense of the mandated tax increase was simply that a federal judge must have the power to implement his orders, even if it required violating "two venerable maxims of the American tradition, 'Taxation without representation is tyranny'" and "'the power to tax involves the power to destroy.'"[23] Clark made sure to mention that the Eighth Circuit had "in the St. Louis desegregation plan recognized that 'the district court's equitable power includes the remedial power to order tax increases or the issuance of bonds.'" His only other justification was that his "plan seeks to be supportive of those high principles which separate our society from those which lack a commitment to human dignity."[24] Clark also felt no need to connect the condition of the KCMSD's facilities to a specific constitutional violation: "The State's argument," he said, "that the present condition of the facilities is not traceable to unlawful segregation is irrelevant."[25]

The black community applauded the true purpose of Judge Clark's plan, to improve education. The *Kansas City Times* reported that "many black parents are relieved . . . that Judge Clark's order was limited to educational improvements rather than plans to end racial isolation by busing."[26] This relief, however, would be brief because Clark's future orders would create an immense magnet-school system that would require an elaborate transportation system to bus children across the city to the appropriate magnet school. The burdens on suburban white students would not be so severe. They would receive door-to-door taxi service.

Clark's tax increase aroused little attention or protest in Kansas City. Because it merely kept the property tax at the previous level, many Kansas City citizens probably did not even notice it. Articles on the case in the local papers barely mentioned the tax increase, and the few articles that did buried it at the end of the story far from the front page.[27]

The Judicial Iron Triangle

The Eighth Circuit Court of Appeals had taken a particular pride in its aggressive approach to desegregation. During the 1970s and 1980s, appointees by Lyndon Johnson and Jimmy Carter dominated and were particularly vigilant in overseeing desegregation cases. In the St. Louis case, as discussed in Chapter 2, the Eighth Circuit overruled the trial judge, James Meredith, for ordering an insufficiently ambitious plan and ordered him to adopt a desegregation plan designed by Gary Orfield. Three Johnson appointees, Donald Lay, Gerald Heaney, and Myron Bright, were especially well known for their strong support of desegregation. In a 1998 tribute to Judge Bright, Lay described how an attorney representing a school board asked the Eighth Circuit's clerk which judges would be hearing his appeal. The clerk told the attorney Lay, Bright, and Heaney. The attorney responded "Oh xxxx" (x's in the original). Lay, Bright, and Heaney became known as the "Oh xxxx" panel among the court's employees.[28] With the addition of Theodore McMillian in 1978 and Richard Arnold in 1980, the Eighth Circuit had a solid majority of judges supporting aggressive desegregation remedies. In 1985, Judge Bright took senior status, which left four very aggressive supporters of desegregation on a circuit with a total of eight judges at the time.

Additionally, three Nixon and Reagan appointees turned out to be relatively strong supporters of desegregation as well. John Gibson, appointed by Reagan in 1982, at times seemed indistinguishable from Democratic appointees. And Donald Ross, appointed in 1970; George Fagg, appointed in 1982; and Roger Wollman, appointed in 1985, were only slightly less aggressive than Gibson. The question with the Eighth Circuit was not whether it was going to require desegregation, but how substantial the remedies would have to be to pass its scrutiny.

With this aggressive appellate court in place, *Missouri v. Jenkins* fell into a pattern from the mid-1980s through the mid-1990s. Benson and the KCMSD would make requests for programs, buildings, and tax increases to Judge Clark; Clark would approve these requests; the state would appeal to the Eighth Circuit; and the appeals court would then uphold Judge Clark's rulings. Only one of Clark's major rulings, an income-tax increase, was overturned by the Eighth Circuit. This process completed its first cycle when the state, the KCMSD, and Benson all appealed parts of Judge Clark's first two orders.

The state appealed the verdict and Clark's initial remedial plan, while the KCMSD and Benson appealed the dismissal of the suburban school districts. The Eighth Circuit, which heard the case en banc, upheld Judge Clark's ruling in a 5-3 decision. It did modify parts of Judge Clark's opinion, however. For instance, it ruled that the KCMSD should have to pay for more of the desegregation costs. In short, the appeals court "affirm[ed] the judgment of the district court and its intradistrict remedy imposed upon the State and the KCMSD with the exceptions we have discussed above that equalize the cost between the State and KCMSD."[29]

Despite the court's 5-3 decision, only four justices agreed with Judge Clark's release of the suburban school districts. Judge Richard Arnold concurred and dissented in part. He argued that Clark erred because "it is not necessary that each school district subjected to an interdistrict remedy have itself committed a constitutional violation."[30] Arnold believed that housing discrimination had interdistrict effects, which justified including the suburban districts in the remedy.

The most forceful dissent came from Judges Heaney, Lay, and McMillian, who thought that Judge Clark's plan was insufficient. Like Judge Arnold's dissent, theirs was leveled at the dismissal of the eleven suburban school districts. Judge Lay, the author of the dissent, began, "A world of rhetoric cannot hide the world of fact. No one can deny that the school systems within the Kansas City metropolitan area were racially segregated before 1954, continued to be segregated after 1954, and that virtually all remain segregated today." Forebodingly, he continued: "It now remains for the people of metropolitan Kansas City to choose whether their community and school systems shall continue to foster an environment of racial separation." "This remedy is fine as far as it goes," he concluded; "however, it falls far short of the relief that should be required under the facts of this case."[31] The Eighth Circuit clearly signaled that Clark needed to be very aggressive. No one urged restraint.

With the Eighth Circuit's decision, Benson knew that even though he had not succeeded in reinstating the suburban school districts, virtually any intradistrict plan he proposed would be approved and upheld. Clark, the Eighth Circuit, and Benson were now a closed system.

If You Build It, They Will Come

When Judge Clark issued his initial remedial order, he also required the KCMSD to conduct a survey to find out what magnet-school themes would be most appealing to suburban- and private-school parents. The results from this survey were not encouraging. Market Information Services, the research firm that conducted the survey for the KCMSD, submitted both quantitative and qualitative reports. Its quantitative report, submitted in January 1986, was based on a telephone survey of 606 randomly selected parents in the KCMSD and suburban districts. According to this survey, the report said, "white parents appear more selective and discriminating regarding school programs than minorities. Thus, Magnet School programs should be selected which create the greatest interest among white parents." The percentages from the survey, however, indicated that white parents were unlikely to enroll their children in magnet schools, at least in the numbers needed to create integration. (See table 4.1.) Seventy-three percent of suburban public school parents, 90 percent of suburban private school parents, and 78 percent of KCMSD private school parents reported that they thought their child's school was excellent or very good.[32]

In March of 1986, Market Information Services filed the qualitative report. This report relied on the surveys and less scientific focus-group reaction and individual interviews. Parents "familiar" with Kansas City's limited magnet-school program expressed "disappointment" with them, calling them a good "concept" but ineffectively implemented. Private school parents expressed a "moderate-to-low overall level of interest" in magnet schools. Only parents in three suburban districts expressed any significant interest, but, the report stated, "it may be anticipated that any enrollment from these areas will be slow."[33] In spite of these results, the school district pursued a magnet plan rather than asking Judge Clark to consider other alternatives.

The school district's leadership, however, was divided about the size of the magnet plan. On one side were Superintendent Claude Perkins and a minority of school board members, who opposed a large magnet-school plan. On the other side were a majority of the school board members led by the board

Table 4.1 Parent Evaluation of Child's Education, 1986

	Total (N=606)	Suburban (White) Public (N=340)	Suburban (White) Private (N=39)	Kansas City District Public (N=182)	Kansas City District Private (N=45)
Excellent	24%	25%	62%	10%	40%
Very Good	40	48	28	27	38
Good	26	22	5	40	18
Fair	9	4	5	20	4
Poor	1	1	—	2	—
Very Poor	1	1	—	1	—

Source: Market Information Services, *Magnet School Survey*, January 13, 1986.

president, Sue Fulson, and Benson, who supported "magnetizing" almost all the district's schools.

Initially, Perkins was responsible for creating the plan. Fulson's bloc on the school board rejected five of Perkins's plans for being too small in scale. Most of these plans proposed turning only five to ten schools into magnet schools.[34] Because Perkins was not going to propose or support a large magnet program, the board voted to ask Daniel Levine and Phale Hale, an educational consultant who was then overseeing a magnet program in Rochester, New York, to design a comprehensive plan for the district.

Shortly after the board brought in Levine and Hale, Judge Clark gave the district further advice about designing its magnet-school program. Reiterating his position that money was no object, on June 16, 1986, Clark wrote, "The long-term goal of this Court's remedial order is to make available to *all* KCMSD students educational opportunities equal to or greater than those presently available in the average Kansas City, Missouri metropolitan school district. In achieving this goal the victims of unconstitutional segregation will be restored to the position they would have occupied absent such conduct, while establishing an environment designed to maintain and attract nonminority enrollment." This order essentially freed Levine and Hale to craft their ideal school district. In less than a month, Levine and Hale, with Benson's help, drew up a $180 million plan that would completely transform the district. Anyone familiar with Levine's recent research would have expected such a plan. Two years earlier Levine co-authored a paper for the U.S. Department of Education that argued that "an emphasis on 'gradual progress' is not appropriate for inner city schools. . . . Some degree of substantial and relatively quick change is necessary in 'difficult' schools if fundamental operating patterns are to be reversed."[35] The court, Levine also found, was the best institution available for creating these dramatic changes.

Dramatic changes were just what Levine and Hale proposed, and they readily admitted that their "design for magnet schools for the KCMSD is quite ambitious."[36] In their "pink" plan (it was printed on pink paper), in order "to avoid the establishment of a two-tier system of schools," they recommended that every high school and middle school and half of the district elementary schools be converted to magnet schools.[37] This conversion would automatically create the need for new facilities to accommodate these special magnet-school themes. It would also immediately add another layer of bureaucracy. To address this issue, Levine and Hale recommended "establishing a new Associate Superintendent position with adequate staff to implement and monitor the program." The plan required a minimum of twenty more central administrators, not including a support staff, just to implement and run the special programs, plus additional administrators at each school. To emphasize the complexity of their plan, Levine and Hale cautioned, "There has to be a great deal of coordination with administrative departments; coordination of education design with facility development; monitoring of construction milestones; development and clarification of staffing and admissions procedures; monitoring of implementation—including reviews of changes and modifications; development of recruitment guidelines; development of public information materials; counseling of students and parents; and review and administration of budgets."[38]

At the elementary and middle school levels, they recommended themes such as computers unlimited, communications and writing, environmental sciences, foreign languages, classical Greek, science and math, and visual and performing arts. At the high school level, they recommended engineering and technology, law and public service, ROTC, business, agribusiness, international studies, and health professions. All of these themes would require special facilities and instructors. Cost was never a consideration. Noticeably absent in the plan and its modifications were phrases such as "if possible" or "if it can be afforded." The total estimated cost for this plan came to $187 million, nearly double the KCMSD's yearly budget.

The hope for this plan, Benson later recalled, was to create schools where everyone would be interested in and excited about the same subject: "We believed that if you put together a science school you will attract kids and their parents who are truly interested in science and are turned on and enthusiastic about science and you will attract teachers over time. If the school beforehand was just a normal school, teachers who don't like science will transfer out and teachers who do like science will transfer in, and so you'll have the perfect conditions. . . . [T]herefore, the school will flower. It will blossom. It will be great."[39] Not surprisingly, the state was less taken with the idea, and it vigorously contested the cost and questioned the potential effectiveness of the KCMSD's magnet-school plan.

The debate proceeded in two stages. The first stage involved the magnet programs themselves. The second stage involved the long-range capital improvements — the special facilities and renovations that the magnet schools would need. At the initial stage, the state argued that the plan was "hastily drafted" and "magnetize[d] too many schools over a short period of time," and it repeated its contention that many of the programs were actually counterproductive to the court's goal of improving students' fundamental skills.[40]

Judge Clark again disregarded the state's criticisms and relied on the KCMSD's educational experts to support his ruling in favor of the KCMSD's magnet-school plan. "In response to the Court's request," Clark wrote, "the KCMSD submitted a long-term magnet-school plan that was the product of extensive research, experience, and planning of nationally respected experts on magnet schools." Based on the expert testimony, Clark said, "the Court believes that the proposed magnet plan is so attractive that it would draw non-minority students from the private schools who have abandoned or avoided the KCMSD, and draw in additional non-minority students from the suburbs."[41] Clark, however, had to know that the evidence presented for such a belief was slender at best. The survey he ordered had shown little parental interest in the proposed magnet schools. The *Kansas City Times* publicized this fact as well, reporting that "parents showed little interest in schools for the performing arts, foreign languages, and military careers."[42] But the underlying problem with the plan was that, as the survey showed, most suburban parents who were supposed to be enticed to send their children to KCMSD schools were more than satisfied with their children's current schools. With such a large number of parents already satisfied, the magnet-school plan had no chance of drawing in the thousands of white students necessary to racially balance the KCMSD, especially given the many unpopular magnet themes.

Clark still approved the plan in its entirety and held the state and the KCMSD "joint and severably liable" for $53 million of the estimated cost of $143 million. This meant that the state would be responsible for any part of the KCMSD's share that the district could not pay for. Clark also ruled that the state was solely liable for the remaining $90 million because it "contributed to, if not precipitated, an atmosphere which prevented the KCMSD from raising the necessary funds to maintain its schools."[43] This, however, was a preliminary ruling. The KCMSD had more work to do on its plan because it wanted to include more capital improvements. Another nine months would transpire before Clark issued his final ruling.

During these intervening months, the state continued its attack on the KCMSD's plan. According to the state, the plan relied "on a demonstrably unrealistic prediction of student enrollments," proposed "funding allocations . . . that virtually absolve[d] the KCMSD and the citizens of the District of their traditional responsibility to support public education," and "would be the waste of substantial funds already expended on renovation of buildings KCMSD now proposes to abandon, and the construction of unneeded facilities that will further tax KCMSD's demonstrated inability to maintain the assets it presently administers."[44] The state repeatedly argued that many, if not most, of the magnet programs were unnecessary and educationally counterproductive. The plan, according to the state, was a transparent attempt to raid the state treasury.

In support of its position, the state first argued that the KCMSD overestimated the number of new students that the magnet-school program would bring into the district. All of the data indicated that the student population would decline in Kansas City at least through the year 2005. But the KCMSD assumed that the plan would draw enough white students into the district to make the overall student population 40 percent nonminority. The KCMSD had predicted that by 1990 there would be 47,107 students in the district even though there were only 35,899 during the 1986–87 school year. The KCMSD obviously expected 11,000 new students to enroll in the district. To accommodate these students, the KCMSD would need a variety of new facilities. The state, once again, pointed out that the magnet themes proposed by the KCMSD were relatively unpopular according to Judge Clark's own survey. "Parents," the state argued, "are considerably more interested in the basics of education than such esoteric concepts as the 'Classical Greek' education and foreign language programs that are currently showcased by KCMSD. In fact, KCMSD has consistently proposed magnet programs that generated low levels of community interest or were not included in the surveys at all."[45]

The state also argued that the KCMSD's plan virtually eliminated the district's duty to finance the education of the children of Kansas City. The KCMSD argued that the state was "the primary constitutional violator" and therefore should bear most of the cost, at least 94 percent, of its capital-improvements program. To the state, this was another blatant attempt on the part of the KCMSD to extract money for physical improvements in the name of desegregation.

The state's final point was that the KCMSD plan called for the demolition of newly renovated buildings in order to build new facilities that would accommodate their special magnet programs. For example, Central High, which had undergone substantial renovation, was to be torn down and replaced with a special facility to house the Classical Greek High School. According to the KCMSD, the magnet theme required a facility with Olympic swimming and diving pools, an indoor track, and a complete gymnastics facility. The state contended that tearing down newly renovated buildings in order to build lavish complexes was a waste of money.

The state had submitted a long-range capital-improvement plan that emphasized more modest improvements and less exotic programs, but Clark summarily dismissed it, finding that a plan that cost $61,074,565 was unsatisfactory compared to the KCMSD's $282,401,915 plan. The state's plan, Clark said, "would result in unsightly floor coverings with unsightly sections of mismatched carpeting and tile, and individual walls possessing different shades of paint." The state also made the mistake of proposing "to replace only those tiles which are loose or damaged with a new tile of similar color" and replacing "only the sections of carpeting which are worn or torn." Clark would not allow this "patch and repair approach" because it would not achieve "suburban comparability or the visual attractiveness sought by the Court."[46]

The state made the mistake of ignoring Judge Clark's precarious position with the Eighth Circuit. Less than a year before, the Eighth Circuit barely upheld Clark's ruling, with the dissenters calling for him to do more. The only way for Clark to keep the suburban districts out of the remedial plan was to provide a significant windfall for the KCMSD. He had made it clear that he wanted a substantial overhaul of the district and that disregarding his wishes irritated him. His tone indicated that he was becoming increasingly frustrated with the state's insensitivity. Its comparatively spartan plan was not helpful.

Individuals on all sides of the case believe that if the state had offered a plan that cost at least half as much as the KCMSD's, Clark might have approved it or possibly split the difference with the KCMSD's plan. University of Missouri professor Eubanks said that significantly lowballing the KCMSD's plan was "bad strategy on the part of the state." The court, he said, "was given two plans, a massive plan by the district and the plaintiff's counsel and a totally inadequate plan by the state. So you've got polar extremes and you've got all this evidence showing how bad the situation is.... If the state had put forward a meaningful response, the state could have saved maybe 300 million dollars."[47] Pete Hutchison of the conservative Landmark Legal Foundation agreed:

> One of the things we always understood around here was that Judge Clark can only rule on what he's presented with. And when the plaintiffs and the school district were presenting him with these outrageous and expensive and dramatic and sweeping plans and the state was just coming in and saying that costs too much and never really advanced a viable alternative and I think that was a mistake.... I don't think he [Judge Clark] had too terribly many options. But you know he did have the option to say you know what, this is not going to work. I mean this is too much. I'm not going to approve this. Go back to the drawing board.[48]

But Clark could hardly tell the KCMSD to start over when he had already held that each day it violated the Constitution did untold harm to the children of Kansas City. A leisurely remedial pace would appear hypocritical.

In the end, Clark seemed taken by the exhaustive and even shocking nature of the plan. His final order approving the KCMSD's plan, which had increased in cost by another $100 million, praised the KCMSD for its comprehensiveness. Clark specifically cited examples such as the Kansas City Technical Center, which would offer "programs ranging from heating and air conditioning to cosmetology to robotics."[49]

These unusual magnet themes were controversial, but the controversy surrounding these schools paled in comparison to that stirred up by Clark's method of funding them. The KCMSD could not provide its share of the funding, so Clark decided that it was necessary to order tax increases once again. He said that he was reluctant to mandate another tax increase but that he must "weigh the constitutional rights of the taxpayers against the constitutional rights of plaintiff students" and that ultimately the "Court is of the opinion that the balance is clearly in favor of the students who are helpless without the aid of this Court."[50]

Clark ultimately ordered two tax increases. The first was an increase in property taxes. The property of residents of the KCMSD was taxed at a rate of $2.05 per $100 of assessed value. Clark nearly doubled that rate to $4.00 per

$100 of assessed value. Hence, a person owning a $75,000 home would owe $3,000 instead of $1,537.50. The second tax increase was an entirely new tax based on where people worked rather than where they lived or owned property. Clark decided to levy an income tax on "residents and non-residents of the KCMSD" who worked within the district. This tax was a "1.5% increase as a surcharge on the Missouri State Income Tax," raising the rate from 6 percent to 7.5 percent. "During the hearing on the liability issue in this case," Clark explained, "there was an abundance of evidence that many residents of the KCMSD left the district and moved to the suburbs because of the district's efforts to integrate its schools but continue to be employed in the district.... [T]he Court has determined that it would be equitable to involve these people in a plan to help defray the district's desegregation expense."[51]

Unlike his previous tax increase, these two prompted a storm of protest in Kansas City. Bill Waris, the Jackson County tax collector, denounced the decision, saying that "this is tyranny" and that "when one man — whether it is King George or Judge Clark — attempts to impose his will on a free citizenry unilaterally we must stand up and be counted."[52] Governor Ashcroft attacked Clark's order as "excessive, exorbitant and extravagant" and vowed "to use every legal means at our disposal to fight this order."[53] This rhetoric reflected a common sentiment in Kansas City. Angry citizens staged several symbolic tea parties, where they dropped tea bags into patriotically decorated boxes, listened to fulminating speeches about tyranny, and sang patriotic songs.[54]

The business community was divided about the tax increases. Some local businessmen, especially contractors, criticized the decision because of its potential to depress economic development. Gary H. Cortes, president of a large contracting company, said, "People will say, 'Why should I build there if I'm being charged these surcharges when I can go somewhere else and not have it.'"[55] But larger corporations such as Hallmark publicly praised Clark and the tax increase and criticized those who opposed them for being callous to the needs of Kansas City's children.

The *Kansas City Times* and *Star*, the morning and afternoon editions of the same paper, supported Clark's tax increases. The *Times* published two editorials on the same day titled "Children's Rights First" and "The Hollow Protesters." Dismissing criticism of the ruling as a "babble of protests," the paper asserted: "Judge Russell G. Clark's last resort to finance rehabilitation of the Kansas City School District is not an easy one. But it is right." The only legitimate concern about the order, according to the *Times*, was "in the case of people whom higher taxes will push into official poverty." "But," it continued, "almost all, particularly fair-weather civic leaders who mouthed platitudes when the district sought approval of higher tax levies, and politicians more worried about their favorite side-show projects than developments of substance, are missing the point. . . . It is government['s] responsibility to fund basic social needs."[56]

This sharp rebuke from the *Star* and *Times* was particularly hypocritical. Throughout the 1970s and 1980s, they ran multiple sensational exposés about mismanagement and waste in the KCMSD administration, incompetent school boards, violent attacks by students on teachers, and unqualified instructors. These sensational stories solidified public opposition to the KCMSD's pleas for more money. Now, however, the paper ignored its own culpability, concluding, "So let the posturing proceed. The very people who have complained loudly about the public schools, and who have shrunk from doing anything constructive about them in the past, now profess shock over a remedy. They do so, knowing full well the remedy is outside their competence and now outside their ability to affect. It's a shabby, destructive performance."[57]

Those looking for a principled defense of Clark's tax increase had to turn to Benson. He had mentioned a property tax increase in his briefs but never proposed an income tax surcharge, and he found defending the income tax surcharge difficult if not impossible.[58] There were too many complications. Shortly after the ruling, Benson said, "Everybody's got questions." One company had asked about how to tax a supervisor "who works only three or four days in his Kansas City office and travels the rest of the month." Benson told the *Kansas City Star*, "There are a million questions like this."[59] Income from savings accounts was also taxed, so if someone worked within the KCMSD but lived outside it, would his income from savings accounts be taxed? Or what if someone lived and worked outside the KCMSD but his bank was inside the KCMSD? Mark Bredemeier of the Landmark Legal Foundation recalled that there were things "that nobody ever thought about" and that there was "no way you could implement something like that fairly." This tax, he said, is the perfect example of why legislatures, not judges, make policy.[60] The accessibility of legislators allows interest groups to point out the problems with implementing such an unusual tax.

The complexity of Clark's income tax forced the Missouri Department of Revenue to hire twelve additional employees just to work on the tax.[61] The *Kansas City Star* warned its readers on its front page, "If you think figuring income taxes is a headache now[,] wait until you see the paper work being cooked up to comply with the court-order surcharge for Kansas City schools. The Missouri Department of Revenue is preparing 10 special forms to collect the 25% increase."[62] The city of Kansas City decided that it would apply the tax to all of its employees. Thomas Lewinsohn, the city's director of personnel, explained, "We basically made the decision that all city employees work out of City Hall and all are subject to Judge Clark's order." The tax also applied to employees at the Kansas City International Airport, which was located far north of the KCMSD. The city gave the astonishing justification that it made this decision to set a good example. Airport employees protested that it was forced charitable giving. The police department, whose employees were also subject to the tax surcharge, said that the tax was too complicated. An employee from its budget department told the *Kansas City Star*, "To tell you the truth, this all came so quickly [that] I'm not sure anyone really knew exactly what to do. We thought we had to start taking it out . . . and we decided we'd take it out for everybody. Until we have definite answers, I don't think we can do any better than that for now."[63] The tax surcharge was doomed from the beginning.[64]

One group that apparently seemed less distressed by the tax increase was Kansas City's black community. Some leaders of the black community were initially optimistic about the magnet plan and tax increases—the *Call* consistently praised both—and incorrectly believed that the plan would not require substantial busing.[65]

Former Kansas City NAACP chairman Jeremiah Cameron, however, maintained a steady attack on the plan, the tax increase, the school board, and the district's teachers. Even before Judge Clark's ruling, Cameron had advised the readers of the *Call* not to expect much from the desegregation case because the school district's problems were the school board and its teachers. "Nearly as often as the clouds form in the skies and the bright stars shine on a dark night," he said, "I have in these columns informed the black community of constant monitoring of the school board meetings, which are mainly 'run' by a group of women from whom that awful woman of the Old Testament, that hater of prophets and good men called Jezebel, could take lessons."[66]

Immediately after Clark's ruling, Cameron asked, "Can a judge—even the Supreme Court—command citizens to take their hard earned dollars and pour them down a sewer—not too harsh a metaphor for this school board, aided and abetted by a well-meaning but educationally imperceptive plaintiff lawyer [Arthur Benson]—in the name of integration? Is it desirable to be integrated on a sinking ship—an educational Titanic?"⁶⁷ A few months later, he wrote:

> Because of the savage resentment aroused in the education establishments—the National Education Association and the American Federation of Teachers especially—most reports refuse to lay the blame where it belongs, at the doors of inept, grossly mistrained and uninspired and uninspiring teachers. . . . It will make little difference whether we put on paper the basic curricula of Secretary [of Education, William] Bennett or build the palaces which Judge Clark believes will cause whites to flock to Kansas City schools, if we continue to let dumb—and I mean dumb—teachers handle the subject matter.⁶⁸

At the moment, Cameron seemed slightly out of step with the black community, but in reality, he was ahead of the curve. Others would shortly echo him.

Judge Clark's rulings generated intense resentment, but protests against him were remarkably civil. Unlike in Boston, no angry mobs of parents threatened violence. Clark did receive angry mail from outraged taxpayers—eventually enough to fill two file drawers—and some contained threats serious enough to require security at his home, but public protest was relatively restrained. Other than the occasional "tea party," most protest was carried on through op-ed pieces and talk radio. Any tangible effort to thwart Clark's plans had to be carried out in the courts.

It would be the state and a local conservative public advocacy law firm, the Landmark Legal Foundation, that would battle it out. The day Judge Clark ordered the tax increases, Landmark attorney Mark Bredemeier announced that he would challenge Clark's order. Landmark asked Judge Clark to name the foundation as an intervenor on behalf of Kansas City's taxpayers, but Clark denied the request. Landmark eventually appealed to the Eighth Circuit to be named intervenor on behalf of over 14,000 Kansas City citizens. Icelean Clark, the president of a black homeowners' association, was their representative plaintiff.

While many taxpayers obviously agreed with Landmark, the firm did face criticism from some of the most influential citizens and corporations in Kansas City. The Hallmark Corporation was initially quite critical. When it came time to pay Clark's taxes, however, Hallmark paid them under protest, which ironically made Landmark their legal representation. If Clark's tax increases were overturned, only individuals and businesses that paid them under protest would receive a refund. Since Landmark represented those protesting the taxes, it would be responsible for disbursing the refunds. In its protest letter, Hallmark said, "We believe the increased tax liability ordered by the U.S. District Court produces an appropriate level of taxation. We are willing and want to pay our fair share of any such tax increase." But, the company continued, because there was the chance the tax increase would be ruled invalid, "we have decided to protest the court-ordered portion of our 1987 property taxes."[69] The Civic Council of Greater Kansas City, which was comprised of presidents and chief executives of large companies in Kansas City, adopted a similar position. The chairman of the Civic Council was Irvine O. Hockaday Jr., president and CEO of Hallmark. The council even filed a brief with the Eighth Circuit saying that Judge Clark's tax increases were appropriate. Their brief acknowledged that many of their corporations paid their taxes under protest but only "in order to discharge fiduciary duties and to protect the interests of these corporations in case the imposition of such taxes is overruled or modified."[70]

A Distinction without a Difference: I

On appeal before the Eighth Circuit, the Landmark Legal Foundation concentrated its arguments on becoming an official intervenor and on Judge Clark's tax increase. The state also contested the tax increase but was more concerned with overturning Clark's remedial orders than his method of funding them. The remedial orders — tax increase or no tax increase — would drain the state's treasury.

Landmark chose not to challenge Clark's remedial orders. The tax increase was Landmark's primary concern. Mark Bredemeier later commented:

> I would argue that all of that scheme [Clark's remedial plan and tax increases] was indefensible.... But from a legal standpoint... the only thing ... that the court can do is require ... that remedy. ... As long as the state of Missouri funds it, which they were griping about it but they were funding it, the courts are not allowed to go any further than that.

Clark, he argued, "would be more empowered to go down to Jefferson City and cordon off the capitol and say we're going to auction off the capitol to pay a portion of the deal." Clark ordered the tax increase, Bredemeier believes, to "deal with the unpopular political decision of having the state and the state general coffers and therefore everybody in the state including people in Cape Girardeau pay for this desegregation case in Kansas City."[71]

Landmark, facing an unsympathetic appellate court, made five general arguments against the tax increases: they violated the constitutional principle of separation of powers, ignored the constitutional principle of federalism, exceeded judicial equity power, violated principles of due process, and violated provisions of the Missouri Constitution and state law.[72] Its strongest specific arguments, and the only ones that ever had a chance of succeeding, were directed at Clark's income tax surcharge. "The income tax surcharge," Landmark argued,

> is both overinclusive and underinclusive in that it automatically penalizes suburban school district residents—citizens who already pay a property tax to support one school district—who earn income within the Kansas City, Missouri School District, all because of purported "white flight" due to court-ordered integration. Yet the District Court already held that these taxpayers were not guilty of constitutional violations. Further, this "remedy" assesses damages against some suburban taxpayers who never lived in, or fled, the district. It punishes those who moved into a suburban district from Omaha or Montreal. It penalizes those born, raised and still living in Independence or Lee's Summit. It even taxes blacks who moved to the suburbs to flee urban crime, congestion and, in some instances, the KCMSD. It punishes those who moved to the suburban districts for reasons altogether unrelated to education or integration. And yet the District Court's classification fails to tax white racists who fled the city to avoid desegregation but now live and work outside the Kansas City school district, perhaps in the suburbs, perhaps in Des Moines.

In short, the income tax surcharge was inapt.

The state reiterated the arguments it presented in district court against the magnet plan and made many of the same arguments as Landmark against the tax increases. Arthur Benson, while most interested in defending Clark's remedies, argued that since Clark had found a constitutional violation and had been upheld by the Eighth Circuit, he had to be able to determine how the remedy should be funded. Denying Clark the power to raise taxes was tantamount to denying the plaintiffs their constitutional right to equal protection under the law.

A five-member panel of the Eighth Circuit upheld Judge Clark, denied Landmark's application to intervene, and denied the state's request for a rehearing en banc. Judge Gibson, joined by Judges Heaney and McMillian, authored the 3-2 opinion. He wrote: "We affirm the judgment of the district court with respect to scope of the remedy as to magnet schools and capital improvements with some slight modifications."[73] These slight modifications left the substance of the plan unchanged. The court dismissed all of the state's arguments against the remedial plan, including its related arguments based on the tenth amendment and the principle of separation of powers." "These doctrines," it asserted "simply have no bearing on the district court's operations in enforcing its judgement."[74] The court offered no further justification for this dismissal.

The court struck down the income tax surcharge as an unjustified expansion of judicial authority. The reversal was not based on constitutional principle, however. Rather, the court held that "the district court has exceeded its authority in ordering the collection of school district revenue from an entirely new source, with all funds delivered to one district for a specified purpose."[75] Other than the fact that it came from a "new source," the majority had no disagreement with the tax.

Two judges, Pasco Bowman and Roger Wollman, dissented from the majority, saying that the case needed to be heard by the entire Eighth Circuit. Judge Bowman wrote, "The sheer immensity of the programs encompassed by the district court's order . . . [is] concededly without parallel in any other school district case. Similarly, in no other case has federal judicial power been used to impose a tax increase in order to provide funding for a desegregation remedy." In his years on the court, he said, "I have not seen a case more deserving than this one of thoughtful consideration by the entire court. The decision as it stands appears to arrogate to the federally [sic] judiciary vast powers that under the Tenth Amendment are reserved to the states or to the people."[76] There would not be a hearing before the entire Eighth Circuit. The next stop for *Missouri v. Jenkins* was the Supreme Court.

A Distinction without a Difference: II

The appeals court's approval of Judge Clark's plan and property tax increase set the stage for an appeal to the Supreme Court. In 1987, Benson had already appealed Clark's dismissal of the suburban school districts in *Milliken I* but was denied certiorari, indicating the Court's unwillingness to reconsider the appropriateness of metropolitanwide busing plans. But the controversy surrounding Judge Clark's tax increases made it likely that the Court would want to hear an appeal on that issue. Because the Eighth Circuit denied Landmark's application to intervene, the state was solely responsible for an appeal to the Supreme Court. It requested certiorari on the tax increases and the remedial plans.[77]

To the state's disappointment, the Supreme Court granted certiorari only on the issue of the property tax increase. To the KCMSD's relief, the Court declined to review whether the scope of Judge Clark's remedial plan was justified. School board president Sue Fulson said the Court's decision "should be a great upper" for the district, which she said was struggling with low morale. "It reaffirms that what we are trying to do is the right thing to do all the way through to the Supreme Court."[78] The obvious loser was the state. If the Supreme Court struck down Clark's tax increases, the state would have to pay more of the KCMSD's share of the remedy. Benson commented that before the case went before the Court, "It might be in their [the state's] interest to say they screwed up" in appealing Clark's rulings.[79]

The state did not change its position, and on October 30, 1989, the Supreme Court heard oral arguments. Justices Scalia and Kennedy seemed most skeptical of Clark's actions. Kennedy went beyond the tax increase and asked KCMSD attorney Allen Snyder if Clark's remedial plan was not "intrusive" and "drastic." And Scalia asked if a remedy should go as far as "to gold plate the schools."[80] Much of the questioning revolved around the technical issue of whether the state filed its appeal in a timely manner. The issue of taxation received less attention than expected, leading Arthur Benson to speculate that the Court might simply rule on whether the state followed the proper procedure.

But the Court did address the issue of judicial taxation. The technically unanimous decision, written by Justice Byron White, held that Judge Clark had no authority to mandate specific tax rates but that he did have the authority to enjoin the state law, Proposition C, and let the district decide a sufficient rate. The district court, White wrote, "could have authorized or required KCMSD to levy property taxes at a rate adequate to fund the desegregation remedy and could have enjoined the operation of state laws that would have prevented KCMSD from exercising this power." This ruling, however, was transparent to most observers of the Court, for there was little difference between Judge Clark setting the tax rate and letting the KCMSD set the tax rate, as long he is enjoining state law. "Authorizing and directing local government institutions to devise and implement remedies," White asserted, "not only protects the function of those institutions but, to the extent possible, also places the responsibility for solutions to the problems of segregation upon those who have themselves created the problems."[81] This defense was inadequate for one reason: the KCMSD had already recommended the tax increase to Judge Clark. It had "devised" and, in a perverted sense, "implemented" the tax increase through Judge Clark. Kansas Citians knew that this ruling would have no effect on what tax increases they faced. In fact, nothing changed. The Court's ruling only made the KCMSD feel more comfortable in recommending tax increases to Judge Clark, which it did shortly after this decision. In July of 1990, three months after the Court's ruling, the *Kansas City Star* reported, "It's official. The Kansas City school board can bypass voters and raise the district's property tax levy by 24 percent."[82] The school board had decided that it needed an extra $68 million in pay raises for all district employees. The school board recommended the tax increase to Judge Clark, who subsequently gave his approval.

The disingenuousness of the Court's decision was not lost on four of its members. Justice Kennedy, joined by Chief Justice Rehnquist and Justices O'Connor and Scalia, wrote an opinion concurring in part and dissenting in part. Kennedy concurred that Judge Clark overstepped his authority by mandating a specific tax increase, but he disagreed that the solution was to let the KCMSD decide how much to raise taxes. "Perhaps the KCMSD's Classical Greek theme schools emphasizing forensics and self-government will provide exemplary training in participatory democracy," he commented derisively. "But if today's dicta become law, such lessons will be of little use to students who grow up to become taxpayers in the KCMSD." The majority's decision, he continued, provided "no obvious limit . . . that would prevent judicial taxation in cases involving prisons, hospitals, or other public institutions."[83] Kennedy believed that, by not granting certiorari on the scope of Judge Clark's remedies, the majority was able to approve Clark's tax increase and his remedial plan. If certiorari had been granted on the scope of the plan, Kennedy believed, the plan would not have survived the Court's scrutiny. The Court had dodged the difficult question on the scope of the remedy and offered a hollow justification for its approval of judicial taxation. But the question remains: Why didn't Kennedy, Rehnquist, O'Connor, and Scalia grant certiorari on the scope of the plan and later lament the Court's decision? Unfortunately, nothing in the written record provides the answer.[84]

The Court's decision prompted an angry response from some members of Congress. Missouri senators Danforth and Bond, both Republicans, for example, immediately proposed a constitutional amendment prohibiting judges from ordering tax increases. However, division within Republican ranks doomed any effort to overturn the Court's decision. Charles Grassley and Trent Lott opposed Danforth and Bond's proposal and suggested passing a statute rather than a more cumbersome amendment. Grassley said, "There is no doubt that Congress has the constitutional power to limit the authority of the federal courts to propose such an extreme judicial remedy as a tax increase on the people. So we do not need a constitutional amendment."[85] This division, combined with Democratic control of Congress, ensured that neither effort was successful. The Supreme Court's distinction without a difference remained official constitutional doctrine.

Conclusion

Judge Clark's victory before the Supreme Court capped a long run of successes. Only once, on the income tax surcharge, had he been overturned on appeal. His success dramatically exhibits the judicial branch's power to command and have those commands carried out. The case also illustrates the important role of appellate courts in shaping judicial policymaking. By the time the Supreme Court ruled in 1990, most of the school buildings in the KCMSD were erected or renovated and all the magnet programs were in operation. An Eighth Circuit that supported aggressive desegregation efforts both compelled Clark to approve monumental remedies and insured that they would be implemented.

From a policy perspective, however, and in keeping with Donald Horowitz's classic argument about the focused nature of the adjudicative process, the most striking aspect of this case is the severe winnowing function the courts perform. Out of all the possible plans to improve the KCMSD, Judge Clark had only two to choose from. There was no range of choices or the possibility of discussion or compromise.

The remedy phase of the case also shows how the courts often exist in an alternate policy universe. The very survey Judge Clark commissioned on magnet schools showed that they had little chance of actually drawing white students into Kansas City. Nevertheless, Clark cited the survey in support of the remedial plan. He seemed to have the power to say that two plus two equals five. Rules and common sense did not apply. There are three possible explanations for Clark's actions: He was either stupid, deceived, or constrained. The first two are not satisfactory. No one suspected him of being the second coming of Oliver Wendell Holmes, but no one questioned his intelligence, either. Certainly few doubted his ability to understand basic survey data. The second explanation fails as well, since the data was so obvious he could not have been deceived. This leaves us with the third option. He was constrained. Limiting his discretion were judicial precedent and the Eighth Circuit Court of Appeals. Shortly after approving the magnet-school plan and the tax increases, Judge Clark told the *Kansas City Times*, "If you read case law, it's rather apparent (what must be done) concerning liability."[86] A few years later, responding to complaints from local taxpayers, he said, "If the public thinks this court is autocratic, it was by reason of direction from the Eighth Circuit Court of Appeals."[87]

5

Waking Up
Implementing an Educational Disaster

After Judge Clark ordered his remedial programs, extraordinary optimism permeated the KCMSD. Since the KCMSD's academic difficulties and racial isolation were the result of inadequate financial resources, the argument went, then Kansas City schools would soon show dramatic improvement in achievement levels and begin drawing thousands of white suburban students into the district because of the remedial program. But such optimism quickly faded. Within a year after Judge Clark ordered the magnet-school plan, everyone but the plan's most enthusiastic supporters knew that it was not going to lead to the improvements initially expected. Year after year the Desegregation Monitoring Committee (DMC) offered harsh assessments of the plan's effects. In desegregation and student achievement, the plan was nothing less than a failure. Student achievement fell and the percentage of minority students increased.

On the other hand, despite delays and mistakes caused by careless oversight, the capital improvements program was far more effective. This chapter examines the results of the remedial plan by comparing the KCMSD's performance in overseeing the capital improvements with its performance in desegregation and student achievement. Unfortunately the effects of the plan were not limited to these areas. The plan exacerbated some of the KCMSD's preexisting problems, including its fiscal irresponsibility and inability to keep or attract competent superintendents. The chapter concludes by exploring the causes of these unintended consequences.

Construction

The DMC was relatively critical of the KCMSD's oversight of the capital improvements plan, routinely chastising the KCMSD for tardiness, mistakes, and even possible corruption. However, in retrospect, the school district performed well. Anyone driving by a Kansas City school will be struck by its extraordinary facilities. The KCMSD had to oversee the complete physical overhaul of the entire school district, so delays were inevitable. What is surprising is that there were not more of them. The district may have been wasteful or extravagant, but just getting everything built was in itself a remarkable accomplishment. This combination of effectiveness and extravagance is best illustrated by the KCMSD's decision to subcontract oversight of the capital improvements and the construction of Central High School.

The PMT

After two years of chaos following Judge Clark's initial order for capital improvements, the wisest decision KCMSD officials made was to hire a Project Management Team (PMT), a group of architects and contractors, to oversee the new construction. The PMT included some of Kansas City's largest and most reputable contracting and architectural firms. The district could never have managed the far more ambitious Long-Range Capital Improvements Plan accompanying the magnet-school plan without the PMT. The PMT was supposed to pay for itself by soliciting bids and overseeing the bidding process and reviewing projects to eliminate waste and keep them under budget. These tasks proved too difficult even for the PMT. Projects consistently ran over budget, usually because of poor planning by KCMSD officials,[1] who regularly changed their construction requests, which then required architects to redesign buildings and contractors to undo or change work that had already been done.

The PMT, along with a watchful state auditor, helped keep corruption, or at least accusations of corruption, to a minimum. In such an expensive endeavor opportunities for unscrupulous behavior abounded. Before the PMT began its oversight, Margarite Kelly, the state auditor, documented a litany of suspicious decisions by the KCMSD, such as a $400,000 project receiving one bid over the telephone. By requiring each project to be competitively bid, the PMT made certain that this did not happen, at least with new projects. It had less control over projects that were already under way. The DMC regularly reported to Judge Clark that the KCMSD was allowing too many "change orders"—revisions to the construction plan and contract. The "massive number" and "financial magnitude" of the change orders caused concern for two reasons.[2] One was that they unnecessarily slowed construction. The second was that the change orders often were not bid upon, which opened the district to accusations of corruption. For instance, the state auditor pointed out that during the renovation of Central Middle School a change order totaling $282,373 was approved without competitive bidding.

Central High School, aka The Taj Mahal

Central High School was the most notable example of how the PMT helped rescue a poorly planned project. According to the Long-Range Magnet School Plan, Central High School's themes would be classical Greek and computers unlimited. The classical Greek theme was based on the notion of "strong mind, strong body." While the initial idea was to require students to learn classical Greek and to participate in athletic activity, the district quickly abandoned the language component. The main thrust of the program was athletics, with some emphasis on democracy and self-government. This change itself indicated that the wildly optimistic predictions of academic excellence were unlikely to come true.

In spite of having spent $1.2 million on renovating the old Central High School building, the KCMSD decided that it was inadequate for supporting a sports-centered curriculum. The renovations included "tuck pointing"—the repairing of mortar between bricks usually reserved for preservation projects—to the tune of $256,484.[3] The district decided to make the new Central High School its showpiece facility, requiring an indoor track, whirlpools, racquetball courts, an Olympic-quality gymnastics center, and a fifty-meter swimming pool with an underwater observation room. Just heating the 650,000-gallon swimming pool would cost $100,000 to $200,000 annually. The total utility costs for the old Central High averaged around $61,000 annually.[4] To accommodate the Computers Unlimited theme, the district also decided that the number of computers should nearly equal the number of students. The new building would also have an astonishing 220 square feet for each of its 1,200 students, compared to less than 140 for most high schools, including those in surrounding districts.[5] Before the PMT stepped in, the budget the KCMSD quoted was $15.2 million. After reviewing the project, the PMT had the unfortunate task of pointing out that the budget needed to be doubled. The construction budget alone was $23.4 million. With equipment, furniture, and site preparation, the total estimated cost was $32 million.

Ironically, despite the extravagance of the building it proposed, the district failed to include in its plan an auditorium large enough to hold the entire student body. In fact, the school's one auditorium could only hold about one-quarter of the students. Willie Bowie, who served as principal of Central High School, believed this omission was a serious impediment to creating a spirit of community necessary for teaching principles of democracy and self-government, which was the theme of the school.[6] However, as Justice Kennedy noted in his 1990 concurring opinion (*Jenkins II*), given the origins of the new building, perhaps self-government was not an appropriate theme.

In hearings before Judge Clark on the PMT's proposed budget, the state called John D. Maher, one of the KCMSD's initial advisers on the magnet school. Maher, who had designed and implemented a physical education magnet school in Cincinnati, testified that special amenities should be secondary to a sound curriculum. His school in Cincinnati, which the KCMSD acknowledged was a success, did not have a swimming pool, a track, or even a football stadium. The state argued that the building was extravagant and directed attention away from academic improvement.[7]

In spite of the construction and maintenance costs, Judge Clark approved the building asserting that "the magnet programs could not be implemented in a lesser facility." The one amenity that he did not approve was a ten-meter diving platform. "The Court is not convinced," he said, "that the desegregative attractiveness of a 10-meter platform outweighs the dangers and costs of construction and liability insurance associated with the platform."[8] Eliminating the platform, however, did not substantially reduce the cost of the facility since the natatorium would have to be redesigned by the architects to make the roof lower and pool shallower. The district decided to eliminate the platform and not alter any of the other designs.

Arthur Benson was ecstatic after Judge Clark's approval, commenting that Central "will be the most extraordinary high school facility in the nation" and that it "will be the most sought after high school in the district."[9] The attorney general's office was not as enthusiastic. Michael Fields, the assistant attorney general overseeing the litigation, dubbed the proposed building the "Taj Mahal."

The project was large, costly, and complicated, but with the oversight of the PMT, the new Central High School opened on schedule in September of 1991. It was indeed the district's showpiece facility. The building, along with its numerous athletic opportunities—the KCMSD even hired the Soviet Union's former Olympic fencing coach—was supposed to entice hundreds of white students into the district. But, as with all the KCMSD's new facilities, after they built it, no one came.

Desegregation

Unlike its oversight of the capital improvements plan, the KCMSD's performance in desegregation was a complete failure. Even those most heavily invested in Judge Clark's program could not report that his plan was successful. Eugene Eubanks, chairman of the DMC, had to report that the programs he had helped design were not working. In fact, the percentage of minority students in Kansas City's schools actually increased after the advent of Judge Clark's program. Each year Eubanks could only present more bad news to Judge Clark. The data from 1987–95 show the plan to be a costly exercise in futility.

In 1988, the first year after the establishment of the magnet schools, the DMC reported a disturbing trend: black students were "returning from private and/or parochial schools to the KCMSD" while there appeared to be no similar return of white students.[10] The percentage of minority students in Kansas City's elementary schools increased from 71.8 percent in 1987 to 73.5 percent. Under any other circumstances, this change would be considered a positive development, since it would indicate increased class-based integration. But since the remedy seemed to be promoting racial isolation, the opposite was the case.

Similar trends prevailed in 1989, and the DMC was clearly losing patience with the KCMSD. The failure to draw white students, according to the DMC, was due to the district's poor recruitment.[11] The DMC was so disheartened that it made a radical proposal, a voucher program. In the summer of 1989, the DMC submitted a twenty-page proposal to Judge Clark asking him to order the state to pay for the tuition and transportation of any KCMSD minority student to any private school in the area. The plan also called for the state to pay for any minority student to attend a suburban public school. This would include paying for tuition and transportation, plus $1,000 per pupil to the suburban school as an enticement to accept students. "It is hoped," the DMC stated, "that dramatic steps, even though some may be costly to the state, will assure that the fundamental rights of black school-children will be elevated above the prejudices of our times that prevent so many young people from taking their rightful place in our society." Arthur Benson, who now says that he is "strongly opposed"[12] to vouchers, at the time said he was "excited" because the plan offered the chance "to get hundreds of kids into integrated settings."[13]

The state naturally opposed the plan because of its cost. No one ever calculated precisely how much the plan would have cost, but the lowest estimates according to the *Kansas City Times* put it at "tens of millions of dollars." When asked to comment about the additional cost, Arthur Benson said, "Cost is not the question at this point."[14] Judge Clark, for once, sided with the state and declined the proposal. Clark consistently refused to compel suburban participation, although he encouraged suburban school districts to "cooperate" with the KCMSD. And if he could not compel suburban participation, vouchers certainly ran afoul of his judicial philosophy.

In 1990, the DMC stepped up its criticism of the district. "The KCMSD's performance in achieving desegregation has not been adequate in any meaningful way," the committee charged. "The overall loss of majority students from KCMSD continues. While individual schools show increased percentages in non-minority students, there are other schools where the percentage of minority students is increasing."[15] The DMC continued citing "ineffective recruitment" as the primary reason for the plan's failure, but it never really offered any suggestions about what the district could have done differently. In fact, much of the responsibility for recruitment had been contracted out to private marketing firms, who, with the munificent desegregation funds at their disposal, put together exceptionally polished advertising campaigns for the district.

In 1991, the DMC offered another discouraging report: "Of the 1,100-plus non-minority students who applied for admission [to the magnet schools], 794 were placed, but only 545 actually showed up." More troubling to the DMC was that the 545 broke down "as 106 high school, 135 middle school, and 304 elementary school" students."[16] White parents appeared willing to send their children to elementary school in the district but not junior high and high school.

One year later, the DMC made a similar report. The *Kansas City Star* reported that the DMC's "review of the 1991–92 school year echoed previous annual reports in its blunt assessment of the school system's shortcomings."[17] The committee said that progress toward integration "continued at an uneven and unacceptably modest pace." The district's goal for the 1992–93 school year was to recruit 2,100 new white students, "but it only received 1,980 applications, and only 715 of those actually enrolled."[18] While the district did successfully recruit over 700 new students, the percentage of minority students in the district was the same as it was in 1986, 74 percent.[19]

More bad news came in 1993. The school district reported that it had recruited 2,138 new white students to its magnet schools, but the DMC scoffed at the district's report. The DMC noted that the district had spent over $900,000 (the average annual amount spent on recruitment since the desegregation plan's inception) to recruit white children the previous year and that, of the 720 new white kindergartners enrolled, 582 of them lived in the district, and many would have attended Kansas City schools anyway. Also, the number of suburban recruits had dropped off from previous years. In 1993, the district gained 632 new students from the suburbs, compared to 794 and 714 students in 1992 and 1991, respectively. Even more distressing was that the district was losing its white students almost as fast as it was gaining them, which meant that even with the addition of its 2,138 new white students, there was no meaningful increase for the district.

In 1994, the *Kansas City Star* reported that one in three suburban white students who attended Kansas City schools during the 1992–93 school year did not return. And, overall, "one in four white students did not come back." Thus, the district had a net gain of forty white students from the year before. With an average yearly recruiting budget of $900,000, each new white student was costing the district $22,500, not including the cost of taxi service to and from each child's suburban home.[20]

The only progress that the district could report in 1994 was that the number of schools in Kansas City with minority student populations of more than 90 percent had decreased from twenty-four in 1985 to just fourteen.[21] But critics noted that this decrease of ten schools hardly justified the $1.3 billion that had already been spent. According to the *Kansas City Star*, demographic data showed that white enrollment, at its lowest, would have been 20 percent in 1994 even without the desegregation effort, whereas, with the desegregation effort it stood at only 25 percent.[22]

In 1995, the Supreme Court dealt a fatal blow to the KCMSD's already unsuccessful desegregation effort. After the state asked the Court to review Clark's plan again, the Court found that he had gone too far. This decision, which is discussed in detail in Chapter 7, urged Judge Clark to bring an end to court control of the KCMSD. After the Supreme Court ruling, minority enrollment in the district rose to a record level of 77.9 percent, from 75.9 percent the year before. In the ten years following Judge Clark's initial decree, minority enrollment in the KCMSD rose by over four percentage points, from 73.6 percent in 1985 to 77.9 percent in 1995.[23] Out of minority enrollment as a whole, the total number of black students had risen by nearly 1,000, from 68.3 percent in 1985 to 68.8 percent in 1995. The only reason the black percentage did not increase more was because of the influx of other minority, mostly Hispanic, students. As table 5.1 shows, from 1984 to 1995, the total black student population rose while the white student population fell.

The reasons for the magnet schools' failure to draw white students are easy to identify. Most importantly, as Judge Clark's polling data showed in 1986,

Table 5.1 KCMSD Student Racial Composition, 1984–1995

Year	Black	White	Other	Total	Percentage Black
1984–85	24,772	9,679	1,808	36,259	68.3
1985–86	24,905	9,611	1,935	36,451	68.3
1986–87	24,709	9,604	1,996	36,309	68.1
1987–88	24,325	9,172	1,932	35,429	68.7
1988–89	24,089	9,145	1,953	35,187	68.5
1989–90	24,059	8,785	2,006	34,850	69.0
1990–91	24,202	8,891	2,005	35,098	69.0
1991–92	24,610	9,297	2,100	36,007	68.3
1992–93	24,817	9,148	2,384	36,349	68.3
1993–94	25,391	9,188	2,559	37,138	68.4
1994–95	25,571	8,965	2,615	37,151	68.8

Source: "Total Student Membership: School Years 1955–56 through 1999–2000," Kansas City, Missouri, School District, Research Office (2000).

the overwhelming majority of suburban white parents were satisfied with their children's education.[24] Even members of the black community doubted that the new programs and buildings would lure white students. For example, Jeremiah Cameron, a former teacher in the district, commented, "It's discourteous to white students to think they will be attracted to pretty buildings.... After they find out that nothing is going on in them they'll go back to the suburbs. White folks want what black folks want, and that's quality education."[25] Cameron's prediction was accurate. Even with multimillion-dollar advertising and recruitment campaigns, such as the one for the New West Magnet School, the KCMSD could not convince white parents to withdraw their children from decent suburban schools and enroll them in the KCMSD.

Besides being satisfied with their current schools, white parents had other reasons for not enrolling their children in the KCMSD. In 1991, the DMC reported to Judge Clark that many of the white students who actually enrolled in the KCMSD transferred by the end of the school year. The KCMSD surveyed these students and their parents to find out why they left. The four top reasons were: "(1) students wanted to stay in neighborhood schools; (2) safety; (3) transportation; and (4) distance from home to school."[26] Since these were essentially the same reasons why many Kansas City parents opposed busing

KCMSD recruitment advertisement

in the seventies, predicting that parents would not want to re-enroll their children in the KCMSD should have been easy.

Safety was a particularly troubling issue for the DMC. In 1992, it reported to Judge Clark that the "security issue relative to providing a safe learning environment for student learning is emerging as a major problem for the implementation of the desegregation plan. During the 1991–92 school year, reports appeared in the media about altercations at one or more of the magnet schools. . . . One could conclude that safety and security could be a negative factor impacting on the desegregative efforts and successes at the secondary magnet schools."[27] The perception, if not reality, that the KCMSD's schools were unsafe clearly hindered the desegregation effort. The school district hired additional security guards to reduce school violence, but the need for the extra security only reinforced the idea that the KCMSD's schools were dangerous.

The safety problem became a citywide scandal when a local advertising executive, Jack Cashill, wrote a scathing article in a local magazine describing what he considered the futility of the desegregation plan. In 1989, the KCMSD had hired Cashill to prepare an advertising campaign to draw suburban white students to Martin Luther King Junior Middle School. The campaign won several awards for excellence, but it failed to attract notable numbers of white students.

After the campaign, in what became known as "The Killing Fields" article, Cashill condemned the magnet program. "The more you learn about King Middle School," he wrote, "the more you wonder what kind of mushrooms its planners ate during the school's conception. . . . Just where were their heads? Had they never talked to a single suburbanite? Did they not have a clue about 41st and Indiana [King's location]? Focus groups reveal that a night-time PTA meeting, smack in the heart of the urban killing fields and miles away from the nearest white suburb, is no one's idea of 'harmony' but everyone's idea of a 'world of difference.'"[28] The magnet-school plan, he believed, was best compared to Vietnam. "As with Vietnam," he said, "we needed a well-intentioned, spectacularly-expensive, overly-engineered boondoggle to show us the limits of our ambition." The "real enemy," he continued, "lies not across a DMZ but in the DMC. For here sit the 'best and brightest,' the architects of the plan itself, the master strategists of the war on, well, if nothing else, the discretionary income and the constitutional rights of the Kansas City homeowner." The solution, he said, was to "demand responsibility from the real *responsibles*—Gene Eubanks and Judge Clark. We ask them to put up their homes as collateral to guarantee the fiscal prudence and marketing wisdom of every magnet school they conceive." "We should actually thank the Judge and Gene," he concluded sarcastically, "for exhausting traditional options — they truly meant well — and giving us five years of public access vaudeville."[29]

Cashill's "Killing Fields" article was, to say the least, controversial, evoking cries of protest from the KCMSD administration and accusations of racism. But few disputed his argument that the plan was bound to fail. Cashill staunchly maintained that almost everyone in Kansas City was critical of the plan and that "some of the most critical people are on the [school] board." As evidence he pointed to a $175,000 contract the board awarded him to do further advertising less than one month after his controversial article appeared.[30]

While safety remained a substantial impediment, an additional recruitment barrier the DMC identified was the complexity of the magnet plan. The DMC detected early in the program that the number of available themes confused many parents. The "mechanism for registering a choice for a child becomes an exercise in balancing of policies and priorities, frankly confusing and intimidating to the most sophisticated parent," the DMC reported in 1988. "The wary parents must inform themselves carefully on the current, and changeable, policies with regard to retention within a theme movement from feeder elementary to middle to high school, availability of places for each category (minority or non-minority) at a given school, and status of siblings in selection."[31] Behind this jargon, which was confusing in its own right, was a simple fact — many parents, both black and white, thought the plan was too complicated. This fact also hinted that many parents suspected that all of these special programs might actually get in the way of their children's education.

The final reason for the plan's failure was the DMC itself. Its constant criticism reinforced the image of the school district as incompetent. Within three months of being formed by Judge Clark, the committee began publicly criticizing the district, and its comments were regularly headlined in the *Kansas City Times* throughout the year.[32] One article in particular described a "heated" meeting between the DMC and district officials, with the DMC accusing the district of "dragging its feet."[33] Two months later an article quoted Eugene Eubanks's comments at the previous night's meeting of the DMC. "What bothers the chair," he said, "is the growing perception on the part of a number of persons who fought a hard battle . . . that a plan that showed great promise and great potential to do great things for the school district may not be implemented in the most efficient way."[34] Each article made the same point: the KCMSD administration was incompetent. For the next ten years Kansas City could expect at least one article a month describing the DMC's frustration with the school district.

Arthur Benson believes that this criticism not only reinforced the public's perception of the school district as incompetent but also contributed to further incompetence. The DMC, he said, exercised immense power "with good intentions and malevolent effects." The DMC meetings were "rancorous" and "not very productive." The DMC "got to the point," Benson said,

> where if there was a problem they would require the school district's upper administration to bring the people in who were responsible for the problem so if somebody had failed to do something about a leaky roof, they bring that administrator in . . . and the monitoring committee, and Gene Eubanks was quite good at this, would grill that administrator unmercifully and some of the administrators just quit. Some of them said, "I'm not going to take this." Others would just withdraw into their shell and so what happened was it communicated a sense of fear among all these mid-level administrators who have these huge responsibilities essentially trying to rebuild the entire school district in a very short period of time. So none of them would take any risks. . . . Everything just ossified and the monitoring committee in a major respect was responsible for the school district slowing into a molasses mode at a time when it needed to be moving quickly.[35]

In fact, the DMC became so intensely critical that administrators, including superintendents, would regularly schedule out-of-town trips to coincide with DMC meetings.

Eugene Eubanks acknowledges that he was exceptionally critical of the school district but defends himself and the DMC by pointing out that their role was to make sure that the funds given to the district by the court were being used appropriately, not to provide emotional support or therapy for district personnel. He also says that there were "serious questions about the competency on the part of the principals," which made vigorous and critical oversight necessary.[36]

To the attorney general's office, the DMC's harsh criticism of the KCMSD provided vindication. Assistant Attorney General Michael Fields had long argued that the KCMSD's main affliction was mismanagement rather than racial isolation. When Eubanks asked him at a DMC meeting if he should censure the KCMSD at the risk of being accused of micromanaging the school district, Fields responded, "Micro-management is better than no management at all."[37]

Student Achievement

While the failure of the plan to attract white students was an immense disappointment to the school district, few would have complained if it had led to the academic improvements its architects predicted. But here the plan was just as unsuccessful.

Disturbing trends were already apparent by 1988. The DMC noted with some consternation that "a few of the non-magnet elementary schools did as well or better" on standardized tests than their "magnetized counterparts."[38] In 1989, the DMC noted that while elementary school test scores were tolerable, middle and high school test scores were "abysmal."[39] The DMC reported in 1990 that the "best interpretation" of testing results was that early grades "showed relatively adequate achievement, with achievement beginning to fall behind national norms after about the second grade," with a "singular drop in achievement" at the sixth grade.[40]

In 1991, the DMC concluded, "In a number of cases the quality of program, level of instruction and facilities combine to make district schools superior to what is available anywhere else in the metropolitan area. . . . But it also must be noted that based on academic performance, the KCMSD . . . continues to offer the worst of education in the Kansas City area." The committee reported that standardized test results showed that district students made less than a year's progress in the 1990 academic year in most academic areas and that "achievement test scores for 1990–91 were abysmal at grades above grade three."[41]

In 1992 the DMC made an even more critical assessment of academic progress. "Desegregation expenditures during the 1991–92 school year in the (district)," it reported, "will exceed $217 million. . . . After seven years, the DMC hoped for and expected better results in [terms of both] desegregation and academic achievement on the part of the (district). These needed improvements and outcomes at this time have not been adequately realized."[42] The committee's report found that students in "eight of the district's 12 grades" were more than "half a year below national norms on standardized tests measuring academic achievement," that high school students were "more than 18 months below national norms," and that sixth-graders, "whose entire educational life [had] been spent in schools benefiting from the desegregation program, remain[ed] one year below national norms in reading."[43] The *Kansas City Star* reported that in 1991–92 scores "actually declined since 1986 in fifth- and sixth-grade language and in fifth-, sixth-, seventh-, and eighth-grade math."[44] Moreover, the *Star* reported, "In grades kindergarten through four, Kansas City students tend[ed] to score above national averages in most subjects, except reading. In all other grades and subjects, they fall below grade level. In addition, Kansas City students are even further behind their peers in Missouri now than they were in 1987." Ironically, five of the "17 traditional elementary schools," which had far fewer resources and no magnet themes, "posted scores above national averages in most grades and subjects."[45]

In 1993 speculation began to mount that generally the desegregation effort and specifically the magnet schools had actually "lowered academic achievement for all students and black students in particular."[46] At a hearing about reapproval of the magnet plan, John Alspaugh, a statistician from the University of Missouri–Columbia, testified for the state that "black students' median reading and math scores declined in most grade level groups between 1987 and 1991 on the Iowa Test of Basic Skills and the Tests of Achievement and Proficiency." Alspaugh also "contended that scores declined in most subjects in grades three, six, eight and 10 on the Missouri Mastery and Achievement Test." Herbert Wahlberg, a professor of educational psychology at the University of Illinois at Chicago, agreed with Alspaugh's conclusions. Previously, Wahlberg "was part of a U.S. Department of Education panel that concluded desegregation nationally has had minimal effect on black student achievement." Wahlberg contended that blacks attending schools with higher concentrations of blacks performed better than blacks attending more integrated schools. The crux of his testimony was exactly what he told Clark in 1985: "Magnet schools often emphasized specialization to the detriment of black students' mastery of basic skills." Rather than special magnet-school programs, Wahlberg "recommended instead a strong concentration on basic college preparatory academic subjects."[47]

Because the district's academic performance was so poor in 1993, district officials started judging academic performance by comparing it to other "large city districts which face[d] similar educational challenges" rather than to national norms.[48] But even when measured by this "big-city standard," the KCMSD was still below average. KCMSD students "were fairly close to average in the fourth, sixth, seventh and eighth grades." By high school, "district reading scores [were] well below" the national, large-city average. By the end of high school, "Kansas City students [were] significantly below average in everything, regardless of whether national or big-city norms [were] used." The DMC looked at the same statistics the district did and reported that "although the District has met with some incremental success at the elementary level over the past eight years of the desegregation plan, the secondary level scores remain disappointingly low." "Even after repeated statements of concern by the (committee) in past year-end reports to the Court," the DMC chided, "the (school district) continues on a path that fails to adequately address the issue of low academic achievement levels."[49]

In 1994, Kansas City's academic problems became a national story. CBS's *60 Minutes* ran a special feature on the school district, exposing the plan's failure to draw white students and improve test scores. While Leslie Stahl, the reporter on the story, exposed both problems in Kansas City, the educational failure caused the most embarrassment. Stahl pointed out that one of the best schools in the district was Martin Luther King Middle School. But King did not receive a new building or a special magnet theme. It offered only a "basic curriculum." The story highlighted this difference between the expensive and ineffective magnet programs and the less expensive but often more effective traditional schools. Clinton Adams, a parent and black activist who was interviewed for the story, told Stahl, "We have not . . . taught kids how to read, write and count effectively, so how the hell [do] they think we're going to be able to teach them foreign languages?"[50] The school district bitterly complained about the story and even filed a complaint with CBS, asserting that some of the story's data was incorrect. But the complaints seemed hollow. The evidence coming from the DMC was overwhelming. After the story ran, the *Kansas City Star* reported that the "'60 Minutes' embarrassment has left nearly everyone unhappy with test scores."[51] To believe that the plan would achieve its goals had become untenable.

There are many possible explanations for the plan's failure to improve student achievement. The favorite target of the DMC was the district administration. According to the DMC, the district failed to effectively implement its programs. Eugene Eubanks, who crafted many of the programs, still maintains that the plan failed because of poor implementation.[52] At times the KCMSD did find it difficult to implement completely new programs, but this was a task no district could implement without some setbacks and delays. The district eventually implemented all of the programs ordered by Judge Clark, and the students were in those programs for several years. The problems with education in Kansas City went much deeper than poor implementation of magnet schools.

The DMC, in fact, pointed out one of the central problems with education in Kansas City. In its 1988 report to Judge Clark, the DMC noted that many of the parents in the KCMSD were not "educationally attentive" or "educationally advantaged" and that they therefore did not know or care about the magnet-school programs. The problem, then, was that "demograph[ic]s show that minority families have a higher representation among the educationally disadvantaged."[53] Because the KCMSD was largely minority, it undoubtedly included many "educationally disadvantaged" parents who were not involved in their children's education. Without close parental supervision it was very difficult for children to take full advantage of the unusual academic options that the magnet plan offered.

Even when there was parental involvement, it often had a negative effect because of the KCMSD's policies. In 1984, for example, the school district adopted a policy allowing failing middle-school students to proceed to the next grade if their parents signed a waiver. One of the leading sponsors of this policy was Sue Fulson, who also happened to be the strongest supporter of the magnet plan on the school board. The school board apparently adopted the policy because large numbers of middle-school students were failing and the district did not know what to do with them. By 1994, one-fifth of all middle-school students in the KCMSD used waivers to advance to the next grade. In signing the waiver, parents explicitly forfeited the right to hold the district "responsible for (the child's) inability to function in higher grades."[54] The message to both students and parents was that achievement did not matter. One middle-school official said, "The waiver system stinks." It made no sense "to give a kid carte blanche to screw up a whole year and all his mom has to do is sign a paper and he goes up."[55] The school board eventually abolished the waiver system in 1995. It is telling, however, that its existence coincided with the magnet-school plan. A plan intended to improve academic achievement was implemented alongside a policy directly undermining achievement. Thousands of middle-school students—4,500 from 1991 to 1994 alone—were pushed through the system without meeting the minimum requirements to pass a grade.

One reason for declining academic achievement directly related to the magnet plan was the school district's inability to attract students and teachers with similar interests to the magnet schools. A goal of the magnet schools was to bring students and teachers who were interested in science, for example, together at science magnet schools. While designing the programs, however, their architects never inquired if teachers would be willing to change schools and if students would choose schools based on their academic interest. Neither teachers nor students behaved as expected. According to Arthur Benson, the students "selected schools on the basis of where their friends were going to school" and they "didn't give a rat's tail about what the theme was at the school."[56] This outcome, however, should have been expected. How else would educationally disadvantaged children with inattentive parents decide where to go to school? According to Eugene Eubanks, many students' test scores "bordered on less than chance."[57] If students had randomly answered the questions, they would have done better. That such students would make a choice based on their academic interests was implausible. Teachers also proved a disappointment. According to Benson, the "teachers didn't want to change." Instead of transferring to schools that matched their interests, most preferred to stay at the schools where they were teaching before the magnet plan. The plan, therefore, failed to create the flourishing islands of like-minded students and teachers Benson expected. Benson readily admits the failure: "Where we had thought this synergy would come together in the schools to create this learning community that would cause the curriculum to evolve and the instruction practices to improve didn't happen."[58]

Judge Clark's plan also failed to improve educational achievement because it emphasized the wrong things: test scores. Clark wanted the KCMSD to improve test scores—in fact, bring them to the national average within four to five years. The remedial plan caused KCMSD teachers to emphasize test-taking skills. Several years into the plan, the district asked John Murphy, a former superintendent of schools for Prince George's County, Maryland, and Charlotte-Mecklenburg, North Carolina, to study the KCMSD for ways to improve its quality of education. He was hired because of his success in improving the academic performance of minority students. The KCMSD had even attempted to hire Murphy twice as a superintendent. He testified to Judge Clark in 1996 that "the focus of instruction in all grades and classrooms observed was drill on specific facts students needed to master in order to score higher on the standardized test." But these tests, he said, only measure a "relatively narrow range of skills," and by concentrating on them "the district actually limited the learning experiences in the classroom." Hence, teaching students how to do well on these tests does not teach them the general skills that enable them to improve in later grades. Thus, the KCMSD showed some improvement in reading in grades one, two, and three but returned to its abysmal rate in later grades. Even at the time the remedial plan was developed, this argument was in circulation. In 1983, for example, Jeanne Chall, a professor of education at Harvard University and a well-known expert on reading development, described the problem this way:

> Pre–Grade 4 reading can be said to represent the oral tradition, in that text rarely goes beyond the language and knowledge that the reader already has through listening, direct experience, TV, and so forth. We can view reading beyond Grade 4 as comprising the literary tradition—when reading matter goes beyond what is already known. Thus, Grade 4 can be seen as the beginning of a long progression in the reading of texts that are ever more complicated, literary, abstract, and technical, and that require more world knowledge and ever more sophisticated language and cognitive abilities to engage in the interpretations and critical reaction required. The materials that are typically read at Grade 4 and beyond change in content, in linguistic complexities, and in cognitive demands.[59]

Hence, drilling students to improve test scores might help in early grades but not in later ones. Around the same time, an education reporter summarized the argument:

> Some education professors who have followed testing trends argue that the narrow focus on the basics in the elementary grades causes an increase in the scores at the lower grades but then results in a decrease in scores at the upper grades. "To read for comprehension and inference, you need broad, general knowledge," says Harry Singer, an education professor at the University of California at Riverside. "Schools have narrowed their curriculum to fit the tests. But they have ignored the general knowledge that makes you a good reader.". . .
>
> Stanford University professor Robert Calfee agrees: "If you concentrate on simple passages in a workbook format, you can get test scores up."[60]

The remedial plan, then, was perverse from the beginning. The children coming into the KCMSD were from "educationally disadvantaged" backgrounds, and the only way the district knew how to raise test scores was by teaching students how to take tests. The KCMSD was in an impossible situation. The DMC would chastise the KCMSD for stagnant test scores, so the district administrators would emphasize improving test scores to their teachers. The teachers would then drill their students on taking standardized tests and neglect teaching them broader skills. This approach in turn would lead to stagnant or declining test scores in later grades, which would lead to further chastisement from the DMC, prompting the cycle to repeat.

Compounding the emphasis on test scores was the quality of instruction. Even Arthur Benson, who had argued before the remedial plan was implemented that the failure of the KCMSD was due to inadequate resources, has said that at least 20 percent of the teaching staff was completely incompetent. While chair of the DMC, Eugene Eubanks looked at the college coursework and SAT scores of the KCMSD's teachers and saw that there were "severe shortcomings on the part of the teachers." Eubanks says that even though Clark gave all of the teachers substantial pay raises and gave them compensation for professional development, apathy remained a serious problem. Many teachers, according to Eubanks, complained to him about having to take on "additional responsibilities like learning."[61] But there was little that could be done about the teaching staff except wait for the incompetent teachers to retire. The teachers' union was an official intervenor in the case, and its contract with the school district prohibited teachers from being removed except in the rarest of circumstances.

A final reason the plan did not lead to academic improvements was that the magnet themes distracted from more pressing educational needs. Students without even basic reading skills in English found themselves immersed in French and Spanish magnet programs. And math and science magnets whisked students away for special field trips and activities before making sure that students had basic math skills. The problem, which the DMC recognized, was that these special programs were designed to attract and help educationally advantaged white children but they were not particularly helpful to children from "educationally disadvantaged" backgrounds. While these special classes, activities, and trips were undoubtedly interesting, they were not what the children of the KCMSD needed most: a sound educational foundation.

Fiscal Irresponsibility

The negative effects of Judge Clark's plan were not limited to the failed desegregation plan and poor student achievement. In 1986 the *Kansas City Star* reported that the KCMSD was "wasteful, top-heavy, and insensitive to the needs of children."[62] This condition worsened with the influx of billions of dollars. In 1991, the DMC reported that district administrators appeared "complacent about their responsibilities to manage their budgets. This attitude has been prevalent in the district since day one of the desegregation plan." The report continued, "The attitude has been prevalent . . . that money is no object and the court will provide all that is necessary, and no one will take any punitive actions if we are sloppy in our work habits. There is no strong feeling of responsibility to manage the funds in a cost-efficient manner."[63] In 1992, the DMC came back with a similar report chastising the district for being wasteful and specifically criticizing the district for its top-heavy, centralized administration. This centralization, Eugene Eubanks noted, "has tended to limit parental and community involvement in the schools, which is totally contradictory to the 'bottom-up' approach required by the Court." The problem with Eubanks's criticism was that Clark might have wanted a "bottom-up" approach but the complexity of his plan required a "top-down" approach. The DMC also said that its members spent "less time evaluating how the district keeps track of its money and more time looking at 'how the District spends its money.'"[64] The DMC constantly questioned the district's spending and always found wastefulness.

There were many instances of questionable behavior on the part of district administrators. For instance, when purchasing new furniture for several schools in 1989, the district decided to go through local dealers rather than buying directly from the manufacturers. The size of the order, valued at over $5 million, meant that the district could have ordered at a discount from manufacturers. The furniture from local vendors cost at least $50,000 more and possibly $100,000 more than it would have cost had the district bought it directly from the manufacturers.[65] The KCMSD offered the justification that it wanted to help small and minority-owned businesses. The district refused to buy furniture from companies that offered discounts to larger distributors, saying that giving discounts to dealers that buy in bulk was unfair and that it wanted a "level playing field." The district also did not provide a list of authorized cab routes to cab companies transporting white students from the suburbs to magnet schools, which led to the state disputing over $200,000 worth of cab fees in 1988.[66] In addition, in 1989, the *Kansas City Star* investigated overcharging by cab companies. It found that the companies "charged for almost twice the mileage that reporters logged while driving between the same schools and homes" and that "some drivers charged the district for trips that were never made and some billed the district twice for one trip."[67] Another comparatively small but emblematic example of this profligate behavior was the district's request for a $43,000 trophy case for Metro High School. Metro had been a vocational school with no full-time students before becoming a magnet school. This meant that it had no trophies. The DMC asked a district administrator why such an expensive trophy case was necessary for a school without trophies. The administrator responded that it was needed to give the school "the atmosphere of a regular high school."⁶⁸

There were four reasons for such irresponsible behavior. First, as discussed in Chapters 3 and 4, the KCMSD had trouble running its finances long before Clark's remedial plan. Most of the problems afflicting the KCMSD could not be resolved by more money or more programs. Rather, these were underlying problems that could only be addressed through a change in philosophy and in the way the district was administered.

Second, even with its enormous preexisting bureaucracy, the influx of money overwhelmed the KCMSD. Clark more than doubled the district's yearly revenue, and this proved too much for the KCMSD to control, use, and keep track of. Only the most naive would say that the district's personnel would not abuse its resources. The KCMSD also could not protect the expensive equipment that it purchased. For example, in 1990 the DMC reported that "several hundred thousand dollars of equipment have mysteriously disappeared in the last couple of years," and in 1997 an audit found that in 1995 over $250,000 worth of district equipment was stolen and in 1996, $180,000 worth. Every year hundreds of thousands of dollars worth of computers, overhead projectors, VCRs, and TVs would disappear.⁶⁹ The remedial plan destroyed any incentive for the KCMSD to keep track of its equipment. Missing equipment could just be replaced with the money supplied by Judge Clark.

Third, Judge Clark's plan required at least another layer of bureaucracy to an already bloated administration just to start and manage the programs. In doing so, the plan promoted the belief that the KCMSD existed for the administrators rather than for the students. A 1990 court-ordered audit by Deloitte & Touche showed that the district spent less than half of its budget, 46 percent, on instruction. Transportation, food services, and central administration consumed the remaining 54 percent.⁷⁰ This percentage spent on non-instructional purposes and on administrative employees was higher than that spent by each of the fourteen other comparable urban districts considered in the audit. The central administration of the KCMSD had 600 employees for a student population of around 36,000.

Finally, by approving virtually every request made by the KCMSD, Clark, as one local columnist put it, "wedged" himself between the people of Kansas City and the KCMSD and made himself the "only patron who really mattered." Therefore, "school officials had no further need to be concerned about public opinion."⁷¹ District officials could be unconcerned about how they spent money because Judge Clark had shown himself to be a most generous and friendly donor. The school district felt free to tear down perfectly good facilities that the community liked in order to build elaborate facilities for special magnet programs. The most controversial example of this was the district's decision to tear down Paseo High School. The school's nearby residents, who were mostly black, considered the old Paseo building a centerpiece of its area and protested its destruction.[72] But Judge Clark sided with district administrators and approved the building's demolition in favor of a performing arts facility at a price of over $20 million.[73]

Superintendents

A virtually universal feature of urban school districts is the short tenure of superintendents. The KCMSD was no different. However, the magnet-school plan created its own set of problems, which further contributed to the KCMSD's difficulty attracting and keeping a qualified superintendent. The tenure of the KCMSD's superintendents was actually close to the urban average of three to four years. The district had two superintendents both serving four years during most of the desegregation plan. However, both of their tenures were marred by conflict with the school board, Arthur Benson, and the DMC.

George Garcia was hired as superintendent in 1986. Before coming to Kansas City he was a deputy superintendent in Brownsville, Texas, and ten years earlier he had been a junior high principal in the KCMSD. Garcia's misfortune was becoming superintendent just after a popular black superintendent, Claude Perkins, was fired after one year because he opposed the magnet plan. The black community, as Chapter 6 discusses in detail, was angry about both Perkins's dismissal and the magnet plan. Garcia had to mollify angry patrons as well as oversee the complete overhaul of the KCMSD. He quickly showed that he was not up to the task, although it is not clear that anyone else would have been, either. According to Arthur Benson, by the 1980s "the principals and many of the teachers [were] subpar."[74] In addition to an ineffectual central administration, Garcia's supporting cast was less than confidence-inspiring, which led to him trying to do everything by himself. Garcia, Benson says, "refused to delegate" and became overwhelmed. The DMC then began routinely chastising Garcia for the failure of the magnet plan. For instance, at one DMC meeting, Eugene Eubanks announced that he had "the gravest concerns" about the district administration and that "it is time for some serious consideration of some alternatives . . . of the structure and administration within the district."[75] And on a panel discussion that was broadcast over talk radio, Eubanks told Garcia that there were "real questions on the monitoring committee and within this community about the quality of leadership and its ability to pull this plan off."[76] This barrage of criticisms then led Garcia to cede authority to the school board. He went from trying to do everything to doing nothing. According to Benson, Sue Fulson, who was president of the board at the time, "ran the school district herself" when "Garcia froze on the job." Not surprisingly, the school board refused to extend Garcia's contract when it expired in 1991. Even though his tenure by all accounts was a failure, many people involved with the KCMSD still speak fondly of him as a person. Benson says that he was a "wonderful guy" and "extraordinarily well-intentioned." And Clinton Adams, a black activist who routinely criticized Garcia while he was superintendent, says that "he was in retrospect a pretty decent educator" and "was probably the best educator we had in this whole line of superintendents."[77]

Garcia's replacement, Walter Marks, inspires no such kind remarks. Like Garcia, Marks took the job under less than auspicious circumstances. Initially the school board had sought out a black superintendent to replace Garcia. Many in the black community believed that a black superintendent would be more responsive to their concerns. The school board rather suddenly changed directions and tried to hire John Murphy, who was white. As superintendent of schools for Prince George's County, Maryland, Murphy had earned a reputation for improving the academic performance of minority students. Murphy declined their offer, taking the superintendent's position in Charlotte instead. But the sudden decision to offer the position to Murphy prompted an angry response from parts of the black community. At the time, Clinton Adams said, "I'm not inclined to work cooperatively with a white superintendent."[78] A group of black leaders and organizations called the Black Agenda Group threatened to shut down the district if Murphy took the job. While Murphy said that he took the position in Charlotte because of the timing of the offer, he also told the *Kansas City Star*, "I'm simply appalled by the fact you would have such bigoted people in the community."[79]

Ten days after offering the position to Murphy, the school board offered the position to Walter Marks. The Black Agenda Group had expended most of its political capital opposing Murphy and could barely muster a word against Marks, who was also white. The school board, with Arthur Benson's encouragement, offered Marks the position because he had run a magnet program in Richmond, California. The board hired him so quickly that his performance in Richmond received little public scrutiny. It turned out that Marks had recently been fired by the school district for running it into bankruptcy. The financial manager for the Richmond district told the *Star*, "He doesn't take advice from the financial experts on his team. If I hired that man, I'll tell you, he would have absolutely no control over any budget." And Bill Honig, California's superintendent of public instruction, said that the KCMSD's hiring Marks without a more thorough background check was a "dereliction of duty" and that "everyone in California is up in arms over this guy." While black leaders were initially subdued, they quickly began questioning the school board's wisdom. Ajamu Webster, a black activist, said, "This guy is obviously someone who has had problems with finances. Why him, when this district is under the gun for accountability?" Even the more restrained NAACP questioned why the school board had rushed to hire him.[80]

Marks's tenure was a disaster. Arthur Benson was an admitted Marks admirer because Marks believed in magnet schools. Benson even criticized the DMC for its strong criticisms of the district administration and having a "penchant for punishment," which he thought was unnecessary with Marks's strong leadership.[81] But Marks's support for magnet schools put him at odds with much of the black community. And his decision to surround himself with highly paid, mostly white assistants created even more hostility. Many in the black community accused him of being a shameless self-promoter incapable of remedying the KCMSD's educational shortcomings. During Marks's first year on the job, Clinton Adams said, "He's more concerned about creating something that will give him some publicity. . . . I have not seen any substantive initiatives designed to improve the quality of education for our children on a day-to-day basis."[82] Most damning, however, was the magnet plan's continued failure to draw white students or improve student achievement under Marks's supervision. Both the black community and the DMC began criticizing his performance.

After three years on the job, Marks told the school board that he was taking an extended medical leave because of an arthritic back and left for his vacation home in Florida. A local TV station, suspicious of his claims, went to Florida and secretly filmed him lifting large boxes and doing construction work on his house. The school board then fired him in February of 1995.[83] Few were sad to see him go. Clinton Adams recalls with an obvious sense of vindication that Marks "was a piece of work. . . . He could sell an icebox to an Eskimo. The guy was just a smooth talker, snake-oil salesman that was only out for Walter Marks."[84]

For Arthur Benson, the failure of Marks and Garcia does not indict the magnet program. "The job clearly could have been done with the right people," he says. "But," he adds, "the right people don't exist in public education."[85]

Conclusion

Despite Judge Clark's remedial plan, the children in the KCMSD remained the victims of a woefully substandard education. There were some exceptions, but they were exceptions that did not prove the rule. Lincoln Academy, for instance, provided, by everyone's admission, an excellent education. It was a college preparatory academy, so it focused on a traditional but very rigorous educational program. It was also housed in the building that, before *Brown v. Board of Education*, was the site of Kansas City's all-black high school. While it received money for renovation, its facilities did not measure up to the state-of-the-art buildings that Central High School boasted. The fact that Lincoln, whose program and facilities seemed positively archaic in comparison to the cutting-edge facilities and programs of its sister schools, offered the best high school education in the district was perhaps the most damning indictment possible of Judge Clark's remedial plan.

The central problem with the plan, as Arthur Benson noted about its effective schools component but could have applied easily to all of it, was that "nobody at that time understood the problems of scaling something up to a district wide remedy."[86] Because no one knew exactly how to implement such a vast program in an effective way, the primary effect of the remedial plan was to compound the district's preexisting problems. The plan concentrated on provocative but educationally unsound magnet themes and programs, led to a costly but failed attempt to attract suburban white students, exacerbated the KCMSD's fiscal carelessness, and prompted the hiring of a superintendent whose only proven qualification was that he "believed" in magnet schools. The one area in which the KCMSD was successful—the capital improvements—was supervised by private contractors with a profit motive. Wherever the KCMSD retained control, disaster followed. The situation could hardly get worse. But it did. As Chapter 6 discusses, the magnet plan alienated the very group it was designed to help: the black community. The plan actually undermined the political support it would have needed to succeed.

This lack of support is directly related to one of more surprising disappointments of *Missouri v. Jenkins*, the fact that the KCMSD could not attract a superintendent with the skills to use the court-ordered resources. One reason, as Arthur Benson recognized, is that such people are rare in public education. But the KCMSD clearly did try to recruit one very capable superintendent, John Murphy. However, Murphy wisely detected the anger in the black community over the plan and removed himself from the search. Had the school district been able to recruit someone of his ability, the plan might not have been the comprehensive failure it turned out to be.

6 Ambivalence and Anger
The Response of Kansas City's African American Community

In 1994 a *Kansas City Star* poll reported that 60 percent of black parents thought that the desegregation program had helped the quality of education for black students and 29 percent thought that it had hurt the quality of education.[1] At first glance, these percentages are not surprising. They should give pause, though, to anyone familiar with the KCMSD before the remedial plan. The physical condition of the district prior to *Missouri v. Jenkins* was squalid. At least after the remedial plan the buildings had reliable heating and air-conditioning, roofs without holes, glass in all the windows, and excrement-free hallways. One would have expected almost everyone to say that the quality of education was better because of the physical improvements alone. That 29 percent believed that the quality of education had deteriorated must be considered surprising. This poll pointed to the ambivalent attitude many in the black community had toward the magnet plan, an attitude that often grew into anger.

Throughout the history of the plan, black community leaders excoriated Judge Clark, Eugene Eubanks, and Arthur Benson—the three men most responsible for bringing $2 billion to the district to improve the educational lot of black children. But the reasons for black ambivalence and hostility are clear. First, community leaders were excluded during the design of the remedial plan. Second, many in the black community never liked the idea of magnet schools. And third, once the magnet schools were in place, the black community objected to their racially insensitive implementation.

But this is not just a story of black dissatisfaction and complaint. Through its intervention in Kansas City, the court gave rise to a new black political force that was powerful enough to seize control of the school board, challenge the magnet plan in court, and return the KCMSD to a system of neighborhood schools. These developments were made possible by a large pool of well-educated black professionals willing to use "scorched earth" political tactics, the legal and financial support of both conservative and liberal white allies, the political and verbal blunders of Arthur Benson, and the vulnerability of the magnet plan to charges of racism. The rise of this movement was the most important consequence of *Missouri v. Jenkins*.

Kansas City Politics

Unlike the rest of the story, black opposition to the magnet plan was largely a political rather than legal battle. Understanding what happened requires a general description of the political terrain—the district leadership, the black community, and the media—black opposition had to navigate during the 1980s and 1990s.

The most important political fact about the KCMSD is that it is a world unto itself. Kansas City's government and the KCMSD are distinct with the mayor and city council rarely meddling in the KCMSD's affairs. City hall in Kansas City has had enough intractable problems of its own. Befitting the hometown of the infamous political boss Tom Pendergast, *George* magazine named Kansas City one of America's ten most corrupt cities in 1999.

Because of the KCMSD's independence, the locus of power in the district has been the school board. Changing policy in the KCMSD requires changing the school board. It helps to remember that it was the school board—not the superintendent, not the black community, and not Arthur Benson—that initiated *Missouri v. Jenkins*. With a total of nine members, the board has six subdistrict representatives and three at-large representatives. For more than three decades, the board has been the center of controversy, the target of unending accusations of corruption and intrigue, with the accusations often divided along racial lines. Even though an overwhelming majority of the district's students have been black, the board generally has had only two to three black board members at a time. Life on the school board has been so unpleasant that in several elections the district has had difficulty finding candidates to run for seats. For example, Sue Fulson, the magnet plan's strongest supporter on the board and president from 1988 to 1992, was first elected in 1982 in an uncontested race in her subdistrict. And low voter turnout was the norm for board elections. Turnover was also fairly high. From 1970 to 2000 the board had sixty-four different members. Despite this neglect, turnover, and rancor, for most of *Missouri v. Jenkins*, the board was remarkably united about the case. From 1976 to 1996, a solid majority of the board supported the litigation and Arthur Benson's handling of it. Benson says that during those years the board "never made the wrong decision" about the case.[2]

Because of the school board's power, the superintendent's office has largely been an appendage of the board. George Hazlett, who retired in 1969, was the last superintendent in the KCMSD with real power. A number of superintendents were fired or forced to resign because of their conflicts with the school board. The board was the superintendent's employer and thus rarely acquiesced during disagreements. A superintendent who did not complain about the board's micromanagement was a rarity.

The KCMSD teachers' union, on the other hand, has occupied a strong (but not invulnerable) position. It was especially effective in securing pay raises from Judge Clark as part of the desegregation plan, which eventually increased their base pay by 44 percent. In addition to pay raises, the union persuaded Judge Clark to pay for professional development programs. It also successfully resisted efforts to implement a system of performance-based pay. In spite of these successes, however, the teachers' union has come under intense scrutiny several times in the last thirty years. After two disastrous strikes, the union had to consent to a no-strike clause in a 1977 contract with the school district. In addition, the union's credibility dramatically fell after substantial pay raises under the desegregation plan failed to translate into better student performance. More money, the union assured Judge Clark, would inevitably lead to better academic achievement. When teachers failed to deliver on this promise, they were soundly criticized by both black activists and Arthur Benson. According to Clinton Adams, the most outspoken black critic of the union,

> The teachers were parties to the lawsuit. They were intervenors in the lawsuit and they got everything they wanted and they did not deliver and they still have not delivered. They said they wanted reduced class sizes. The judge ordered reduced class sizes. They said they wanted better pay because their salaries weren't competitive. They couldn't get and keep good people. The judge made that controversial ruling when he increased their salaries. They said they needed shorter hours, so the judge cut back the number of periods they worked and gave them more planning time. They said they needed more training. The judge ordered more training and paid them to go to the training. I've never seen anything like that. In my profession we have to take fifteen hours of CLE (continuing legal education) every year. We have to pay for it. . . . He gave them all that and they still have not shown the professionalism, dedication, or ability to accomplish their goals or to meet the challenge.[3]

Overall, Adams believes that at least 50 percent of the teachers were "not focused, rather vacuous, totally devoid of intellectual capacity, ill suited for the mission at hand" while Arthur Benson maintains that only 20 percent of the teachers were "totally incompetent."[4]

Obviously, the major patron of the KCMSD was and is the black community. While Arthur Benson and Judge Clark always referred to the black community, or at least its children, as a single group with a single set of interests, it was and is far from monolithic. There are, of course, the traditional mainstream organizations such as the local NAACP and Southern Christian Leadership Conference (SCLC). However, they have had little money and their power generally comes from their name recognition. Kansas City also has a black political machine, Freedom Inc., which has been quite successful at getting its candidates elected to the school board, city council, and state legislature and at turning out the black vote for statewide elections. Black pastors are also a significant force, and their power often comes from the fact that many in their congregations hold critical positions in the school district. The Reverend Emmanuel Cleaver, a former mayor, had in the 1990s over 200 teachers in his congregation. To this day, the school board will not meet on Wednesday nights because it is Baptist Training Union night. There are also more self-described "radical" groups of black separatists, such as the Black United Front, who criticize the NAACP and SCLC for being too moderate. The black community has also shown what Tocqueville called the gift of association. Ad hoc groups routinely form for particular causes. Several groups formed just because of the desegregation case. The most important of these was the Coalition for Educational and Economic Justice (CEEJ), led by Clinton Adams.

These civic- and issue-oriented organizations cannot be counted on to speak with a unanimous voice. For example, a perennial issue in the KCMSD has been whether a superintendent must be black to be hired. The black pastors have generally argued for hiring only black superintendents, while the NAACP, CEEJ, and SCLC have varied their positions over time. An additional source of contention has been the teachers' union. Activists like Clinton Adams have been deeply critical of the teachers' union, while the black pastors have tended to attack those who attack the union. The largest employers of middle-class blacks in Kansas City are the post office and the KCMSD. Many of these district employees also attend Kansas City's black churches. As a result, the black pastors, according to Arthur Benson, vigorously protected the employment of their church members.[5] But in spite of these differences there were nevertheless several times when the major black organizations were united in opposition to the magnet-school plan.

The other major force in KCMSD politics is the media. Traditionally, the *Kansas City Star* has been the dominant media outlet in Kansas City.[6] Generally, if you want to get your issue reported on television, you have to be mentioned in the *Star*. According to Clinton Adams, the *Star* is "the only game in town."[7] But the avenue to the *Star* for black activists has been the *Call*, Kansas City's oldest black newspaper. Community mobilization has traditionally started with the *Call*. After the *Call* reports that an issue has the support of the black community, the *Star* will then take notice. Since the editorial board of the *Star* has been left/liberal-leaning and very much a supporter of Arthur Benson, however, getting the newspaper to recognize black opposition to desegregation as more than just the work of a few malcontents proved to be one of the most difficult tasks facing black activists.

"Somebody's kids have to go through the meat grinder"

Almost from its inception, Judge Clark's magnet-school plan provoked hostility in the black community. Two things quickly polarized opinions. The first was an unfortunate comment made by Arthur Benson. The second was the firing of Superintendent Claude Perkins.

As the magnet plan was being designed during the mid-1980s, Arthur Benson and supportive school board members held a series of meetings with parents to answer questions about the proposed programs and facilities. At one meeting, many parents expressed concern about the disruptive nature of the plan and how it would affect their children. Benson responded, "Somebody's kids have to go through the meat grinder." This comment raised concerns among many parents, both black and white. Pete Nugent, a parent who attended the meeting, said Benson "rode roughshod over us."[8] To many Kansas Citians, Benson's comment indicated a callousness and unhealthy paternalism toward patrons of the school district.

The second event was the firing of Superintendent Claude Perkins. The school board hired Perkins in the late summer of 1985 after Eugene Eubanks's term as interim superintendent expired. It was Perkins's first superintendent position after previously serving as an assistant superintendent in Richmond, Virginia. It was just prior to Perkins's hiring that Judge Clark ordered the KCMSD to develop a magnet-school plan. Perkins, along with the only two black school board members, Julia Hill and the Reverend Bob Stephens, favored a modest magnet-school program, arguing that a large magnet program would be too disruptive for the school district. Perkins, who also was black, seemed to be well liked and trusted by the black community. The local NAACP and SCLC, along with the socially and politically powerful black pastors, supported his approach to Judge Clark's order.

But Perkins was opposed by a majority of the school board and Arthur Benson, who wanted a much larger magnet plan. The school board and Benson won. Because Perkins opposed the board's plan, it was only a matter of time before it fired him or forced him to resign. Black community leaders knew that the board was trying to remove Perkins and decided to take preemptive action. At one closed school board meeting, thirty-five black pastors and community leaders broke in and told the board not to fire Perkins and called the magnet-school plan "too ambitious."[9] That same week another group of black ministers threatened to boycott the public schools by asking their church members to keep their children home. One minister said, "I can't understand why the Board selected a superintendent and after a year they want to get rid of him. Is there something wrong with the superintendent or is there something wrong with the board?"[10] The threats, however, had little effect. The school board forced Perkins to resign. The black leadership was outraged. At a series of meetings drawing hundreds of parents, black community leaders called for the entire school board to resign. The local branch of the NAACP sent a letter to the state commissioner of education requesting an audit of the school district. It sent a second letter to Judge Clark, saying that the "black community does not support the long-range magnet school plan which board membership approved."[11] Julia Hill, board member and former chair of the local NAACP, retaliated by publicizing how much the school district spent on consultants for the magnet-school plan. From May 18 to June 17 of 1986, she revealed, the district spent $77,000 on consultants' fees. She also made special note of the alcohol tab of Phale Hale, the person the school board had hired to help design the magnet-school plan, after it rejected several plans submitted by Claude Perkins. In a two-week period while working on the magnet plan, Hale billed the school district for six trips to cocktail lounges to the tune of $180. While not much money, it symbolized to parents the school district's inability to use its resources appropriately.

Perkins's forced resignation appeared to be the result of a paternalistic school board not letting the black community make decisions for itself.[12] After Perkins's resignation, the NAACP continued opposing the magnet-school system. In a 1988 letter to Judge Clark, the NAACP requested a meeting with him and asked him to scale back the magnet plan, calling it "too ambitious, costly, and a misuse of personnel resources."[13] It said more resources should be devoted to training teachers and administrators. The NAACP only requested this meeting after it tried to express its concerns to the DMC and the school board but was rejected by both. Clark also rejected the requests.

Black leaders became increasingly convinced that their community was not being heard on the issue. Jeremiah Cameron, former president of the local NAACP, summarized the feeling of many critics of the plan when he attacked Eugene Eubanks, Judge Clark, and Arthur Benson in a letter to the *Kansas City Star*:

> The insufferable arrogance of Eugene Eubanks, who runs the Desegregation Monitoring Committee as if it were a plantation to which he holds fee simple, is not surprising. Lawyer Arthur Benson can address the entire committee whenever he pleases, but this arrogant professor invokes his interpretation of Judge Clark's intent to prevent the NAACP, which really has been in the forefront of school desegregation and integration, from telling the committee that black people are sorely displeased with the mire and inconveniences that this whole plan has dragged public education into. And Eubanks calls himself a professor of education. Indeed.
>
> The public should know that some in the School of Education of UMKC, which Eubanks formerly headed, have more than a little vested interest in the wild—and expensive—plans adopted by the school board and approved by the monitoring committee. Eubanks really has a conflict of interest—guess who devised some of these plans? And it is surprising that a federal judge would not have recognized this. No wonder he does not want a whole committee to hear criticisms of plans so dear to his heart. That they are proving a dismal failure is the least of this educator's concerns.[14]

Even though largely ignored by Benson and Eubanks, the NAACP maintained its criticisms of the magnet plan. In 1990, the school board began considering a proposal by Arthur Benson to convert the remaining traditional elementary schools into magnet schools. Once again, black civic organizations vigorously opposed the proposal. Ronald Finley, then president of the Kansas City branch of the NAACP, told the school board, "I'm not sure we've got it right so far, so I wonder where the logic is for expanding it." And Nelson Thompson, a member of the SLCL, told the board, "The black community is tired. We're fed up, but we're not giving up. We're back to say, 'We told you so.' Please listen to us this time."[15]

For their part, some black parents decided to express their dissatisfaction by asking for vouchers. A group of black parents sued to have desegregation funds pay for their children to attend private schools. Their motion said, "Extreme racial imbalance continues in the (Kansas City) schools, despite the well-intended and costly plans to reduce it."[16] The suit noted that there were 3,800 seats available in area private schools and that a rigid quota system ordered by Judge Clark prevented many black students from attending their magnet school of choice. The parents maintained that paying for students to attend private schools would be less expensive and more effective than the magnet plan. Judge Clark, however, dismissed the case saying that he was unwilling to "require the state to subsidize private education."[17] The parents' appeal to the Eighth Circuit met with no greater success.

Black parents continued to express their dissatisfaction with the plan and to question its effectiveness throughout the early 1990s. One black parent told the *Kansas City Star*, "I'm not sure the magnet schools are the remedy.... We ought to have reading-'riting-'rithmetic magnet schools."[18]

"The Movement"

While the very idea of the magnet plan was coolly received in the black community, the way Judge Clark carried it out generated outright hostility. In fact, the plan's implementation created permanent black opposition to the magnet-school plan. A group of black parents and community activists, loosely organized as the Coalition for Educational and Economic Justice, worked solely to undermine the magnet-school plan, a campaign they later dubbed "The Movement." Often criticized as malcontents and ruffians, these activists could not be dismissed as mere obstructionists. While attacking the magnet-school plan, they offered proposals of their own to improve the quality of education in Kansas City. And they were not critical of judicial intervention. They admitted that money made available by the court was helpful; however, they believed it could be used in a more effective and less demeaning way. Benson's insistence that "the legal goal has to be . . . to eliminate the effects of segregated schools" indicated to the CEEJ that Benson thought black children could not learn unless surrounded by white children.[19] This logic seemed convoluted and degrading to them. The goal of the CEEJ was to force Benson and the school district to focus on education rather than integration.

The de facto leader of the CEEJ was the eminently quotable Clinton Adams, a local attorney and lifelong resident of Kansas City. Adams was dissatisfied with his son's parochial school education, so when his daughter was entering elementary school just as the magnet plan was starting, he decided to enroll her in a magnet school close to home. But after visiting the school, Adams transferred her to a different magnet school, one of the best elementary schools in the district. His experience with the first elementary school made him suspicious of the magnet plan's ability to create meaningful changes in the school district. He determined that the quality of the teachers, not the theme of a particular magnet school, was the crucial factor in the quality of his daughter's education. Adams's experience prompted him, along with other like-minded black parents, to try to get involved with the school district. "When my daughter got involved in the public school system, I got involved as a parent," he explained. "One of the things that cajoled me was that there really were no black people involved in this implementation of the desegregation plan. People in the community, with whom I associated and worked, nobody knew anything about the desegregation plan. So I took it upon myself to become as knowledgeable as I possibly could and try to promote [and] foster community involvement, parental involvement in the desegregation plan and implementation of the desegregation plan."[20] The people Adams began working with, however, were not typical KCMSD parents. Most were middle- to upper-income professionals. For example, the other leaders of the CEEJ were Ed Newsome, a lawyer who worked in real estate appraising and development; Bill Grace, the director of the W. E. B. DuBois Learning Center; and Ajamu Webster, a local engineer. Their educational background and economic status gave them greater confidence and ability to oppose Arthur Benson than the average parent.

Initially concerned that the black community was not involved in the design and implementation of the magnet-school plan, Adams eventually concluded that the plan was actually harmful for the black children of Kansas City. A quota system that Judge Clark ordered confirmed this view.

Strange Bedfellows

Under Clark's plan each magnet school had a rigid quota system. For every six black students, there had to be four white students. This quota system was based on total enrollment in a school rather than the total number of seats. Hence, if a school had 1,000 total seats but had 240 white students, only 400 black students could attend that school. Because the district could not come close to filling all of the "white" seats in the magnet schools, many black children could not attend the magnet school of their choice, even though space was available in the school. The quota system was so rigid that in the middle and high schools, which were all magnet schools, the district became concerned about being able to find space for all of its black students. In 1989, there were over 7,000 black students on waiting lists for magnet schools even though there were thousands of available seats. Adding insult to injury was KCMSD's advertising campaign, which touted the magnet schools as the "best education in Kansas City."[21] While the magnet themes were not necessarily enticing to some parents, they knew that the magnet schools had more resources, newer facilities, and smaller class sizes. Many black parents became so exasperated that they decided to list their children as white in order to enroll their children in a preferred magnet school. For instance, one mother told *Time* that she "was lucky to get her [daughter] into this school. . . . Well, not lucky—I lied. She didn't get in the first time, so I applied again and said she was white."[22]

These quotas and the penalties they imposed on minority children infuriated the black community. Several black community organizations, including Freedom Inc., the Black Chamber of Commerce, the Kansas City Chapter of the Southern Christian Leadership Conference, the W. E. B. DuBois Learning Center, the Black United Front, the Minority Contractors Association, and the Coalition for Educational and Economic Justice, along with a group of parents, decided to file a suit requesting that the quotas be overturned. The parents needed legal representation, however, and the civic organizations could not finance the suit on their own. Clinton Adams decided that there was one organization that had sufficient funds, would provide good representation, and would demonstrate the anger of the black community, the Landmark Legal Foundation. In addition to having challenged Judge Clark's tax increases in court, Landmark's president, Mark Levin, was a close personal friend of Rush Limbaugh. Adams contacted Mark Bredemeier, who was then overseeing Landmark's legal challenge to Judge Clark's tax increases. When asked what led him to Bredemeier, Adams says, "I knew Mark through politics. He was active in Republican politics and I was involved in Democratic politics. We had a common issue basically. They thought it was unfair for black kids to be denied equal access to the schools and we thought it was unfair and we needed good legal representation. Mark Bredemeier is a real bright guy, real good lawyer. They had resources, we didn't and they were willing to represent us."[23] With Landmark's attorneys, who Bredemeier says had been "tagged as racists and for segregation," working with Kansas City's most prominent black leaders to oppose parts of Judge Clark's plan, no one could deny the deep animosity felt toward the magnet-school plan.[24] Arthur Benson, however, refused to support relaxing the racial quotas, which further alienated him from the black community.

In the summer of 1989, Landmark, with black civic organizations submitting an amicus brief, sued on behalf of the black parents to overturn the quotas. Judge Clark, however, dismissed the motion. He wrote that the "court views the 60 percent/40 percent racial guidelines as a steadfast magnet school admissions requirement and refuses to depart, even slightly, from this requirement. . . . To hold otherwise would jeopardize the possibility of ever desegregating the Kansas City School District." Clark acknowledged that at least one hundred black high school students (in reality there were hundreds more) would not be able to attend the magnet school of their choice in 1989. He was still "convinced that such a result is in the best interests of all current and future students in the district." Clark also said that the Landmark Legal Foundation represented interests that were adverse to the black students and, hence, must be dismissed as the parents' legal counsel.[25]

Landmark and Clinton Adams responded quickly by switching counsel. Landmark represented the amicus group of civic organizations, and the civic organizations' attorney, Kit Carson Roque, represented the parents. One week after Clark's dismissal, Landmark and Roque refiled their motions, which fiercely attacked the magnet-school plan and Arthur Benson. "Mr. Benson," Roque wrote, "has made public statements . . . voicing unequivocally his unwillingness to listen or represent the interests of the black community."[26] Landmark's amicus brief called the KCMSD's white recruitment "a monumental failure" and charged that "the Court's goals of remedying past constitutional violations have been frustrated by the KCMSD's ineptness." Kansas City's black children, it said, had "once again . . . fallen victim to a dual school system in Kansas City." The quota system "herded" minority children "into neglected traditional schools," while "millions of dollars are showered upon magnet schools which will sit with empty desks during school hours."[27]

Arthur Benson maintained his support for the quotas, and black community leaders continued holding meetings to criticize him. The criticism worked. Less than a month after Judge Clark first denied the motion, Benson changed his mind and filed a brief asking Judge Clark to relax the quotas. He said, "Blacks must not be denied the educational advantages of components of this desegregation plan just because whites do not care to take advantage of them." Clinton Adams, while pointing out that he still had deep disagreements with Benson, was obviously satisfied with this reversal. "We're glad to see that Mr. Benson has come around to our way of thinking," he said, "and that he's taken steps to see that black students are not denied access to magnet schools.... It seems to be an indication by Mr. Benson that ... we were right all along."[28]

Judge Clark eventually capitulated as well. In an admission that desegregation was not going to occur, he relaxed the quotas in 1990—one year after his decision to maintain the "60/40" ratio.[29] However, his initial decision had solidified in the minds of many black parents and community leaders that Clark, Benson, and the magnet-school system were not benefiting their community.

A Permanent Campaign

Having decided that black students' gaining access to the magnet schools was not enough, the CEEJ began a campaign on both political and legal fronts to eliminate the magnet schools, remove Arthur Benson as class counsel, and eventually take over the school board. Initially dismissed as a fringe group by the *Kansas City Star*, a majority of the school board, Arthur Benson, and Eugene Eubanks, the CEEJ became a powerful and feared political force that would eventually force a return to neighborhood schools.

Not everyone in the black community supported this move to a permanent campaign, although most of the disagreement centered around the CEEJ's tactics rather than its positions. The local branch of the NAACP, for example, often criticized the CEEJ for being unnecessarily inflammatory. It took particular issue with the CEEJ calling supporters of the magnet plan "misguided Aryans."[30] However, the SCLC and Freedom Inc. maintained their support for the CEEJ and its tactics. Responding to repeated critical stories in the *Kansas City Star*, Clinton Adams and the presidents of Freedom Inc. and the SCLC wrote to the newspaper, "Much has been written on the pages of this newspaper about the Coalition for Educational and Economic Justice. From the slant of the news coverage and the tone of the opinions it is apparent that we do and say things that the guardians of racial privilege don't like.... [But] myopic reporting, vapid editorials and gaseous commentaries cannot cover up the facts. Despite massive expenditures, the KCMSD is failing to serve the educational needs of this community."[31] Adams agrees that he was often strident but maintains that given the black community's exclusion during the plan's creation and implementation, he had no reason to expect Benson and the school board to listen to him without some "histrionics."[32]

After Judge Clark dismissed the CEEJ's request to relax the magnet-school quotas, its members decided the organization needed a more systematic plan of attack and held a retreat to plan its strategy. The stated goal was to "take control of the Kansas City Missouri School District."[33] Their strategy for achieving this goal involved several steps: the removal of hostile district personnel, grassroots activism through weekly community meetings, media exposure, and continued legal action.

Following this retreat, the CEEJ began what can best be described as a scorched-earth campaign against the school board, Arthur Benson, and the district administration. To those unaware of their plans, the CEEJ's actions seemed to be the product of thoughtless malcontents intent only on gaining attention through the most disruptive means possible. For instance, CEEJ members regularly took over school board meetings, and it was not unusual to see pictures of irate CEEJ members seizing microphones at board meetings gracing the pages of the *Kansas City Star*.

But, considering the actions of Arthur Benson and the school board, these tactics seemed justified to many parents. Convincing parents that programs in agribusiness, Slavic studies, and environmental science did not address their children's educational needs was not difficult. Benson and the school board lost what remained of their credibility when they proposed turning a traditional elementary school, D. A. Holmes, which was located in the heart of the black community, into an "Asian studies" magnet school. Bill Grace, a member of CEEJ and founder of the W. E. B. DuBois Learning Center, called the idea "an insult." At a school board meeting Grace asked the board if the Asian studies program was "another example of your racist white supremacy attitude."[34] Arthur Benson tried to dismiss Grace as a "narrow minded ideologue" who did not represent the majority opinion in the black community. Benson's position was difficult to maintain, however, when hundreds of parents regularly attended school board meetings and CEEJ rallies to protest the new program.[35]

Asian studies was only the most controversial theme proposed. There were others, such as Slavic studies, which also left parents perplexed and angered. The school board and Benson decided to try to accommodate the protesters by changing these programs to "multicultural" and "world" studies programs.

To reveal what they considered the racist assumptions behind the new programs, the CEEJ urged parents to request an Afrocentric magnet school, knowing that Benson would oppose it. To show their seriousness, the CEEJ designed a comprehensive proposal for an Afrocentric school. In this proposal, the CEEJ attacked the "multicultural" programs, saying that "the impact of African Americans cannot be ignored or disguised under the banner of 'multicultural' education or 'world/global' studies. It deserves the same level of respect to exist as a primary focal point as an Asian studies magnet proposal."[36] As expected, Arthur Benson opposed their proposal because it was not "desegregatively" attractive. But once again, pressure from the black community forced him to capitulate. Benson decided that he could support one African-themed elementary school but no more. However, the damage was already done. To black parents, the double standard was obvious. If Asian and Slavic studies were educationally beneficial, why not African studies?

After the Asian studies debacle, the CEEJ began their attack in earnest, holding weekly rallies to criticize the magnet plan and generate parental support for African-centered education. The CEEJ regularly distributed fliers denouncing Benson, the school board, and district personnel. The tone of these fliers was often harsh and inflammatory, making appeals to racial animus. The CEEJ believed these tactics were necessary because of the way that black community leaders had been ignored. The CEEJ even hired students at a local art institute to draw cartoons for fliers. The school district gave them ample material to work with. District Superintendent Walter Marks was always a convenient target because of his strong support for magnet schools. Art Rainwater, the associate superintendent for instruction, was also an easy target because he had said that he was willing to sacrifice the education of a generation of students in order to get the magnet-school system working properly. The CEEJ relished reminding parents of his statement at every available opportunity.

The CEEJ wanted to force Judge Clark to consider an alternative to the magnet program. In 1992, when Clark was deciding whether to convert all the remaining traditional elementary schools into magnet schools, the CEEJ filed a counterproposal to turn them, along with several magnet junior high and high schools, into "community-based" schools, which would essentially be neighborhood schools supported by substantial resources. In its proposal, the CEEJ expressed its support for the parts of Clark's remedial plan that provided funds for basic education. However, it argued that the "principal barometer for determining unitary status MUST be academic achievement levels and related factors such as college matriculation, graduation, retention, expulsion, and dropout rates, NOT arbitrary and insignificant racial quotas." To continue supporting the magnet-school plan would mean implicitly retaining racist assumptions about black children. "If white students who attend overwhelmingly white schools in environments that some consider racially isolated can succeed and excel," they argued, "our children can reach similar levels if given adequate facilities, effective curriculum and instruction, developmental support mechanisms, and culturally relevant materials. Those who believe otherwise adhere to the notion that whites are inherently intellectually superior to African Americans."[37] Additionally, the CEEJ said that no substantial integration would ever occur until black students began performing at levels comparable to those of suburban white students. White parents would not send their children to schools with underperforming peers. Community-based schools, the argument ran, would substantially improve black student performance, making white parents more willing to return to the KCMSD.

These community-based schools would have an African-centered curriculum that also emphasized improving basic skills in reading and math. "The vestiges of 'separate but equal,'" it said, "cannot be removed without curriculum equity for those who have been victimized by culturally biased education." A central part of the proposed plan was a strategy for providing a system of support for children that the CEEJ acknowledged tended to come from disadvantaged homes and neighborhoods. The plan called for hiring psychologists, home social workers, parent "outreach" coordinators, mentors, and nutritional specialists at each school. These personnel would "empower parents, especially those with relatively little or no formal education, to become more competent at stimulating the intellectual development of their children."[38] The goal of the plan, Clinton Adams later said, was "to provide support that they [students] might not have at home."[39]

Like the CEEJ's other proposals, this one received cool treatment from Arthur Benson and had no chance of being adopted by Judge Clark. If he had adopted the plan, he would have tacitly admitted that the magnet-school plan was misguided from the beginning. The CEEJ was able to stop Benson's plan to expand and extend the magnet program, however. Clinton Adams had said that to continue "Benson's Boondoggle and Fulson's Folly in the light of the plan's failures would be lunacy."[40] Judge Clark partially agreed, refusing to expand the magnet program and extending it for only two years—far less than the ten Benson had requested.

The CEEJ continued to push to eliminate the magnet program and to implement alternative programs, adopting two strategies. The first was to elect a slate of sympathetic candidates to the school board. The second was to remove Benson as plaintiff's counsel.

Edward Newsome was the first member of the CEEJ to decide to run for the school board. A Kansas City real estate appraiser, Newsome describes himself as a "Johnny come lately" to the CEEJ because he did not get involved until 1992, when his son enrolled in the school district. What really drew him to the cause, he says, was "how the school district was treating some of its black professionals . . . because it seemed like everything there was run primarily by white upper management and there were no blacks . . . who were very qualified in key positions."[41] Once involved, Newsome quickly became one of the CEEJ's most prominent members. Some of his speeches before the school board were scathing, equaling the rhetorical flourishes of Adams. In November of 1992 Newsome told the school board,

> Our community is concerned about the leadership in the KCMSD and the lack of African American involvement at the administrative level with the LRMP [Long-Range Magnet Plan]. This leadership embodies white-male privilege, white-male dominance, and white-male control. This is one that reflects the white supremacy (an oxymoron) views of the unenlightened Walter Marks, who is only comfortable with obsequious, deferential, and unconscious Negroes. They are views that embody the philosophy of this despicable, bigoted, Art Rainwater who is willing to sacrifice a whole generation of young African American children who are eager, ready, and willing to learn, if given a fair and honest chance. Art Rainwater, the George Wallace, the Lester Maddox, and the David Duke of the KCMSD. Art Rainwater, the shielded and protected reject of other districts. They are views that embody the "false Messiahiac" Arthur Benson who self-proclaims to be the one and only real representative, the only real "great white" hope for little Black boys and little Black girls.[42]

Over the next two years, Newsome continued this rhetorical assault and increased his profile in Kansas City.

In 1994, Newsome approached Edward Nutter, a white wealthy Kansas City mortgage banker, about supporting his campaign for a position on the school board. Newsome had known Nutter professionally for twenty years and was well aware that Nutter regularly contributed to the Democratic Party at the local and national levels. Nutter was not universally popular in Kansas City and was referred to by some Kansas Citians as a "Kingmaker" and as its "first citizen." Despite the criticism, Nutter remained extraordinarily powerful. His handpicked mayoral candidate, Emmanuel Cleaver, for example, was elected Kansas City's first black mayor in 1991.

After hearing Newsome's plan for the KCMSD, Nutter agreed to finance his campaign. He also told Newsome to consider fielding a slate of candidates, which Nutter would also finance. Having a voting majority on the school board would be the only way to change the direction of the school district.

Newsome recruited a slate of candidates who ran on a platform of returning the KCMSD to a system of neighborhood schools. They were John Rios, a compliance analyst; Patricia Kurtz, a part-time high school teacher; and John Still, a twenty-seven-year-old self-employed interior decorator. Since the majority of voters in the KCMSD were white, Newsome's success depended on attracting support across racial lines. John Rios, who was Hispanic, was the only other minority candidate on the slate besides Newsome. All but Still, who was running in a subdistrict against twelve-year board member Sue Fulson, were running for at-large seats. Clinton Adams also decided to run, but because he was known as the most outspoken member of the CEEJ, he was not part of Newsome's slate of candidates. The *Kansas City Star* commented favorably on all of Newsome's recruits but dismissed Newsome as a "'rabble-rouser' undeserving of endorsement."[43] Despite the unfavorable press, Newsome won, along with the rest of his slate. John Still's victory was especially significant since he had defeated Sue Fulson, who was the board's most outspoken proponent of the magnet plan. Her loss indicated how much the public had lost confidence in the remedial plan.

Clinton Adams ran in a largely black district and expected to do well, but some of the most powerful forces in Kansas City politics opposed his candidacy. Darwin Curls, whose brother was a former president of Kansas City's black political machine Freedom Inc., ran against Adams. Many women also opposed him, and the organization Concerned Women Against Violence was formed just to oppose his candidacy. The group held a rally shortly before the election condemning Adams for his "disrespectful, hateful attitude toward women." Reflecting a very common position, one of the featured speakers at the rally praised Adams for his views on education but said his personality made him unfit to serve on the school board.[44] The editors of the *Kansas City Star* also condemned Adams's candidacy, saying that his election "could spell chaos for the school district" because he "is a dishonest bully" who likes to "inject race" into debates about school district policy.[45] Rich Hood, the *Star*'s editorial page editor, said, "Adams['s] crude outbursts and threatening of district employees has overshadowed his sometimes sound ideas on needed changes in the schools."[46] Darwin Curls co-opted many of Adams's "sound ideas," such as increased support for "traditional" schools. Curls, whose brother routinely praised Adams, had the advantage of appearing to share Adams's position without the controversial personality. The result of the election was a fairly easy victory for Curls.

Adams's loss turned out to be crucial. With only a four-person voting block on the nine-member school board, Newsome fell one vote short in his bid to be president. Curls supported the previous president of the school board, Julia Hill, even though he indicated during the campaign that he supported many of Newsome's positions.[47]

After failing to take over the school board, the CEEJ turned to a legal challenge to Arthur Benson's status as class counsel. In late 1994, on behalf of several parents, Adams filed a motion before Judge Clark requesting that Benson be replaced. The brief said that Arthur Benson now "seemed to blame the victims for their plight," since he recently argued that "'poor kids are from dysfunctional families'" and that their "'families are not involved in their education.'" But the most important reason, Adams said, for replacing Benson was that "all critical decisions relative to the educational interests of the African American children have been made without meaningful input from the victims or their parents [and that] . . . little has been done by the parties to remedy the most crippling and incapacitating vestige of 'low achievement' and 'general attitude of inferiority among blacks.'"[48] The motion failed. Clark and the Eighth Circuit denied that the interests of black parents had been ignored throughout the case.

However, by the time the Eighth Circuit denied Adams's motion, the CEEJ had something almost as important, control of the school board. It had taken two years for Adams's motion to be finally dismissed by the Eighth Circuit, and another school board election had intervened. In this election, Newsome and his allies won a majority of seats, and one week later Newsome was elected school board president. Instead of being a political outsider, the CEEJ now had a seat at the table. Not surprisingly, its tactics changed. Ed Newsome had to show he could do something constructive with his newfound authority. In addition to control of the school board, Newsome had a powerful ally, the Supreme Court. As Chapter 7 discusses, the Court's 1995 opinion gave Newsome considerable leverage to undo much of the remedial plan.

Conclusion

The experience of Kansas City's black community was not unusual for a group affected by a judicial decision in a class action suit. In fact, it is common for plaintiffs' attorneys to pursue "objectives that clashed with the wishes of many of those in whose name they litigated."[49] Being excluded forced the black community to go to extreme lengths to be heard on a case ostensibly litigated on its behalf. In 1990, after growing frustration with the desegregation plan, Clinton Adams suggested this redefinition of desegregation and integration: "Many people use desegregation and integration interchangeably. That's a mistake . . . . Desegregation is the process of removing the vestiges of segregated schools: lack of adequate resources, deteriorating buildings, inadequate supplies and a generally undereducated teaching force. Correcting those wrongs is the process of desegregation. Integration is merely mixing the races in a setting. . . . Our pursuit is desegregation to improve the quality of education."[50] The redefinition, while at odds with judicial doctrine, resonated with Kansas City's black community. The exclusion of their leaders from the plan's development and the exclusion of their children from its magnet schools generated deep hostility to the idea of integration. A majority would have undoubtedly preferred that the money be spent on improving fundamental education rather than exotic magnet themes and programs. The unfortunate consequence of the magnet-school plan was anger and disillusionment in the community it was meant to serve. Throughout the remedial plan, black community leaders predicted that it would fail either to improve student achievement or to draw suburban white students. And they were right.

But this is not an entirely discouraging story. The unintended consequence of Judge Clark's intervention was the creation of a new black political force that mobilized black parents, established coalitions across political and racial lines, and reasserted common sense against the far-fetched theories of educational experts. Black parents saw that they could force changes and did not have to be the complacent victims of a dysfunctional school board and administration. By 1995, few people were talking about what would be attractive to suburban white students. Arthur Benson was forced to recognize that the very community he claimed to represent deeply opposed his emphasis on attracting white students. He needed to shift his focus to the wishes of the black community. The CEEJ had changed the terms of the debate and by doing so won the political war.

While it is certainly encouraging to see a grassroots movement effect change through the political process, it is distressing that the black community was excluded from the legal process and could not influence the framing of the remedial decree. Of course, forces in addition to the nature of class action lawsuits were at work. The remedies preferred by the black community were at odds with both Supreme Court precedents and the Eighth Circuit Court of Appeals. This placed the black community in precisely the opposite position it was in prior to *Brown v. Board of Education*. Then, the black community found itself disempowered because of the political process and was forced to resort to the courts for protection. In *Missouri v. Jenkins* the political process was its only avenue of influence.

7

The Last Days of Desegregation?

Time magazine's April 29, 1996, front cover forebodingly read, "Back to Segregation." The issue's lead article was largely devoted to Judge Clark's desegregation effort. The article documented the magnet plan's many failures and paid substantial attention to the complaints of black critics such as Clinton Adams, who told *Time*, "The most egregious injustice is the situation where suburban white kids get priority over resident African American kids, who are the adjudicated victims of segregation. That's atrocious. Just try to achieve some kind of mythical benefit that black kids will receive by sitting next to a white kid." At the time the article was published, however, there had been a substantial change in the case. For the first time, Judge Clark's authority seemed threatened. *Time* speculated, "When the history of court-ordered school desegregation is written, Kansas City may go down as its Waterloo."[1] This was a mere six years after the Supreme Court upheld Judge Clark's authority to require tax increases. During those years, Judge Clark experienced an extremely fast fall from grace.

As Judge Clark's plan faltered during the early 1990s, the state continued its opposition, unsuccessfully appealing nearly every major order to the Eighth Circuit. The Eighth Circuit remained a reliable ally of Clark, but there were signs that the Supreme Court was changing its position on desegregation. Two Supreme Court decisions suggested that an appeal by the state might be successful. In these cases, *Board of Education of Oklahoma City v. Dowell* (1991) and *Freeman v. Pitts* (1992), the Supreme Court reasserted a distinction between de facto and de jure segregation and indicated that it wanted federal judges to begin withdrawing supervision over school districts. These two cases, along with the failure of Clark's plan to produce desirable results, gave the state hope that it might be successful on a return trip to the Supreme Court. The Court agreed to hear the case again in 1995. Its ruling in *Jenkins III* would be a fatal blow to the magnet-school plan.

Board of Education of Oklahoma City v. Dowell

During the 1980s the Supreme Court gave no rulings on desegregation. In some ways, this reflected the uneasy accommodation it had reached in the 1970s. But in others it reflected the deeply controversial nature of desegregation. In addition, the Reagan and Bush administrations' Justice Department had actively pursued a policy of terminating desegregation cases. That policy was successful in the early 1990s, starting with the Court's decision in *Board of Education of Oklahoma City v. Dowell*.[2]

The Oklahoma City School District had been under judicial oversight since 1972 when ordered to adopt a busing plan. The district maintained the busing plan until 1984, when the school board determined that demographic changes were leading to increased burdens on inner-city black children. The district decided to largely abandon the plan and return to a primarily neighborhood-based attendance policy. The new policy received the support of black members of the school board, black teachers, and black members of the PTA. To ensure that the plan met constitutional standards, while the board set up the new attendance zones, the school board consulted with the Office of Civil Rights in Dallas.[3] Meanwhile, the original plaintiffs in the suit from 1972 who opposed abandoning the busing plan asked the district court to reinstate it. The district court ruled against the plaintiffs, asserting that the school district had achieved unitary status.[4] On appeal, the school district lost, with the appellate court remanding the case back to the district court. Back in district court, the school board won once again. In a sharply worded opinion, the district court pointed out the limitations of remedying the segregation in Oklahoma City:

> Plaintiffs are . . . proposing that this court perpetuate a remedy which cannot correct the condition they object to—residential segregation. . . . Under plaintiffs' rationale, this court should continue the busing of young students in Oklahoma City until such time as racial balance exists in all neighborhoods. Yet, plaintiffs do not suggest how the school district should go about creating this balance or what kind of order this court could enter that might, as a practical matter, have chance of changing the present patterns of residential segregation. . . . For the plaintiffs to claim that the [district's plan] is a step toward a dual school system is ludicrous and absurd.[5]

The appeals court, however, once again reversed the district court decision, arguing that the school district was still under the court injunction to maintain unitary status for student attendance and remanding the case to the district court to fashion another busing plan.[6]

Angered by the appellate court's decision, the school board appealed to the Supreme Court, which granted certiorari. In 1991, the Supreme Court ruled on the case, reversing the decision of the appeals court but without affirming the finding of the district court. Chief Justice Rehnquist stated, "We think that the preferable course is to remand the case to that court so that it may decide, in accordance with this opinion, whether the Board made a sufficient showing of constitutional compliance as of 1985, when the SRP [the neighborhood attendance policy] was adopted, to allow the injunction to be dissolved."[7] Although the case was technically remanded, the district court's previous rulings guaranteed that it would reaffirm its initial finding. The majority's decision indicated that the Court was reasserting a distinction between de jure and de facto segregation; however, the decision provided little guidance for lower courts on how to distinguish between vestiges of de jure segregation and current de facto segregation.

Freeman v. Pitts

Like *Dowell*, *Freeman v. Pitts* involved a conflict between a district court and an appellate court over the removal of judicial supervision. The Dekalb County School System (DCSS), just outside of Atlanta, had undergone massive demographic changes since it first came under judicial supervision in 1969. In 1986, the school board requested that the district court dismiss the case. The district court found that the board was compliant in four of six *Green* factors and granted partial removal of judicial oversight. On appeal, however, the appellate court overturned the district court's ruling, saying that judicial supervision must be maintained until all six *Green* factors had been met.

The board appealed to the Supreme Court, which overruled the appeals court's finding that a district court could not incrementally remove supervision. Writing for a unanimous Court, Justice Kennedy stated that a "federal court in a school desegregation case has the discretion to order an incremental or partial withdrawal of its supervision and control. This discretion derives both from the constitutional authority which justified its intervention in the first instance and its ultimate objectives in formulating the decree."[8] Kennedy went on to give further guidelines for lower courts in deciding whether they could withdraw supervision. These factors became known as the three-part *Freeman* test. Kennedy wrote:

> Among the factors which must inform the sound discretion of the court in ordering partial withdrawal are the following: whether there has been full and satisfactory compliance with the decree in those aspects of the system where supervision is to be withdrawn; whether retention of judicial control is necessary or practicable to achieve compliance with the decree in other facets of the school system; and whether the school district has demonstrated, to the public and to the parents and students of the once disfavored race, its good-faith commitment to the whole of the court's decree and to those provisions of the law and the Constitution that were the predicate for judicial intervention in the first instance.[9]

These guidelines do not actually give much guidance, but they certainly sent a message to lower courts that the time had come to start withdrawing supervision.

While these guidelines were vague, Kennedy was clear that the DCSS was not required to desegregate when segregation resulted from demographic trends. In fact, he noted that the DCSS had achieved unitary status in 1969 when it closed all of its formerly de jure black schools. "Racial balance is not to be achieved for its own sake," Kennedy argued. "It is to be pursued when racial imbalance has been caused by a constitutional violation." He went on to directly attack the notion that de facto segregation warrants judicial relief:

> Where resegregation is not a product of state action, but of private choices, it does not have constitutional implications. It is beyond the authority and beyond the practical ability of the federal courts to try to counteract these kinds of continuous and massive demographic shifts. To attempt such results would require ongoing and never-ending supervision by the courts of school districts simply because they were once de jure segregated. Residential housing choices, and their attendant effects on the racial composition of schools, present an ever-changing pattern, one difficult to address through judicial remedies.[10]

This statement was a clear warning to district court judges that segregation itself was not unconstitutional and that they should not attempt to undo segregation that is only tenuously related to past discrimination.

Dowell and *Freeman* were not unnoticed in Missouri. These cases indicated to the Missouri attorney general's office, which was desperate to stop hemorrhaging money to Kansas City, that the Supreme Court was much more amenable to considering desegregation cases.

Jenkins III: Judge Clark's "Waterloo"

While the Court's message was clear in *Dowell* and *Freeman*, Judge Clark seemed to ignore it. At the same time that the Court instructed judges to begin withdrawing supervision of school districts, Judge Clark expanded his control in Kansas City. In a series of decisions, Clark ordered pay increases for instructional and noninstructional personnel, tax increases to pay for the higher salaries, and a two-year extension of the magnet-school plan.

Clark's 1987 decision had provided a small pay raise for teachers. In 1990 Clark decided to provide more significant raises to make the KCMSD "desegregatively attractive." Based on the 1990 Supreme Court decision, the school board could recommend tax increases, which Judge Clark would have to approve. The school board decided its teachers needed, at a cost of $68 million, an across-the-board 20 percent base pay increase along with additional "step" increases based on experience. To pay for these raises, the district requested and Clark approved a 24 percent increase in the property tax levy, raising it from $4.00 to $4.96 per $100 of assessed property value.[11] The salary increases were supposed to expire and return to their previous levels in 1992, so the KCMSD and the Kansas City chapter of the American Federation of Teachers (AFT) requested that Judge Clark reapprove them for the 1992–93 school year. The state argued that the salary increases had neither improved the quality of education in the KCMSD nor helped to draw better teachers to the KCMSD. Other factors, it argued, such as safety and the KCMSD's reputation for perpetual incompetence, kept better teachers from moving to Kansas City. The KCMSD and the AFT responded that they needed higher salaries to attract and retain better personnel. Clark sided with the district and the teachers' union, ruling that the salaries would remain at the previous judicially increased level for the 1992–93 school year.[12]

The issue reappeared in 1993, with the KCMSD and AFT asking for a raise in addition to the one Clark reapproved in 1992. This time, though, they asked for increases for both instructional and noninstructional personnel. Clark, once again, sided with the KCMSD and AFT and ordered, on top of the reauthorized 1990 increases, another 20 percent base pay increase for teachers, additional "step" increases, and smaller raises for other personnel. Thus,

164   THE LAST DAYS OF DESEGREGATION?

from 1987 to 1993, Kansas City teachers had seen in their base pay alone an increase of 44 percent at a cost of $200 million.[13]

Even though the state continued accumulating legal losses at a shocking rate, it was becoming more confident, even arrogant, in its arguments before Clark. In late 1992, Clark began to review whether or not he should continue the Long-Range Magnet Plan (LRMP). The state argued that under *Freeman* the district had already achieved partial unitary status and should, therefore, be relieved of its obligations in several areas. In briefs submitted to Judge Clark, the state hinted not so subtly that the Supreme Court wanted judges to return control of school districts to local school boards. Relying on *Dowell* and *Freeman* to remind Judge Clark that desegregation plans were supposed to be temporary measures, the state argued that the "results obtained after more than seven years of implementation by the KCMSD and the utilization of more than one billion dollars provide no justification even for continuation, much less expansion, of the LRMP."[14] Scornfully attacking the centerpiece of Clark's judicial career would doubtlessly anger him. The state apparently had accepted that Clark would rule against it. Now, however, the attorney general's office had reason to hope for a successful appeal to the Supreme Court.

Clark ruled that the LRMP should be continued for at least two more years. This was not what Arthur Benson had hoped for. Benson had requested an extension of ten years and an expansion of the program that would have converted all the remaining traditional schools (half of the elementary schools) into magnet schools. By this time, Clark had grown at least somewhat wary of Benson's requests and predictions. For the moment, he could only justify two additional years. This was a moral victory for the state, but the aspersions it cast on Judge Clark's plan did not go unnoticed. Clark chastised the state for "*never* offer[ing] the Court a viable, even tenable, alternative" and being "extremely antagonistic in its approach to effecting the desegregation of the KCMSD."[15]

Meanwhile, Missouri had elected a new attorney general, Jay Nixon, a Democratic state senator who opposed the desegregation orders just as vigorously as his Republican predecessor.[16] In fact, after Judge Clark ordered pay increases and an extension of the LRMP, Nixon immediately appealed to the Eighth Circuit with an obvious eye toward an appeal to the Supreme Court. The Eighth Circuit, once again, affirmed Judge Clark's ruling. But instead of simply upholding Clark's decisions, the Eighth Circuit instituted a new standard for judging the success of a desegregation plan: student achievement.

Clark had said that improving student achievement was one of his goals but never that it constituted a standard for determining when judicial supervision should end. Previously, improved student achievement was considered a by-product of desegregation, not a constitutional mandate. The Eighth Circuit, however, said that the "success of the quality of education programs must be measured by their effect on the students, particularly those who have been the victims of segregation. It will take time to remedy the system-wide reduction in student achievement in the KCMSD schools."[17] Judge Clark could thus continue his programs indefinitely, since student achievement showed no sign of improvement. Such a standard also strangely implied the fact that thousands of white students enrolling in the KCMSD would not be considered desegregation.

In 1994 the state petitioned for certiorari to the Supreme Court on two issues: whether Judge Clark could order the pay increase and whether the KCMSD could remain under Judge Clark's supervision until the district's students reached some as-yet-unidentified level on standardized tests. The Court agreed to hear the case in 1995.

In an op-ed article in the *Kansas City Star*, Attorney General Jay Nixon explained why he had decided to appeal to the Supreme Court: "I have chosen to challenge the court's [Eighth Circuit's] ruling because, if upheld, it would hold the state to a standard higher than has ever been presented in any case in the country." And it also "would require schools to overcome factors over which they have little or no control."[18] In oral arguments before the Court on January 11, 1995, the state reiterated those points and its arguments against mandated pay raises. In opposition, NAACP Legal Defense Fund attorney Theodore Shaw presented Arthur Benson's case, maintaining that previous segregation must have affected student achievement and therefore should be a relevant consideration when deciding to end judicial supervision.[19] The arguments presented to the Court were not new on either side. The only major difference from the 1990 case was the composition of the Court. David Souter had replaced William Brennan, Clarence Thomas had replaced Thurgood Marshall, Ruth Bader Ginsburg had replaced Byron White, and Stephen Breyer had replaced Harry Blackmun. Souter, Ginsburg, and Breyer were expected to vote as their predecessors had. Souter, who conservatives had hoped would be a conservative stalwart, turned out to be much closer to Brennan than to any conservatives on the Court. This made Thomas's replacement of Thurgood Marshall the only meaningful change in the Court's composition. Rehnquist, Kennedy, Scalia, and O'Connor apparently had a crucial fifth vote. Based on the justices' questions, observers expected a sharply divided court.

The 5-4 ruling met those expectations. But this time, Judge Clark and Arthur Benson found themselves on the losing side of an appellate decision. Writing for the majority, Chief Justice Rehnquist ruled that the salary increases constituted an interdistrict remedy for an intradistrict violation of *Milliken* (see Chapter 1) because the increases were designed to draw teachers, staff, and students from the suburban school districts. "This interdistrict goal," Rehnquist wrote, "is beyond the scope of the intradistrict violation identified by the District Court. In effect, the District Court has devised a remedy to accomplish indirectly what it admittedly lacks the remedial authority to mandate directly: the interdistrict transfer of students."[20] Luring personnel and students from the suburbs was in fact a form of punishment against suburban school districts, which had not committed any constitutional violation. In its decision, the majority also urged Judge Clark to expeditiously end judicial supervision in Kansas City. Chief Justice Rehnquist wrote, "The District Court must bear in mind that its end purpose is not only 'to remedy the violation' to the extent practicable, but also 'to restore state and local authorities to the control of a school system that is operating in compliance with the Constitution.'"[21] The Court emphasized that the more the KCMSD became dependent on state funding, the more it became dependent on the district court—an undesirable and unconstitutional effect. Finally, Rehnquist stressed the difference between de jure and de facto segregation: "Just as demographic changes independent of de jure segregation will affect the racial composition of student assignments so too will numerous external factors beyond the control of the KCMSD and the state affect minority student achievement. So long as these external factors are not the result of segregation, they do not figure in the remedial calculus."[22] The Court plainly signaled that low student achievement would be difficult to attribute to de jure segregation, although it left the possibility open. The message to Judge Clark was quite clear: return control to the KCMSD quickly.

In his concurring opinion Justice Thomas was even more outspoken against the assumptions inherent in the judicial attack on de facto segregation: "'Racial isolation' itself is not a harm; only state-enforced segregation is. After all, if separation itself is a harm, and if integration therefore is the only way that blacks can receive a proper education, then there must be something inferior about blacks. Under this theory, segregation injures blacks because blacks, when left on their own, cannot achieve. To my way of thinking, that conclusion is the result of a jurisprudence based upon a theory of black inferiority."[23] Thomas also chastised Clark for "experiment[ing] with the education of the KCMSD's black youth" and for contributing to "stereotypes" of black inferiority. He then questioned Clark's reliance on psychological and educational experts who provided "misleading assistance" about what constitutes harm and how it can be remedied. Thomas finally addressed the issue of equity and how the courts had expanded it in order to "eradicate segregation" and in the end trampled on the constitutional principles of federalism and the separation of powers. The Supreme Court, he believed, should reassert the old restrictions on the use of equity power in order to keep judges from prescribing wildly inapt remedies for complex social problems.[24]

The four dissenters vigorously attacked the majority's opinion, with Justices Souter and Ginsburg filing opinions. Justice Souter's primary criticism was that the Court did not review the scope of the district court's remedies when the Court first granted certiorari in 1988, arguing that this lack of review "lulled the respondents into addressing the case without sufficient attention to the foundational issue." While he disagreed with Rehnquist's opinion, he gave no indication that the project undertaken by Judge Clark would be justified now. Justice Ginsburg, however, seemed open to future judicial remedies for de facto segregation. In her short dissent, she pointed out that Missouri had a long history of legally enforced segregation and implied that the current racial makeup of Kansas City was attributable to this past. She said that in 1984 the school district was "sorely in need" of integration based simply on the fact that it was 68.3 percent black.[25]

The most important part of the majority's ruling was the prohibition on voluntary methods of drawing white students and teachers from the suburbs. Remedial programs relying on voluntary means of attracting suburban white students would no longer be in the judicial toolkit. Consequently, with increasing white flight from urban communities, the courts were left with few options for promoting integration. In communities with a 70–80 percent minority student population, busing would be useless and magnet programs intended to voluntarily draw white students would be unconstitutional.

The End of Desegregation?

The *New York Times* called the Court's decision the work of a "constitutional wrecking crew" that ignored the reality that "America is far from overcoming more than two centuries of bigotry."[26] The reaction in Kansas City was decidedly different. Many patrons of the KCMSD, including several members of the school board, applauded the Court's decision. At the time of the Court's decision, Edward Newsome, parent, black activist, and prominent member of the Coalition for Educational and Economic Justice (CEEJ), was on the cusp of wresting control of the board from supporters of the magnet plan and would shortly begin negotiations with the state to end the state's involvement. Newsome, who wanted to return control of the KCMSD back to the district, told *Time*, "I welcomed the Supreme Court decision. I saw it as an opportunity for the first time in years to focus on removing the vestiges of segregation."[27] The sooner the case ended, the sooner he could implement his reforms. The Supreme Court's decision had raised the hope that the DMC would no longer be watching over the district and chastising administrators and board members.

Following the Supreme Court ruling, the state, smelling blood, filed a motion asking Judge Clark to grant unitary status. But Clark was unwilling to completely surrender. His ruling on the motion revealed a disillusioned, and even bitter, judge attempting to salvage what he could of the case and subverting the will of the Supreme Court. The contrast with his opinions during the 1980s, which applied the law in a straightforward and unemotional tone, is striking. The tenor of this opinion indicated that Clark was angry that the Court had changed the rules. He had faithfully applied the Court's precedents in the 1980s, and those precedents had pushed him into the educational catastrophe, and undoubtedly personal embarrassment, of *Missouri v. Jenkins*.

Clark's opinion had three parts. In the first part, Clark denied unitary status in all areas except for extracurricular activities and struck back at the Supreme Court's 1995 ruling. The Supreme Court, he said, "strained legal reasoning" when it examined "both the scope of the remedy and the voluntary interdistrict remedy prescribed by this Court."[28] The state's request for unitary status, he believed, was "fueled" by its victory before the Supreme Court. But to justify his decision Clark at least had to appear to follow the Supreme Court's "strained" ruling. He noted that the Court told him to "sharply limit" but not eliminate his reliance on test scores. Because the Supreme Court left a small opening, Clark decided that the KCMSD's student achievement level still had to increase before judicial control could end. Relying on a baffling use of regression analysis, Clark tried to demonstrate that at least 26 percent of the achievement gap between white and black students was due to unconstitutional segregation. The KCMSD's expert witnesses had found in 1987 that prior de jure segregation was responsible for much of the underachievement in Kansas City. Therefore, Clark concluded that prior segregation must still be responsible for some of the gap in spite of his own ambitious efforts. The ruling gave the KCMSD three years to close this gap and attain unitary status, but it was clear that the achievement gap could not be reduced by 26 percent in that amount of time. Also, since both minority and nonminority students could be expected to improve at the same rate with better teaching, the achievement gap would not be reduced. All students would improve; hence, the gap would remain. Desegregation was no longer even a nominal goal of judicial oversight. Student achievement was the only justification left for judicial control.

In the second part of his ruling, Clark approved an agreement between the state of Missouri and the KCMSD that would end the state's involvement with the case. Immediately after being elected school board president in 1996, Ed Newsome negotiated a withdrawal agreement with Attorney General Jay Nixon. Newsome said the reason for ending the state's involvement "was that it was difficult—almost impossible—to focus our attention on educating the children from the courtroom." Every time the board wanted to make changes from curriculum to personnel they "would have to go back and get a court order."[29] Under the agreement the state would pay the KCMSD $314 million over three years, after which its obligations would end. Arthur Benson immediately denounced the agreement, calling it "an agreement that politicians would love and parents and students and educators should detest." He saw no way for the KCMSD to be financially viable without state funding in perpetuity.[30] Clark, however, sided with the state and the KCMSD, saying that "any remaining obligation of the State to the children of Kansas City may be discharged by the payment of the funds provided for in the agreement."[31]

Judge Clark devoted the final part of his order to an extended and at times vitriolic attack on the KCMSD. He criticized the KCMSD's lack of a "comprehensive, integrated educational and instructional plan," inept "staff development," "ongoing administrative instability," and the "lavish" size of the "administrative budget." Clark noted that the KCMSD's student-teacher ratio of 12.7 to 1 for the 1993–94 school year was significantly lower than that of ten comparable school districts, such as the Montgomery County School District, Alabama, and the Stockton City District in California, which were 17.7 to 1 and 23.1 to 1, respectively. As well, 1993 per-pupil spending in Kansas City, at $8,315, which excluded expenditures on capital improvements, was nearly double that of all the comparable districts. And by 1995, the school district was spending $10,308 per pupil. But the "lavish" administrative budget meant that much of that money never made it to the students, a point Clark made by comparing the size of the administrative staff in the KCMSD to that of the Springfield, Missouri, School District (SMSD). While the KCMSD's enrollment was one-third larger than Springfield's, its administrative staff was anywhere from two to ten times as large. Springfield had 3 employees in its accounting department while the KCMSD had 63. There were 219 maintenance and custodial employees in the SMSD, compared to 531 in the KCMSD, and Springfield employed 5 people in its data processing department versus Kansas City's 42. Clark called these disparities "alarming even taking the desegregation staffing into account and factors that the KCMSD must face that the Springfield District does not, such as a large minority enrollment."[32] What was most interesting about this piece of judicial venting was that Judge Clark essentially made the same charges against the KCMSD that the state had made back in 1983 during the initial trial. Even the KCMSD's most gracious benefactor had become disillusioned with the district he had tried to save.

This would be Judge Clark's last decision in the case. After issuing this ruling he stepped down, leaving the end of the case to an "exit judge." Although his goal had been to reduce the disparity in educational achievement between black and white students, he later confessed that he did not know "if the disparity ... can ever be eliminated. Probably not."[33]

The End of *Missouri v. Jenkins*

The case was reassigned by lottery to Judge Dean Whipple. A Reagan appointee and Missouri native, Judge Whipple was expected to be less supportive of the desegregation effort. He did, however, have a reputation for "taking over floundering public agencies." He took over the Kansas City Housing Authority and the Missouri Division of Family Services, for example, but only "reluctantly," after they "failed to respond to complaints about how they were run."[34] The KCMSD seemed to fit the criteria for a "floundering public agency," making it unclear whether his preference for restraint or his intolerance of incompetence would guide him in the case. Initially, his intolerance of incompetence drove his decisions.

A month after assuming control of the case, Whipple said that he might name a special master to oversee the KCMSD and even asked all the parties to submit names of candidates for the position. To Whipple's surprise, the school board was outraged at the proposition. He knew that Ed Newsome, president of the school board, was in the process of cutting millions of dollars from the district's budget and closing many schools. A special master, Whipple thought, would give Newsome "someone to blame." But Newsome told Whipple, "We're not looking for a scapegoat or any political cover. We are willing to face the challenge."[35] Instead of appointing a special master, Judge Whipple decided to expand the authority of the DMC and reduce its number from twelve members to three. The KCMSD would "retain final decision-making authority," according to Whipple, but the DMC would "participate in the day-to-day decision-making process and in the creative process of restructuring the District to pursue academic achievement and racial integration within practicable means."[36]

Several major developments followed Whipple's inauspicious start, which culminated with the termination of the case. The first was a return to neighborhood schools. Under Newsome's direction, and with the support of black and Hispanic community leaders, the KCMSD school board voted to return to a largely neighborhood-based system.[37] According to Newsome, educational and financial reasons guided this return to neighborhood attendance boundaries. The school board and most parents believed that the long distances children had to travel to attend the appropriate magnet school were detrimental to their education. In addition, many parents, especially the poorer ones, had neither the time nor the money to travel across town to attend school functions. "There were some families with four or five children that went to four or five different schools with four or five school buses pulling up in front of their house every morning," Newsome said later. "If you have a parent, maybe a one-parent family, even a two-parent family with two cars it's difficult. But many parents did not have even one car to get across town. So that relationship between parents and schools was severed by the magnet school system."[38] Financially, the school district could not justify the millions of dollars in transportation costs the magnet system required. Newsome estimated that the school district would reduce its busing costs by half, nearly $20 million in savings, after returning to a neighborhood system.

A second development was a permanent increase in the KCMSD property taxes. When judicial supervision ended, the property tax rate would roll back from $4.96 per $100 of assessed value to $2.75. With no state money coming in after 2000, the KCMSD would lose an additional $80 million a year in tax revenue if the case ended. The Missouri legislature decided to remedy the situation by placing a constitutional amendment before Missouri in April of 1998 that would allow the KCMSD school board, rather than the voters, to set the tax rate at $4.95. Amendment 3 (as it was called) received little attention. Almost everyone assumed that it would pass because the rest of Missouri was still angry for having to subsidize the desegregation plan for thirteen years. During the early 1990s Missouri's desegregation expenses in St. Louis and Kansas City comprised close to 10 percent of the state budget. In 1994, Missouri spent more on desegregation than its prison system, court system, highway patrol, and state fire marshal combined.[39] The money being poured into Kansas City diverted money from other—especially rural—school districts. Many districts had to slash athletic programs, freeze pay for teachers, and eliminate full-day kindergarten. The resentment this situation generated carried the day, with Missouri voters overwhelmingly—nearly two to one—approving Amendment 3.[40]

A third development was the establishment of charter schools. The Missouri legislature passed a law permitting charter schools in St. Louis and Kansas City, starting in the 1999-2000 school year. Since their inception, charter schools have been immensely popular in Kansas City. In 1999, fifteen charter schools opened, enrolling 4,500 students. Most of those students came from the KCMSD, whose enrollment dropped from 34,525 students in the 1998-99 school year to 30,688 students the 1999-2000 school year.[41] Two more charter schools opened in 2000, increasing the charter school enrollment to 5,600 students. At the same time, the KCMSD's enrollment declined once again, to 29,945.[42] This precipitous drop in enrollment reflected the deep disaffection and disillusionment parents had toward the KCMSD. Many of the charter schools showed no better results than their KCMSD counterparts, but seats were quickly filled.

The popularity of charter schools created severe problems for the KCMSD through a loss of money and teachers. State aid in Missouri is based on numbers of students, so money for departed pupils went to the charter schools rather than the KCMSD. In the charter schools' first year alone the KCMSD lost $15 million in state aid.[43] The KCMSD also had difficulty staffing its classrooms because many teachers left for charter schools. This was especially true of high school foreign language instructors. Charter schools offered the allure of greater freedom and more-committed students and the added bonus of more parent involvement since parents who send their children to charter schools presumably take a greater interest in their child's education than other parents.[44]

In November of 1999 Judge Whipple issued a surprise ruling. Earlier in the year the Missouri Department of Education had stripped the KCMSD of its accreditation because of poor student performance, and the school district had asked Judge Whipple to reinstate it. Instead, Whipple ruled that everything possible had been done to remedy the prior constitutional violations and therefore the school district should be left to its own devices. Starkly summarizing the past forty years, he said, "Despite the expenditure of vast sums, the prolonged oversight of a federal court and its appointees, the efforts of multiple parties, and the passage of forty years since the end of official *de jure* segregation in Kansas City, Missouri, the KCMSD still struggles to provide an adequate education to its pupils."[45] The simple message of his order was that in light of all that had been tried before, there was nothing more to be gained from his continued oversight. And with the return of neighborhood schools, no one was even attempting to "desegregate" the KCMSD. The last paragraph of the decision said what many thought would never be said, "This case is dismissed."

But it would not be dismissed. Arthur Benson appealed, once again, to the Eighth Circuit, arguing that the KCMSD still needed judicial oversight. The Eighth Circuit agreed with Benson and overturned Judge Whipple in May of 2000. The en banc eleven-member panel split 6-5. The rationale for overturning Judge Whipple was that he had not held a hearing over the issue of unitary status. The majority also said that the KCMSD had to adequately implement plans in five areas: classroom practices, professional development, assessment, accountability, and curriculum. Of course, the KCMSD ever "satisfactorily" implementing any of these plans was a dubious proposition, so the decision kept the case open-ended.[46] However, the language of the opinion indicated that to muster a majority, the judges who strongly favored judicial oversight had moderated their rhetoric. In fact, Judge Roger L. Wollman, a Reagan appointee, said he joined the majority only to require a hearing on unitary status.

The dissenters did not dissent quietly. Judge Arlen Beam, a Reagan appointee, wrote for the minority. He derided the judicial efforts to salvage the KCMSD and even argued that the courts had been responsible for exacerbating the KCMSD's educational deficiencies:

After twenty-three years of federal court supervision, the education program of the Kansas City Missouri School District (KCMSD) is in shambles. Its students remain as racially isolated as when the first remedial order was entered by the district court on June 14, 1985. Student scores as measured by routine and regularly administered standardized tests have remained static or have declined and this occurred even though over two-billion tax dollars have been spent since 1985 on the remedial plan alone, with total educational spending averaging more than $9,000 per student per year (in addition to millions of dollars in capital expenditures). I am confident that this average per pupil amount is well above that spent by any other school district in Missouri for the same period. Until 1996, attorneys for the Jenkins class freely roamed the classrooms, hallways and playgrounds monitoring, observing, talking and projecting themselves into the work and educational lives of school principals, faculty, staff, and students. Until very recently, a Desegregation Monitoring Committee under the direct control of the district court involved itself in the day-to-day activities of the school system. Unremarkably, the Office of Superintendent of Schools, the supposed chief executive of the school system, has been a revolving door[,] and once the office was empty for a significant period of time. Finally, the State has now designated the KCMSD as unaccredited.[47]

This was the strongest criticism ever made by a federal judge against the desegregation plan. This was not an encouraging sign for Arthur Benson. It showed the Eighth Circuit's increasing impatience with his efforts.

Judge Whipple finally succeeded in terminating the case in 2003. When it finally came, the end seemed anticlimactic. After conducting a hearing on unitary status, he ruled that the district had complied with Judge Clark's final ruling from 1997 and that the district had done everything practicable to eliminate the vestiges of prior segregation. Arthur Benson, of course, opposed granting unitary status, but Whipple held that to "accept Plaintiffs' invitation to continue Court supervision over the KCMSD would involve this Court in issues with which it has no business. . . . Taken to its logical end, Plaintiffs would have this Court serve as a super-school board perpetually reviewing educational programs implemented in the KCMSD."[48] Benson did not appeal.

Still an Educational Titanic

When the case ended in 2003, the KCMSD had the same problems it had in 1977. Most importantly, the district administration continued what Jack Cashill called its "public access vaudeville" and remained hopelessly ineffective. School board members did not have either the will or the political capital to make meaningful changes.[49] When board members made tough decisions, they were punished. An example of this was Ed Newsome. Judge Whipple had offered him the political cover of a special master, which Newsome declined, saying that he and his allies on the board were willing to make the tough but unpopular decisions needed to improve the KCMSD. He should have accepted Judge Whipple's offer.

After leading the return to neighborhood schools, Newsome then had to make decisions about school closings. The KCMSD could no longer afford or justify keeping many of its schools open when only half their seats were filled. School closings are always politically dangerous affairs because large numbers of constituents are invariably adversely affected. School board members often become sacrificial lambs. This happened with Newsome. Even though his neighborhood-schools initiative was popular, his school closings created deep animosity among many parents. Much of this was Newsome's fault. The same combative attitude he had while opposing the magnet-school system often carried over during his tenure as president of the school board. He came to be seen as authoritarian and uncaring toward the concerns of parents. As a result he was not reelected to the school board in 1998, coming in third in a race for two at-large seats.

Since Newsome's departure the school board has become even more rancorous, with coalitions constantly shifting and factions emerging and quickly dissolving. In 2000, the situation on the board had degenerated to the point that there weren't enough candidates to fill several seats. The KCMSD even resorted to advertising for candidates.

The school board's problems have been exceeded only by those in the superintendent's office. After Walter Marks was fired for running off to Florida in 1992 under the pretext of a medical leave, the KCMSD has been a revolving door for interim and full-time superintendents. The first of the full-time superintendents, Henry Williams, former superintendent of schools in Little Rock, was hired in 1996. Ed Newsome's first choice was John Murphy, but when he declined the offer, Newsome pushed for Williams, an African American and a strong supporter of neighborhood schools. In the rush to hire Williams, however, no one could do much research on his past.

Williams's tenure, which lasted only two years, was a disaster from the beginning. The *Kansas City Star* reported that within "two months of his arrival . . . Henry Williams was already having second thoughts about his decision to take the job as superintendent." His time in Kansas City was marred by "frequent tangles with the Desegregation Monitoring Committee, various school board members and desegregation lawyer Arthur A. Benson." As a consequence, he had very little time to do anything other than fight political battles. He also made things difficult for himself by moving out of the district, which his contract prohibited.[50] His quick temper also led him to a very public confrontation with Arthur Benson. At a hearing before Judge Whipple, Benson accused Williams of giving his girlfriend's sister a district job, among other acts of nepotism. After the hearing and in front of the local television cameras, Williams called Benson a "punk."[51] The board eventually decided to buy out his contract for nearly $200,000.[52]

Williams's replacement had his own share of difficulties. Like Williams, Benjamin Demps was not the first or even second choice of the school board. The first two choices withdrew their names from consideration. Demps, who had been an administrator for thirty-five years in the Federal Aviation Administration and then served three years as director of the Oklahoma Department of Human Services, had no experience in public education. When the KCMSD approached him, he was "semi-retired" and operated an aviation consulting business.[53]

His tenure was marked by controversy, but most of it not of his own making. The day Demps signed his contract with the district, Judge Whipple warned him about the school board. At a public hearing discussing Demps's forthcoming move, at which the school board was in attendance, Whipple said, "I'm sorry to tell you, this school board has a bad record, a bad history of meddling in administration, particularly in personnel and contract matters. There are land mines you should be aware of."[54]

In October of 1999, two months into Demps's tenure, an unexpected land mine exploded. The Missouri Board of Education stripped the KCMSD of its accreditation, making it, out of 524, the state's only unaccredited school district. If in two years the school district did not improve its performance in student achievement, graduation, and attendance, among other categories, the board of education warned, the state would assume control of the district.[55]

Demps also had serious conflicts with the school board and Clinton Adams, who, while not on the board, remained a feared presence in school district politics. In one instance, a board member who considered himself a supporter of Demps sent a memo to the rest of the board saying he had noticed "the superintendent's tendency to lie" about personnel matters and as a result had been recording his conversations with Demps.[56] And Demps's proposal for Saturday school for poorly performing students was particularly vexing to Adams, who later commented, "If you're not being successful Monday through Friday what makes you think adding half a day on Saturday is

THE LAST DAYS OF DESEGREGATION?   177

going to do anything. The same teachers, teaching the same kids, the same material, in the same way. It's just logical reasoning."[57] Demps, however, deserved some sympathy. He was trying to do what $2 billion could not. Almost everything else had been tried. Why not Saturday school?

Demps's problems with the school board deteriorated beyond the point of repair in the spring of 2001. His relations with the school board were so poor that he wrote a letter to the DMC, which by now had been reduced to one person, pleading for help. Demps argued that the school board's "micromanagement" had hindered his ability to reform the district. In particular, the board's decisions to limit his spending authority and to require the district's outside counsel to report to the board rather than to him, he said, were made "solely to undermine and diminish [his] ability to manage" the KCMSD. In a new low, even for the KCMSD, Charles McClain, the DMC monitor, ordered the school board and Demps into mediation.[58]

The conflict escalated a few weeks later when Demps visited members of the Missouri House Education Committee in Springfield. He told them that the school board opposed his effort to decentralize control of the schools and to implement a system of "site based management" because some friends of board members stood to lose authority and even jobs under his proposal. Demps recommended to the committee that the State Board of Education immediately take control of the school district.[59] The school board was furious and voted to reprimand Demps at the same time that they were undergoing court-ordered mediation. After a couple weeks of unfruitful mediation, Demps withdrew. In response, the board fired him in a 5-4 vote and named the executive director of the district, Bernard Taylor, as interim superintendent.[60] The next day, however, a furious Judge Whipple reinstated Demps and instructed the school board "to refrain from interfering in any way with the operations of the Kansas City Missouri School District and the decision-making authority of Superintendent Demps and his staff until further order of this Court."[61]

The school board immediately appealed to the Eighth Circuit. At the same time, one of the dissenting board members filed suit against the school board, charging that the meeting where Demps was fired violated state law because not enough notice was given. Demps, however, resolved the situation for everyone by resigning four days after Whipple reinstated him. He said that he had "concluded that the governance of this district is fundamentally and fatally flawed. It is broken, and it cannot be fixed."[62]

The school board then renamed Bernard Taylor as interim superintendent and within a few weeks made him full-time superintendent. A few days after Demps resigned, Judge Whipple hauled the school board into court for a tongue-lashing, which one board member shrugged off as "a lecture just like usual."[63] Two months later, Judge Whipple instructed his monitor to hire investigators to look into micromanagement and patronage in the KCMSD.[64] A week later he instructed a local district attorney to give the school board a tutorial on malfeasance of office, saying that they should be aware of its meaning.[65]

Throughout this fiasco, Arthur Benson advocated an unusual position: judicial restraint. He believed that when the court ordered mediation between the board and Demps, Whipple was "on dangerous ground."[66] And when Whipple reinstated Demps as superintendent, Benson called the action "sweeping and overly broad" and even joined the appeal to the Eighth Circuit.[67] Why he opposed this aggressive judicial action is unclear. His reason for keeping the case open was to retain the threat of judicial sanction on the school district to ensure the implementation of educational reforms. In fact, Demps had been in the process of implementing many of the reforms Benson wanted when his problems with the school board escalated. In the controversy over mediation, Benson even credited Demps with making substantial improvements to the district. His sudden desire for restraint was something of a mystery.

Bernard Taylor's tenure, while longer than his immediate predecessor's, did not produce significant improvements in the district. Although the district gained provisional accreditation while he was superintendent, it failed to receive full accreditation. During his five years in the office, enrollment continued to decline, standing at less than 26,000 in 2005. Charter schools continued to attract students. Over 6,000 students attended charter schools during the 2005–6 school year, much to the chagrin of the KCMSD. To help save money, Taylor proposed closing several schools. The school board naturally opposed his suggestions and as a result declined to renew his contract after the 2005–6 school year.

In a final irony, the district and Arthur Benson joined forces to ask Judge Whipple to reopen *Missouri v. Jenkins* when the state said that it would allow the school district to keep $800 in funding per charter school student to help pay off $300 million in court-ordered bonds. The Missouri legislature authorized the state Board of Fund Commissioners to stop providing this cash, which was generated through local property taxes, if it determined that the KCMSD had enough revenue to pay off its bonds. When the commissioners did curtail this funding in April of 2005, Benson and the district petitioned the court to reopen the case and prevent the state from giving the funds directly to the charter schools.[68] Judge Whipple sided with Benson and the KCMSD, holding that the state must allow the district to keep these funds until Judge Clark's court-ordered bonds are retired in 2014.[69] However, Whipple's previous decision to grant the district unitary status remains in effect and, therefore, the district is not under judicial supervision.

While a small victory for the district, few would think that being able to keep these funds will resolve the district's fundamental financial problems. The school board simply lacks the political will to make difficult, but necessary, financial decisions. The *Kansas City Star* summarized the problem in 2006: "Part of the long-term answer to the financial stresses is a workable downsizing plan. The 63 school buildings serving kindergarten through 12th grade have an average occupancy rate of 64 percent. That's simply not cost-effective."[70] But after documenting more than thirty-five years of mismanagement, neither the *Star* nor anyone else should be surprised.

In retrospect, the magnet plan simply allowed the KCMSD to delay making difficult decisions about school closures in a district with steadily declining enrollment. Because the plan assumed that thousands of students would be drawn into the district, the school district kept open all of its schools when it needed to seriously consider how to close many of them. Given the board's historic dysfunction, even a gradual process would have been traumatic. But now the district faces making large numbers of closures in a short period of time, which seems to have exacerbated the board's inability to make thoughtful and prudent decisions.

Conclusion

Shortly before his retirement, Thurgood Marshall offered a dissenting opinion in *Dowell* criticizing the Court's direction on school desegregation. To Justice Marshall, racial isolation promotes the message of racial inferiority even if state action has not caused the isolation. Accordingly, Oklahoma City's prior legally enforced segregation made any current segregation unacceptable: "Consistent with the mandate of *Brown I*, our cases have imposed on school districts an unconditional duty to eliminate any condition that perpetuates the message of racial inferiority inherent in the policy of state-sponsored segregation. The racial identifiability of a district's schools is such a condition."[71] This opinion starkly contrasts with Clarence Thomas's concurring opinion in *Jenkins III*: "'Racial isolation' itself is not a harm; only state-enforced segregation is. After all, if separation itself is a harm, and if integration therefore is the only way that blacks can receive a proper education, then there must be something inferior about blacks." Black leaders in Kansas City essentially agreed with Thomas.

When the Supreme Court handed down its decision in *Jenkins III*, an entire era of judicial history ended. Remarkably, as Gary Orfield and Susan Eaton note in their book *Dismantling Desegregation: The Quiet Reversal of Brown v. Board of Education*, it ended quietly.[72] Their title certainly is misleading on one point, however. *Brown* has in no way been reversed. To say so would trivialize the abuses of the Jim Crow South. But the program that *Brown* launched has certainly faded and faded quietly. What happened in Kansas City helps explain why: the black community no longer believed that the courts could solve their problems. In fact, the courts and the black community disagreed on what the problems were. Legal doctrine asserted that the problem was racial isolation. The black community asserted that it was substandard education, which was ingloriously exemplified by the KCMSD's mismanagement and unqualified teachers.[73] The interests of the black community in Kansas City had simply outpaced Court doctrine.

Conclusion

Missouri v. Jenkins was the extreme case in an extreme category of judicial policymaking. What was simple in *Brown* was wildly complicated when it reached Kansas City. Comparing desegregation to abortion, another prominent judicial venture into policymaking, helps illustrate why things became so complex. With *Roe v. Wade*, the Supreme Court immediately removed legal obstacles to abortion. This was the desired outcome for a very large constituency. In fact, protecting *Roe* remains the agreed-upon goal for prochoice advocates. But with desegregation, there was dissension within the constituency that desegregation was supposed to assist. In Kansas City, this dissension often came from national civil rights organizations and local black parents and community groups. Thus, in the end, those on the receiving end of the court's assistance, black parents, were confused about what the court was actually trying to accomplish. Desegregation was supposed to help them. When it seemed to harm them, they reacted against it.

Beyond the political disagreements involved, desegregation became complicated because of the magnitude of the project. The effort to desegregate America's schools brought the courts directly into the daily lives of millions of Americans. Thousands of school districts with millions of students came under judicial supervision. Federal judges were often responsible for deciding where a child attended school, who his or her teacher or principal was, and how long his or her ride to school would take. Many parents made decisions about where to live based on court-ordered desegregation plans. Judicial action prompted middle-class white and black parents to flee to the suburbs for reasons ranging from shameless bigotry to legitimate concern about lengthy bus rides across town. *Missouri v. Jenkins* occupies the culminating but paradoxical position in this history. It was the most aggressive use of judicial power to attempt to desegregate a school system, but it was aggressive so that it could be less controversial. The hope was that voluntary methods, the "carrot" rather than the "stick," would blunt the harsh edge of forced busing.[1] White parents would participate in desegregation only if they chose to.

These voluntary methods proved costly, leading to judicially mandated taxation and the complete renovation of an urban school district.

While Kansas City experienced none of Boston's violence in reaction to busing, the results were still discouraging. After more than nineteen years of judicial supervision and more than $2 billion spent, Kansas City remains largely segregated. A 2002 study by the Harvard Civil Rights Project found that the KCMSD was one of the most racially isolated school districts in the country. This finding is especially distressing when Kansas City's level of racial isolation is compared to that of other cities with magnet-school plans. For instance, Kansas City's "exposure index," which measures black students' exposure to white students, was lower than that of Cincinnati and Milwaukee, both of whose magnet-school plans were much less ambitious than Kansas City's.[2]

The story of *Missouri v. Jenkins*, then, is a depressing but compelling one. Its legacies include huge financial expenditures, toxic racial politics, an increasingly dysfunctional school board, educationally deprived students, and disillusioned parents. The purpose of this book has been not to gawk morbidly at Kansas City's misfortune but rather to answer questions about both judicial policymaking and urban education in the hope that the lessons learned in Kansas City can be used to avoid similar disasters elsewhere.

Judicial Policymaking

What can a single case tell us about the general issue of judicial capacity to make effective policy? *Missouri v. Jenkins* was obviously unusual, so why not dismiss it as a random outlier? The fact is, however, that it is not so unusual. The case was the culmination of a series of decisions by the Supreme Court—*Green v. New Kent County School Board*, *Swann v. Charlotte-Mecklenburg School Board*, *Keyes v. Denver School District*, and *Milliken v. Bradley*—and of the interpretation of those decisions by the Eighth Circuit Court of Appeals. *Green*, *Swann*, and *Keyes* required judges to combat statistical racial isolation, while *Milliken* eliminated metropolitanwide remedies. When small-scale voluntary methods failed to produce integration, judges had to turn to more aggressive options. *Missouri v. Jenkins* was a logical result of this process. Given the doctrinal box Judge Clark was in, the decision can be seen as a reasonable result or outcome, and not the bizarre creation of an ambitious and idiosyncratic judge. It does not necessarily follow, however, that if Judge Clark had been free to order a metropolitanwide remedy he would have been any more successful. White and middle-class flight would still have taken place. Most of the expansion of the metropolitan Kansas City area over the past fifty years occurred on the Kansas side of the border, and because of the Eleventh Amendment Judge Clark could not have compelled suburban Kansas school districts' participation. In short, being compelled to do something significant about racial isolation in Kansas City put Judge Clark in a virtually impossible situation. There were some decisions that could have reduced the animosity of the black community. For instance, Judge Clark did not have to order attendance quotas for schools. But little could have been done to actually alleviate the racial isolation of the district.

The claim might also be made that the failure of *Missouri v. Jenkins* was the fault of an idiosyncratic appellate court: no other appellate court required remedies like those in Kansas City. But this explanation is unsatisfactory as well because the Eighth Circuit's interpretation of Supreme Court precedent was entirely reasonable. In the mid-1970s judges across the country began requiring school districts to build magnet schools to draw white students from surrounding districts. The Eighth Circuit simply said that if smaller voluntary plans did not work, because of Supreme Court rulings, judges had to try something more comprehensive and more costly. This approach was hardly a radical departure from judicial practice. The Supreme Court had many opportunities to restrain the Eighth Circuit but waited until 1995 to do so. Surely the Eighth Circuit cannot be blamed for aggressively but reasonably interpreting Supreme Court precedent. The Eighth Circuit, though, can be faulted for routinely resorting to the most unhelpful legalism when the remedial plan was obviously failing to create desegregation or improve education in Kansas City. Essentially the court said that "we have determined that there was a constitutional violation, and we have determined that this is the appropriate way to remedy that violation, so even if the policy is a failure, the law demands it because we have said it demands it."

The Supreme Court, by providing guidance, which its institutional role requires, removed flexibility when there was little to begin with. As the Court "muddled through," an expression Malcolm Feeley and Edward Rubin aptly apply to the act of judicial policymaking, it wandered into a doctrinal dead end.[3] Judge Clark, one could say, was "innocent" by reason of institutional incapacity. Where there needs to be flexibility, there is rigidity; where there needs to be discussion, there is adversarial conflict; and where there needs to be compromise, there is a zero-sum game. In this case, a fundamentally conservative decision-making process (conservative because it was precedent-bound) produced a radical result, lying outside the bounds that would have been set either by politics or by common sense.

Missouri v. Jenkins illustrates the need to distinguish between mature and emergent fields of judicial policymaking. The case shows the difficulties of judicial policymaking in a mature policy area in which precedents have already been established and sustained. Even if the courts manage to make effective policy in an emerging policy area, eventually precedents will accumulate and calcify, denying judges the needed flexibility to deal with divergent circumstances.

This point adds a critical element to the critique of judicial policymaking. Legal rules and precedents are by their nature abstract. Precedent cannot consider the particular facts of a future situation. In essence, courts cannot exercise prudential judgment, which follows particulars. Even though courts are supposed to determine the facts of the case, if those facts do not match what the precedent says, then the precedent trumps the facts. For example, Kansas City's schools were segregated for a variety of complicated economic, social, psychological, and political reasons. Those were the facts. But precedent, or judicial theory, if you will, said that segregation persisted for one simple reason: state-sanctioned racism from decades before.

But showing that the courts have difficulty making public policy does not show that they are less effective at it than other institutions. Critiques of judicial policymaking, therefore, cannot proceed on the implausible assumption that other institutions make policy in a flawless manner. Judging institutional capacity is always comparative. Local, state, and national democratic institutions make ineffective public policy all the time. Certainly Kansas City's local government failed miserably in providing education for its children. Could the courts then be the lesser of two evils? Maybe it has virtues that counterbalance failures like *Missouri v. Jenkins*?

The primary virtue offered in the courts' defense is that they have the freedom to try policies that democratic institutions cannot. Perhaps it is a sign that democratic institutions have failed because they will not try something new or costly. The problem with this contention is that when a judge comes up with an idea that no one else would have considered, the idea will likely garner little public support. And when a judge's actions go beyond basic legal requirements—when, for example, a judge moves from striking down laws that support segregated schools to ordering wholesale plans for improving education—public support may be precisely what is needed if there is to be any chance of implementing a successful policy. Striking down laws requires power; remedying a failing educational system requires something more elusive, consent and consensus. The idea that a judge could reform a large, deeply entrenched, deeply troubled public organization without the mobilization of public support seems myopic. At the very least, a local school system would not be able to spend such an extraordinary sum of money unless someone else was required to provide it. While local, especially urban, democratic institutions are hardly paragons of policymaking effectiveness, they at least must remain open to alternative ideas about what should be done to improve education.

Educational Policy

Missouri v. Jenkins also forces us to ask the question, "If $2 billion could not improve urban education, then what can?" Of course, we cannot fully answer this question here. But a few of the lessons learned from the failure of policymaking in this case may at least provide some insights into approaches and policies that are *not* likely to work in resolving the current crisis in the KCMSD.

The KCMSD's educational problems were not fundamentally monetary. A quick glance at the district's per-pupil expenditures demonstrates this. In the 1996–97 school year, the district spent $9,407 per student. Adjusted for cost of living, this amount exceeded the per-pupil expenditures of any of the nation's 280 largest school districts—a point that Judge Clark belatedly and angrily made in his final ruling. The KCMSD's problems were much deeper than a lack of funds. Arthur Benson, who admirably has not attempted to whitewash the plan's failures, admits this. "We've done the easy and expensive things," he commented. "What remains now are the relatively inexpensive but extraordinarily difficult things to accomplish and that's to change how teachers teach and kids learn and buildings are organized and administered."[4] Changing teaching methods, school management, and district administration are far more difficult tasks than building new buildings and establishing new programs. These problems are political, conceptual, and organizational, not financial, in nature.[5]

The issue of textbooks illustrates this point. Before the remedial plan, the school district had a shortage of textbooks, and as the plan drew to a close, it confronted another shortage of textbooks. Why? The reason was not money but administration. The school district had purchased all the textbooks it needed, but because of chaos in its purchasing department, the textbooks were stored in a warehouse in Chicago. "They may not have had the capacity to get them distributed," Clinton Adams commented. "But at least they had them." The district employees, according to Adams, have "the resources that they need." The difficulty is making sure they are "getting distributed."[6]

Many of the problems afflicting urban education can be traced to school districts' political and institutional arrangements, which give incentives to school boards and superintendents to institute quick reforms that do not challenge established interests.[7] The KCMSD is no exception. In the 1970s and early 1980s, a new superintendent would come in with a "new" plan to rescue the city's schools. The plan would fail. The school board would fire the superintendent and then commission a study to come up with another plan. That plan would fail as well. *Missouri v. Jenkins* was the continuation of this failed policy strategy by judicial means. Even with the aggressive oversight of a federal judge, the KCMSD's problems persisted. A dysfunctional organization given all the money it asks for will likely use that money in a dysfunctional way. Fixing the "root causes" of the problem—poor administration and poor instruction—should be the place to start.

But knowing the origins of a problem is much different from knowing how to solve it. What can be done to bring about meaningful political and administrative change in the KCMSD? While there is no simple answer to this question, several institutional reforms have been proposed to improve the district's performance. Expanding charter schools is a reform already well under way. Charter school enrollment increases each year. In the 2005–6 school year, one in five students in Kansas City attended a charter school. Given their growth and ability to operate separately from the KCMSD, charter schools should continue to erode the district's attendance. Parents obviously welcome the opportunity to have some measure of control over their children's education, so few are concerned by this.

Kansas City's Southwest High School is a particularly instructive example of the changes brought on by charter schools. Southwest was the school on which Judge Clark bestowed a model United Nations with simultaneous translation capability. For several decades after its creation in 1925, to serve the "country club district" of Kansas City, Southwest was considered one of the best public schools in the country. By the time *Missouri v. Jenkins* began, it was in a severe state of decline. By 1998, with state funding coming to an end, the KCMSD could not justify keeping open the sparsely attended school. The district shuttered the building. In 2001, a popular charter school, Southwest Charter School, moved into the facility.[8]

Other proposed reforms, for a variety of reasons, are less likely to be adopted. And in such a deeply troubled school district, it is unclear how many of these would actually help. One proposal is to change the way the school board is elected. Currently, three of nine members are elected to at-large seats while the other six represent subdistricts. A recommendation supported by everyone from Arthur Benson to Republican members of the state legislature is to make all the seats at-large. The argument behind the proposal is the same argument "Federalist No. 10" outlines for a large republic. Expanding the area of representation forces representatives to work across political divisions for the common good. According to Arthur Benson, the subdistrict representatives "tend to each have their own particular interests and those school board members tend to represent just the interests of that subdistrict not the district as a whole and so they tend to divide up against each other."[9] Benson makes this argument even though the subdistrict representatives on the board provided his base of support while a coalition of several at-large members eventually undermined this support.[10] In spite of this, Benson believes that if all the members had to run at-large, they would be more likely to form coalitions and stop acting out of parochial interests. But black leaders strongly oppose this proposal. They argue that without subdistrict representatives from black areas, there would be little or no black representation on the school board since the voting population in the KCMSD remains majority white.[11] Without support from the black community this idea is unlikely to be adopted.

Another proposed reform is to dissolve the KCMSD and have parts of it absorbed by surrounding school districts. This plan at times has received a great deal of support in the Missouri legislature from both Republicans and Democrats. The surrounding school districts all seem to be functioning well, but they want nothing to do with the KCMSD out of fear that its problems will infect their districts. The KCMSD is almost seen as a contagiously sick patient who needs to be quarantined. This view holds true even in the case of some local black leaders, such as former mayor Emmanuel Cleaver. Also, some activists, such as Clinton Adams, oppose dissolving the district because they believe it would send the message that blacks cannot effectively manage their own institutions.

The proposed reform most unlikely to receive support is a voucher program. Although some black parents are in favor of vouchers — several filed suit asking Judge Clark for money for vouchers to avoid having to send their children to magnet schools — there is little support for the idea among black community leaders. Those with the political skill necessary to push for vouchers, Clinton Adams, for example, oppose them. Adams and Newsome even have reservations about charter schools.

The final reform proposed and the one most likely to be implemented is a state takeover. In 2007, the state board of education took over the St. Louis school district, which rivaled Kansas City in both its level of dysfunction and in the cost of its desegregation efforts.[12] In 2000, the state board of education removed the KCMSD's accreditation. For accreditation to be reinstated, state policy requires improvement in many areas, including student test scores, graduation rates, and truancy levels, within two years of losing accreditation. The school district barely managed to make the necessary improvements and narrowly avoided a state takeover in 2002. It could easily lose its accreditation again and face receivership. What the state would do after a takeover is unknown. It could replace the school board and superintendent and install its own. It could also follow the example of Philadelphia and contract school management out to private companies. Regardless, a state takeover might be the only way to attack the decades-long mismanagement of the KCMSD. Only someone outside Kansas City without friends or political obligations could change such a deeply entrenched system.

Missouri v. Jenkins and American Politics

Missouri v. Jenkins illustrates the two contradictory impulses toward centralization and local control in American politics. The KCMSD and Arthur Benson turned to the national government through the courts to remedy Kansas City's educational problems, but at the same time this prompted a backlash and calls for local control from the very group the courts were supposed to be helping. The case provides a powerful—and perhaps culminating—example of the judicialization of politics and administration in the second half of the twentieth century. The extreme nature of the case—raising taxes, rebuilding the district, and setting district policy—indicates the extensiveness of judicial policymaking. Other than the Supreme Court's 1995 decision, Judge Clark's remedies withstood every challenge. The ease with which he carried out his policies is striking. Because of *Missouri v. Jenkins*, judges officially have the power to require local and state governments to raise taxes. While, previously, judicial remedies might have led to increased taxes, judges avoided mandating them as a violation of separation of powers. The Court essentially assumed in its 1990 decision, however, that judges had to have the power to fund their remedies through tax increases.

But while *Missouri v. Jenkins* shows the increased centralization of policy-making through the judiciary—or the courts' absorption into the administrative state—it also shows that there remains a very deep attachment to local institutions and democratic governance. Even though Kansas City's minority children were the victims in the case, many black community members refused to accept the educational prescriptions offered by the court. Community activists and leaders demanded that their views be heard and addressed. The billions of dollars spent on their behalf did not eliminate their desire for control and responsibility. In fact, the judicial intervention strengthened this desire. And the reforms black leaders proposed—in marked contrast to those implemented by the courts—were educationally sensible. They did not assume that the fundamental problems of the district could be financed away in a river of money.

In fact, because of the black community's willingness to assert its competence, the news about education in Kansas City is not entirely bad. J. S. Chick, the Afrocentric magnet school that the black community demanded, has been one of the best-performing elementary schools in the district and the state. The school, which is 99.6 percent black and is housed in one of the district's oldest buildings, routinely surpasses district achievement levels. In 2005, 48 percent of its students were rated "advanced or proficient" in math, according to the Missouri Assessment Program. For the KCMSD, the average was 16 percent, and for the state it was 43 percent. In science, 45.7 percent of J. S. Chick's students were advanced and proficient compared to 17.8 percent in the district and 53.4 percent statewide.[13] While other Afrocentric schools have not had J. S. Chick's success, the school has shown that when given the opportunity, black teachers, students, and administrators can succeed.

The black community's protectiveness over local prerogatives and its willingness to mobilize was a surprising demonstration of the gift of political association. If J. S. Chick's success can be replicated in other schools, prompting this initiative might be *Missouri v. Jenkins*'s most lasting contribution to education in Kansas City.

Viewed through the lens of the black community's civic engagement, the legacy of *Missouri v. Jenkins* is not completely negative. It can instead be seen as a sign of social progress. In the early twentieth century the NAACP was forced to turn to the courts because the political process was unresponsive to the violation of minority rights. By the late twentieth century, the local black community in Kansas City was able to turn to the political process when it believed the courts were violating minority rights. In a political regime such as ours, which is premised on self-government, when a previously disenfranchised group protects itself through the political process, there is reason to be hopeful.

Notes

Introduction

1. Because of declining enrollment, the Kansas City, Missouri, School District (KCMSD) had to close Southwest in 1998. The facility went unused until a charter school moved into the building in 2001.
2. 347 U.S. 483 (1954).
3. 163 U.S. 537 (1896).
4. 349 U.S. 294 (1955).
5. *Green v. New Kent County School Board*, 391 U.S. 430 (1968).
6. *Keyes v. Denver School District*, 413 U.S. 189 (1973).
7. 418 U.S. 717 (1974).
8. Some treatments have in fact missed important features of the case. For instance, Wendy Parker, in "The Supreme Court and Public Law Remedies: A Tale of Two Kansas Cities" 50 *Hastings Law Journal* 475 (1999), provides an interesting and often helpful comparison of the desegregation cases in Kansas City, Kansas and Missouri. However, she contends that one of the nominal defendants, the KCMSD, controlled the creation of the remedial plan in *Missouri v. Jenkins*, which then helps explain its peculiar results. In fact, the plaintiff's attorney played the primary role in creating the remedial plan even though the school district officially submitted it to the court.
9. See, for example, James Anthony Ben, "*Missouri v. Jenkins*: Yet Another Complicated Chapter in the Desegregation Saga," *University of Miami Law Review* 51 (1997): 1221; Douglas J. Brocker, "Taxation Without Representation: The Judicial Usurpation of the Power to Tax in *Missouri v. Jenkins*," *North Carolina Law Review* 69 (1991): 741; and Deborah E. Beck, "School Choice: A Method for Desegregating an Inner City School District," *California Law Review* 81 (1993): 1029.
10. *Missouri v. Jenkins*, 495 U.S. 33 (1990).
11. Brutus, "Essay XI," in *The Anti-Federalist*, ed. Herbert Storing (Chicago: University of Chicago Press, 1985), 167.
12. "Federalist No. 78," in *The Federalist Papers*, ed. Clinton Rossiter (New York: Mentor, 1961), 465.

Chapter One

1. Some would cite the advent of the "Brandeis brief" in 1908 as the starting point for social science–based judicial policymaking. While the importance of the Brandeis brief should not be underestimated, it clearly pales in comparison to the use of social science brought about by *Brown*. In *Brown*, the Court placed efficacious public policy on the same plane as constitutional considerations. *Brown*, one could say, institutionalized what the Brandeis brief began.

2. For a compelling reevaluation of the claim that Roosevelt induced the "switch," see Barry Cushman, *Rethinking the New Deal Court: The Structure of a Constitutional Revolution* (New York: Oxford University Press, 1998). Cushman argues that the Court's switch was the result of evolving internal constitutional doctrines rather than external political pressure. Regardless of its origins, the switch did seem to institutionalize the progressive view that the Court was to be subservient to the political branches, especially on economic policy.
3. See Abram Chayes, "The Role of the Judge in Public Law Litigation," *Harvard Law Review* 89 (1976): 1281.
4. Donald L. Horowitz, *The Courts and Social Policy* (Washington, D.C.: Brookings Institution Press, 1977).
5. Gerald N. Rosenberg, *The Hollow Hope: Can Courts Bring About Social Change?* (Chicago: University of Chicago Press, 1991), 2–3.
6. For a variety of perspectives on judicial policymaking in addition to Chayes, Horowitz, and Rosenberg, see Alexander M. Bickel, *The Supreme Court and the Idea of Progress* (New Haven: Yale University Press, 1978); Nathan Glazer, "Should Judges Administer Social Services?" *The Public Interest* 50 (1978): 64–80; Michael A. Rebell and Arthur R. Block, *Educational Policy Making and the Courts: An Empirical Study of Judicial Activism* (Chicago: University of Chicago Press, 1982); Owen M. Fiss, "Foreword: The Forms of Justice," *Harvard Law Review* 91 (1979): 1–58; R. Shep Melnick, *Regulation and the Courts: The Case of the Clean Air Act* (Washington, D.C.: Brooking Institution Press, 1983); Phillip Cooper, *Hard Judicial Choices: Federal District Court Judges and State and Local Officials* (Oxford: Oxford University Press, 1988); Bradley C. Canon and Charles A. Johnson, *Judicial Policies: Implementation and Impact*, 2d ed. (Washington, D.C.: Congressional Quarterly Press, 1999); Malcolm M. Feeley and Edward L. Rubin, *Judicial Policy Making and the Modern State: How the Courts Reformed America's Prisons* (New York: Cambridge University Press, 1998); and Ross Sandler and David Schoenbrod, *Democracy by Decree: What Happens When Courts Run Government* (New Haven: Yale University Press, 2003).
7. These arguments can be traced to Lon Fuller, who argued that policy problems are "polycentric" and therefore poorly suited for bimodal adjudication. Fuller first outlined this argument in an unpublished paper in the 1950s. The paper was published posthumously. See Lon Fuller, "The Forms and Limits of Adjudication," *Harvard Law Review* 92 (1978): 354–409.
8. Rosenberg, *Hollow Hope*, 35–36.
9. For criticism of Rosenberg, see Malcolm M. Feeley, "Hollow Hopes, Flypapers, and Metaphors," *Law and Social Inquiry* 17 (1992): 745; David Schultz and Stephen Gottlieb, eds., *Leveraging the Law: Using the Courts to Achieve Social Change* (New York: Peter Lang, 1998); Michael W. McCann, *Rights at Work: Pay Equity Reform and the Politics of Legal Mobilization* (Chicago: University of Chicago Press, 1994); and Neal Devins, "Judicial Matters," *California Law Review* 80 (1992): 1027.
10. See, for instance, David E. Klein and Robert J. Hume, "Fear of Reversal as an Explanation of Lower Court Compliance," *Law and Society Review* 37 (2003): 579.

Studies measuring lower court compliance tend to find that compliance is the rule. Klein and Hume discuss this literature and offer additional reasons for compliance beyond "fear of reversal," such as wanting "to reach legally sound decisions" (ibid., 602).

11 See Feeley and Rubin, *Judicial Policy Making*, chap. 7.
12 *Brown v. Board of Education of Topeka Kansas*, 347 U.S. 483 (1954), at 493.
13 Ibid., at 494.
14 The Court's reliance on social science was the source of intense controversy. In *What Brown v. Board of Education Should Have Said*, ed. Jack Balkin (New York: New York University Press, 2002), prominent legal scholars of various political persuasions were asked to rewrite *Brown*. In an example of implicit agreement, all of the contributors assiduously avoided relying on the psychological evidence of Footnote 11.
15 *Brown v. Board of Education of Topeka II*, 349 U.S. 294 (1955), at 299.
16 Ibid., at 301.
17 Ibid., at 300.
18 Data from Lee Epstein, Jeffrey A. Segal, Harold J. Spaeth, and Thomas G. Walker, *The Supreme Court Compendium: Data, Decisions, and Developments*, 2d ed. (Washington, D.C.: Congressional Quarterly Press, 1996), Table 9-4.
19 Rosenberg, *Hollow Hope*, 52.
20 Gary Orfield, *The Reconstruction of Southern Education* (New York: John Wiley & Sons, 1969), 79.
21 Alexander Bickel, "Forcing Desegregation through Title VI," *New Republic*, April 9, 1966, 8–9.
22 U.S. Commission on Civil Rights, *Survey of School Desegregation in Southern and Border States, 1965–1966* (Washington, D.C.: U.S. Government Printing Office, 1966), 2.
23 For a thorough history of the effects of Title VI, see Stephen C. Halpern, *On the Limits of the Law: The Ironic Legacy of Title VI of the 1964 Civil Rights Act* (Baltimore: Johns Hopkins University Press, 1995).
24 J. Harvie Wilkinson, *From Brown to Bakke: The Supreme Court and School Integration, 1954–1978* (New York: Oxford University Press, 1979), 107.
25 See ibid., 109.
26 391 U.S. 430 (1968).
27 Ibid., at 437, 438.
28 Epstein, Segal, Spaeth, and Walker, *Supreme Court Compendium*, Table 9-4.
29 402 U.S. 1 (1971).
30 Ibid., at 26.
31 David J. Armor, *Forced Justice: School Desegregation and the Law* (New York: Oxford University Press, 1995), 37.
32 413 U.S. 189 (1973), at 213, 214.
33 Gary Orfield, *Must We Bus? Segregation and National Policy* (Washington, D.C.: Brookings Institution Press, 1978), 24.
34 418 U.S. 717 (1974).

35 For evidence that public opposition to busing influenced the Court's decision in *Milliken I*, see James E. Ryan and Michael Heise, "The Political Economy of School Choice," *Yale Law Journal* 111 (2002): 2052–56.
36 411 U.S. 1 (1973), at 35.
37 433 U.S. 267 (1977).
38 Daniel U. Levine and Robert J. Havighurst, *Society and Education*, 8th ed. (Boston: Allyn and Bacon, 1992), chap. 9.
39 For example, *Hart and Wechsler's the Federal Courts and the Federal System, 5th (University Casebook Series*)* (Foundation Press, 1973) said the question of standing "is the question of whether the litigant . . . is a sufficiently appropriate representative of other interested persons . . . to warrant recognizing him as entitled to invoke the court's decision" (136).
40 This problem is even more acute, or absurd, in environmental litigation. Who, after all, gets to speak for nature? Justice William O. Douglas notoriously argued in a dissent from *Sierra Club v. Morton* that "public concern for protecting nature's ecological equilibrium should lead to the conferral of standing upon environmental objects to sue for their own preservation" (*Sierra Club v. Morton*, 405 U.S. 727 [1972]). The contemporary debate over the proper way to manage national forests immediately raises questions about whether trees have a single set of interests. Should forests be thinned to limit the damage of forest fires? Should controlled burns be used? Should some trees be cleared to allow other species to grow? Even more difficult, then, is who gets to represent the trees, which apparently do not have a single stable set of preferences?
41 Louis L. Jaffe, "Standing Again," *Harvard Law Review* 84 (1971): 633.
42 This is not a problem in the "traditional" model of litigation, where the interests of plaintiffs are almost always monetary.
43 Owen M. Fiss, "Foreword: The Forms of Justice," *Harvard Law Review* 91 (1979): 25.
44 Robert Kagan, *Adversarial Legalism: The American Way of Law* (Cambridge: Harvard University Press, 2003), 224.
45 Jeremy Rabkin, *Judicial Compulsions: How Public Law Distorts Public Policy* (New York: Basic Books, 1989), 43.
46 Sandler and Schoenbrod, *Democracy by Decree*, 124, 133.
47 Christine H. Rossell, "The Convergence of Black and White Attitudes on School Desegregation Issues," in *Redefining Equality*, ed. Neal Devins and Davison M. Douglas (New York: Oxford University Press, 1998), 120.
48 *Massachusetts v. Mellon*, 262 U.S. 447 (1923) at 487.
49 351 F. Supp. 636 (D.C. Cir., 1972).
50 This failure to certify the plaintiffs of *Adams* as a class would go unrecognized by the court until the 1980s. See chapter five of Rabkin's *Judicial Compulsions* for a comprehensive history of the *Adams* litigation.
51 *Adams v. Richardson*, 356 F. Supp. 92 (D.C. Cir., 1973).

Chapter Two

1. Albert P. Marshall, "Racial Integration in Education in Missouri," *Journal of Negro Education* 25 (1956): 289.
2. Shirl Kasper, "Kansas City in the 60s: A Tide of Change," *Kansas City Star*, August 9, 1998, A1.
3. The important word is "relatively." Kansas City was certainly not a racial utopia. Violence and racism were a significant part of its history, just less significant than in the Deep South. For a thorough analysis of this history, see Sherry Lamb Schirmer, *A City Divided: The Racial Landscape of Kansas City, 1900–1960* (Columbia: University of Missouri Press, 2002).
4. 1847 Mo. Laws 103.
5. Missouri Constitution (1865), art. IX, sec. 2.
6. *General Statutes of the State of Missouri*, 1866, chap. 46, sec. 20.
7. Missouri Constitution (1945), art. IX, sec. 1(a).
8. William E. Parrish et al., *Missouri: The Heart of the Nation* (St. Louis: Forum Press, 1980), 297.
9. Monroe Billington, "Public School Integration in Missouri, 1954-64," *Journal of Negro Education* 35 (1966): 252–62.
10. See Boyd F. Carroll, "Dalton Rules State May End Segregation in Schools at Once," *St. Louis Post Dispatch*, July 1, 1954, 3A.
11. *Report of the United States Commission on Civil Rights, 1959* (Washington, D.C.: U.S. Government Printing Office, 1959), 205.
12. *U.S. Commission on Civil Rights 1963 Staff Report on Public Education* (Washington, D.C.: U.S. Government Printing Office, 1963), 27–28.
13. "Report Card: Progress of the States Toward School Desegregation," *Time*, September 19, 1955, 25.
14. Henry Lee Moon, "Desegregation at Work: Progress and Problems," *The Nation*, December 18, 1954, 527.
15. Charles R. T. Crumpley, "How We Got Here: Court Rulings, White Flight, School District's Tragic Past Brings Traumatic Solution," *Kansas City Star*, May 8, 1994, A1.
16. See Reed Sarrat, *The Ordeal of Desegregation: The First Decade* (New York: Harper and Row, 1966), 80.
17. Ibid.
18. "Everything's Up to Date in Kansas City," *Time*, July 28, 1961, 38.
19. Marshall, "Racial Integration in Education," 289–98.
20. "43 Integrated Schools," *The Call*, September 23, 1955, 20.
21. "Kansas City Trouble," *Time*, January 17, 1958.
22. Ibid.
23. "Everything's Up to Date," 38.
24. Ibid.
25. Gregory S. Reeves, "Black Families Join K.C. White Flight," *Kansas City Star*, May 8, 1994, A12.
26. *Jenkins v. State of Mo.*, 593 F. Supp. 1485 (W.D. Mo. 1984).

27 Crumpley, "How We Got Here."
28 *Jenkins v. State of Mo.* (1984).
29 For a comprehensive treatment of Kansas City's residential segregation, see Schirmer, *City Divided*.
30 See Peter William Moran, "Difficult from the Start: Implementing the *Brown* Decision in the Kansas City, Missouri, Public Schools," *Equity and Excellence in Education* 37 (2004): 278. For a very thorough history of the school board's response to *Brown*, see Moran's *Race, Law, and the Desegregation of Public Schools* (New York: LFB Scholarly Publishing, 2005).
31 Crumpley, "How We Got Here."
32 Ibid.
33 *Jenkins v. State of Mo.* (1984).
34 See Moran, "Difficult from the Start," 279.
35 Ibid.
36 For evidence of civil rights organizations' support of "color-blind" policies until the early 1960s, see Eleanor Wolf, *Trial and Error: The Detroit School Desegregation Case* (Detroit: Wayne State University Press, 1981), 336 n. 35.
37 See Billington, "Public School Integration," 261-62.
38 Quoted in *U.S. Commission on Civil Rights 1964 Staff Report on Public Education* (Washington, D.C.: U.S. Government Printing Office, 1964), 147.
39 Quoted in Eric Juhnke, "A City Awakened: The Kansas City Race Riot of 1968," *Gateway Heritage* 20 (Winter 1999-2000): 33.
40 Ibid., quoted at 36.
41 In addition to Juhnke, see Joel Rhodes, "It Finally Happened Here: The 1968 Riot in Kansas City, Missouri," *Missouri Historical Review* 91 (1997): 295-315.
42 Crumpley, "How We Got Here."
43 *Jenkins v. State of Mo.* (1984).
44 Crumpley, "How We Got Here."
45 Author interview with John Duncan, KCMSD historian, Kansas City, Mo., January 23, 2001 (hereafter Duncan interview).
46 "Transcript of the Meeting of the Council for United Action," July 19, 1967, in Arthur Benson Papers, KC 250, Western Historical Manuscript Collection, Kansas City, Mo., Box 440 (hereafter Benson Papers).
47 *Southern Christian Leadership Conference v. Kansas City, Missouri School District*, Complaint for Injunctive Relief and Damages, January 26, 1973, 12.
48 Andrew C. Miller, "Growing Black Divisiveness Over Desegregation Issue," *Kansas City Times*, December 21, 1974, B4.
49 Daniel U. Levine and Jeanie Keeny Meyer, "Level and Rate of Desegregation and White Enrollment Decline in a Big City School System," *Social Problems* 24 (1977): 451-62.
50 Kansas City, Missouri, School District Annual Desegregation Reports, Benson Papers, Box 314.
51 "Progress of Desegregation by Schools: 1955-56 Through 1965-66," Benson Papers, Box 314.

52 Barry Garron, "Officials Tell of Damage to Schools during Strike," *Kansas City Times*, April 1, 1974, A1.
53 Barry Garron, "Teacher Strike Sends Parents Here District-Hopping," *Kansas City Star*, April 21, 1974, A1.
54 "Hints of School-Strike Irritate Mayor Wheeler," *Kansas City Star*, June 17, 1974, B3.
55 Andrew C. Miller, "Hudson Says Strike Vote Date Near," *Kansas City Star*, March 28, 1975, A3.
56 "127 Teachers Arrested in School Disturbances," *Kansas City Star*, April 7, 1977, A1.
57 Barry Garron, "Union Votes to Go Back to Classes," *Kansas City Star*, May 9, 1977, A9.
58 Duncan interview.
59 Crumpley, "How We Got Here."
60 402 U.S. 1 (1971).
61 Ibid.
62 *Adams et al. v. Richardson et al.*, 356 F. Supp. 92 (D.C. Cir. 1973).
63 "Chronology," *Kansas City Times*, September 1, 1977, B4.
64 Ibid.
65 Ibid.
66 Andrew C. Miller, "Parents Favor Desegregation, Not Bussing Plan," *Kansas City Times*, September 3, 1977, A1.
67 Bill Turque, "In the City: Black Parents View Plan for Desegregation as Mindless Shuffling of Children's Bodies," *Kansas City Times*, August 28, 1977, A1.
68 Barry Garron, "School District a Casualty of Change," *Kansas City Star*, February 8, 1976, A1.
69 Andrew C. Miller, "Details of Desegregation Plan," *Kansas City Star*, March 28, 1977, A1.
70 Stephen E. Winn, "'White Flight' Cripples Efforts in This Area," *Kansas City Star*, February 13, 1979, A1.
71 Fred Schecker, "Figures Make KC District Appear to Be Resegregating," *Kansas City Star*, November 15, 1981, A1.
72 Fred Schecker, "Parents Contend Central Area Is Being Sacrificed: Students Drawn Away to Balance Other Schools," *Kansas City Star*, November 16, 1981, A10.
73 "Chronology."
74 391 U.S. 430 (1968).
75 413 U.S. 189 (1973).
76 Stephen E. Winn, "Effect on Suit Here Unclear to Lawyers," *Kansas City Star*, July 3, 1979, A4.
77 418 U.S. 717 (1974).
78 Complaint for Declaratory and Injunctive Relief at 11, May 26, 1977, *School District of Kansas City v. State of Mo.*, 460 F. Supp. 421 (W.D. Mo. 1978).
79 Ibid., 12.
80 Ibid., 14–15.

81 Ibid., 25.
82 Ibid., 26.
83 Ibid., 27.
84 Andrew C. Miller, "Judge Asked to Eliminate Himself from School Suit," *Kansas City Times*, September 20, 1977, A1.
85 *School Dist. of Kansas City, Mo. v. State of Mo.*, 438 F. Supp. 830 (W.D. Mo. 1977).
86 Karen Uhlenhuth, "That Judge Named Clark," *Kansas City Star*, November 17, 1990, E1.
87 Daniel U. Levine and Rayna F. Levine, "Practicalities Impede Desegregation," *Kansas City Star*, July 24, 1977, D4.
88 *School District of Kansas City v. State of Mo.*, 460 F. Supp. 421 (W.D. Mo. 1978), at 441.
89 Stephen E. Winn, "School-District Supports Its Own Prosecution," *Kansas City Star*, July 4, 1979, A3.
90 Stephen E. Winn, "Who Will Pick Up Race Suit? Groups Eye Suit," *Kansas City Times*, October 11, 1978, B1.
91 *Liddell v. Caldwell*, 546 F.2d 768 (8th Cir. 1976).
92 *Adams v. United States*, 620 F.2d 1277 (8th Cir. 1980), at 1285.
93 Orfield has played a large and controversial role in the history of desegregation. He frequently served as an expert witness for plaintiffs in desegregation. Currently he directs the Harvard Project on Desegregation. From this position he has been a consistent critic of "resegregation" and has argued that America has turned its back on *Brown v. Board of Education*.
94 *Adams v. United States*, at 1285.
95 Phillip O'Connor and Lynn Horsley, "Guardian or Glory Hound? Arthur A. Benson II Has Been Called Many Things during KC Schools Case," *Kansas City Star*, July 14, 1996, A1.
96 Donna Stewart, "Attorney Didn't Hesitate to Take Desegregation Case," *The Call*, March 2–8, 1984, 22.
97 O'Connor and Horsley, "Guardian or Glory Hound?"
98 Arthur Benson, "A Tribute to Kamau Agyei (Carroll L. Jenkins)," *The Call*, December 19–25, 1986, 16.
99 Jack Cashill, "Bombs Away," <<http://www.cashill.com/natl_general/bomsaway4.htm>> (accessed April 24, 2007). Cashill achieved some level of fame, or infamy, in Thomas Frank's, *What's the Matter with Kansas* (New York: Henry Holt, 2004). In response, Cashill is writing a book titled *What's the Matter with California*.

Chapter Three

1 Author interview with Clinton Adams, Kansas City, Missouri, January 18, 2001 (hereafter Adams interview).
2 "Kansas City Schools: Problems that Persist," *Kansas City Star*, May 16, 1983, A6; Jeremiah Cameron, "Judge Clark's Ruling," *The Call*, October 1–8, 1987, 18.
3 Faye A. Silas, "District's Master Plan Is Mystery to Teachers," *Kansas City Star*, October 29, 1981, B1.

4 Ibid.
5 "District Decisions Filter to the Students: Effects of Budget and Personnel Cuts Felt in the Classroom," *Kansas City Star*, May 8, 1983, A7.
6 "Why Another Study?" *The Call*, March 16–22, 1984, 20.
7 Walter Burks, "Why Aren't Kansas City's Public Schools Working?" *Kansas City Town Squire*, May 1983, 24.
8 Missouri law required that a tax levy receive approval from a two-thirds majority of voters. Prior to 1969, it took a simple majority to pass a tax levy.
9 Jeremiah Cameron, "A Better School Board," *The Call*, January 13–19, 1984, 5.
10 Author interview with Arthur Benson, plaintiff's attorney, Kansas City, Mo., January 17, 2001 (hereafter Benson interview).
11 Deposition of A. H. Kilpatrick, *Jenkins v. State of Mo.*, 593 F. Supp. 1485 (W.D. Mo. 1984), transcript at 66, Arthur Benson Papers, KC 250, Western Historical Manuscript Collection, Kansas City, Mo., Folder 162 (hereafter Benson Papers).
12 Benson interview.
13 Ibid.
14 *Jenkins et al. v. State et al.*, 593 F. Supp. 1485 (W.D. Mo. 1984), "Plaintiff's Response to School District Defendant's Memorandum and Suggestions to Conserve Trial Time and to the Federal Defendant's Memorandum," filed October 31, 1983, 7, 21–23.
15 Ibid.
16 Letter to Arthur Benson from Theodore M. Shaw, June 22, 1984, Benson Papers, Box 355.
17 D. F. Stewart, "Plaintiffs to End Case on Monday in School Desegregation Trial," *The Call*, March 2–8, 1984, 22.
18 Benson interview.
19 *Jenkins et al. v. State et al.* (1984), "Plaintiffs' Suggestions in Response to Defendants' Rule 41(b) Motions," filed March 26, 1984, 87.
20 Ibid., 123–28.
21 Deposition of Henry Poindexter, *Jenkins v. State*, 593 F. Supp. 1485 (W.D. Mo. 1984), Deposition at 25, Benson Papers, Folder 168.
22 Deposition of James Hazlett, *Jenkins v. State*, 593 F. Supp. 1485 (W.D. Mo. 1984), transcript at 57–58, Benson Papers, Folder 151.
23 "Plaintiffs' Suggestions," 103.
24 Ibid., 107.
25 Ibid., 97.
26 Donna Stewart, "Attorney Didn't Hesitate to Take Desegregation Case," *The Call*, March 2–8, 1984, 22.
27 Codified as R.S. Mo. ß 165.563 (1959).
28 "Plaintiffs' Suggestions," 92–93.
29 Ibid., 95.
30 Ibid., 92–93.
31 Author interview with Mark Bredemeier, former attorney, Landmark Legal Foundation, Kansas City, Mo., January 24, 2001 (hereafter Bredemeier interview).

32 *Jenkins et al. v. State et al.* (1984), "KCMSD Trial Brief," filed March 5, 1984, 28.
33 *Jenkins et al. v. State et al.* (1984), "Defendant United States Department of Education's Suggestions in Support of Rule 41(b) Motion to Dismiss," filed October 17, 1983, 10.
34 *Jenkins et al. v. State et al.* (1984), "Memorandum of the Department of Housing and Urban Development in Support of Their Motion for Dismissal Under Rule 41(b) of the Federal Rules of Civil Procedure," filed March 14, 1984, 30.
35 *Jenkins et al. v. State et al.* (1984), "Memorandum Submitted by Missouri School District Defendants, Showing that Under Missouri Law School Districts are Separate and Autonomous Political Entities," filed October 17, 1983, 8-9.
36 Ibid., 10.
37 *Jenkins et al. v. State et al.* (1984), "Pretrial Brief Submitted by the Missouri School District Defendants (Excluding KCMSD)," filed October 17, 1983, 7.
38 Ibid., 10-11.
39 Ibid., 71.
40 *Jenkins et al. v. State et al.* (1984), "State Defendant Suggested Findings of Fact and Conclusions of Law," filed June 28, 1984, 8.
41 Ibid., 37.
42 Ibid., 54, 60.
43 Ibid., 11.
44 Ibid., 31-32.
45 Ibid., 34-35.
46 Ibid., 37, 70.
47 Louis Blue, "U.S. Judge Deals Blow to Metro Desegregation Plan," *The Call*, June 8-14, 1984, 1.
48 James S. Kunen, "The End of Integration," *Time*, April 29, 1996, 41.
49 Ibid.
50 418 U.S. 717.
51 *Jenkins v. State of Mo.* (1984), at 1488.
52 Ibid.
53 Ibid., at 1490, 1491.
54 Ibid., at 1503.
55 Ibid., at 1493.
56 Stephen E. Winn, "Effect on Suit Here Unclear to Lawyers," *Kansas City Star*, July 3, 1979, A4.
57 *Jenkins v. State of Mo.* (1984), at 1492.
58 Ibid., at 1493.
59 Ibid., at 1492.
60 Ibid., at 1503.
61 163 U.S. 537.
62 Author interview with Pete Hutchison, attorney, Landmark Legal Foundation, Kansas City, Mo., January 23, 2001 (hereafter Hutchison interview).
63 Benson interview.
64 Hutchison interview.

65 Lynn Byczynski, "Judge's Desegregation Ruling Leaves Solution Unclear," *Kansas City Times*, September 18, 1984, A1.
66 *Jenkins v. State of Mo.* (1984).
67 Byczynski, "Judge's Desegregation Ruling," A1.
68 See Paul Ciotti, "Money and School Performance: Lessons from the Kansas City Desegregation Experiment," Cato Policy Analysis No. 298 (March 16, 1998), <<http://www.cato.org/pubs/pas/pa-298.pdf>> (accessed April 23, 2007).

Chapter Four

1 Author's interview with Arthur Benson, plaintiff's attorney, Kansas City, Mo., January 17, 2001 (hereafter Benson interview).
2 Ibid.
3 Tom Mirga, "Kansas City Desegregation Proposal Shelved," *Education Week*, February 6, 1985.
4 "Judge Orders School Board to Submit a New Deseg Plan," *The Call*, February 1–7, 1985, 1.
5 Lynn Byczynski, "KC's Blacks Split on School Desegregation," *Kansas City Times*, December 19, 1984, B2.
6 Benson interview.
7 For an overview of the effective schools literature, see Susan J. Rosenholtz, "Effective Schools: Interpreting the Evidence," *American Journal of Education* 93 (1985): 352–88, and Stewart C. Purkey and Marshall S. Smith, "Effective Schools: A Review," *Elementary School Journal* 83 (1983): 426–52.
8 Kansas City Missouri School District Desegregation Implementation Plan, Submitted by State Defendants at 2, April 29, 1985, *Jenkins v. State of Mo.*, 593 F. Supp. 1485 (W.D. Mo. 1984).
9 110 S. Ct. 2841 (1990).
10 109 S. Ct. 3040 (1989).
11 For a fuller discussion of Webster and his ambitions, see Tony Mauro, "I'm From Missouri—Litigate Me," *The Recorder*, March 27, 1991, 7.
12 Transcript of Record at 24,453, *Jenkins v. State of Mo.*, 639 F. Supp. 19 (W.D. Mo. 1985), May 10, 1985.
13 Benson interview.
14 Transcript of Record at 23076–77, *Jenkins v. State of Mo.* (1985), May 2, 1985.
15 *Jenkins v. State of Mo.* (1985), at 25.
16 Ibid.
17 Benson interview.
18 Ibid.
19 *Jenkins v. State of Mo.* (1985), at 24.
20 Ibid., at 34.
21 Author interview with Eugene Eubanks, former chairman, Desegregation Monitoring Committee; professor, University of Missouri–Kansas City, January 16, 2000 (hereafter Eubanks interview).
22 Ibid.

23 *Jenkins v. State of Mo.* (1985), at 45.
24 Ibid.
25 Ibid., at 40.
26 Lynn Byczynski, "KC District Hopes to End Racial Isolation," *Kansas City Times*, September 4, 1985, A1.
27 Jeff Taylor, "School Reaction Mixed," *Kansas City Times*, June 15, 1985, A1.
28 Donald P. Lay, "Tribute: Judge Myron Bright," 83 *Minnesota Law Review* 225. Lay does not reveal what the xxxx's stand for. There appear to be several potential candidates.
29 *Jenkins by Agyei v. State of Mo.*, 807 F.2d 657 (8th Cir. 1986), at 686.
30 Ibid., at 688.
31 Ibid., at 695, 712.
32 Market Information Services, *Magnet School Survey*, January 13, 1986, 12.
33 Market Information Services, *A Qualitative Report on Attitudes Toward Magnet Schools*, March 3, 1986, 1-2.
34 Lynn Byczynski, "KC School Board Rejects Magnet Plan," *Kansas City Times*, April 23, 1986, A1.
35 Bruce R. Hare and Daniel U. Levine, "Toward Effective Desegregated Schools," United States Department of Education (Washington, D.C.: U.S. Government Printing Office, August 1984), 79.
36 *Jenkins v. State of Mo.*, 672 F. Supp. 400 (W.D. Mo. 1987), "Kansas City, Missouri School District Long-Range Magnet School Plan," July 28, 1986, 21.
37 Ibid., 2.
38 Ibid., 21, 22.
39 Benson interview.
40 *Jenkins v. Missouri*, 1986 U.S. Dist. Lexis 17819.
41 Ibid., at 2, 5.
42 Lynn Byczynski, "KC School, State Delays Draw Fire: Lack of Progress on Magnet Project Angers Committee," *Kansas City Times*, January 17, 1986, A1.
43 *Jenkins v. Missouri*, 1986 U.S. Dist. Lexis 17819, at 6.
44 *Jenkins v. State of Mo.* (1987), at 404, "Opposition of the State of Missouri to KCMSD Motion for Approval of Long-Range Capital Improvement Plan," May 6, 1987, 2-3.
45 Ibid., 17, 18.
46 *Jenkins v. State of Mo.* (1987), at 404.
47 Eubanks interview.
48 Author interview with Pete Hutchison, attorney, Landmark Legal Foundation, Kansas City, Mo., January 23, 2001 (hereafter Hutchison interview).
49 *Jenkins v. State of Mo.* (1987), at 406.
50 Ibid., at 412.
51 Ibid.
52 Steven Farnsworth, "School Tax Order Is Denounced," *Kansas City Times*, September 17, 1987, A1.
53 Steven Farnsworth, "Conservative Group Vows to Challenge Judge's Order," *Kansas City Times*, September 24, 1987, B2.

54 Beverly Potter, "Independence 'Tea Party' Signals Opposition to Judge's Tax Ruling," *Kansas City Times*, September 22, 1987, B1.
55 Debra Skodack and Victoria Sizemore Long, "Businessmen Fear School Tax Could Hurt KC Economy," *Kansas City Times*, September 17, 1987, C2.
56 "Children's Rights First," *Kansas City Times*, September 18, 1987, A14.
57 Ibid.
58 Along with the KCMSD, the Kansas City Federation of Teachers had also asked Judge Clark to raise taxes. In a brief filed with Judge Clark, the union accused the voters of Kansas City of "turn[ing] their backs on the children of their district." The 2-1 vote against the most recent tax levy, the brief stated, was at least partly due to "racial prejudice." As evidence, they cited a Taxpayer Defense League pamphlet in which the league argued that desegregation was impossible because 75 percent of the KCMSD's students were minority and that Clark's remedial programs that were funded by the tax increases would never work. See Lynn Byczynski, "KC Teachers Urge Judge to Boost Taxes," *Kansas City Times*, February 12, 1986, B1.
59 Michael Mansur, "Complexities May Force Tax Order Back to Courts," *Kansas City Star*, September 18, 1987, A1.
60 Author interview with Mark Bredemeier, former attorney, Landmark Legal Foundation, Kansas City, Mo., January 24, 2001 (hereafter Bredemeier interview).
61 Tim O'Connor, "School Tax Refund Plan Detailed: Kansans Get Extra Break on Unconstitutional Surcharge," *Kansas City Times*, January 5, 1989, A7.
62 Gregory S. Reeves, "State's New Torment: Form KC-1," *Kansas City Star*, January 26, 1988, A1.
63 Michael Mansur, "Employees Object to School Tax: Surcharge Taken from City Workers," *Kansas City Star*, November 19, 1987, A1.
64 Further complicating the issue of the tax surcharge the announcement that KCMSD placed in the *Kansas City Star* notifying individuals of the new income tax contained a "clip out remittance form with an incorrect zip code." The zip code, 85105, did not exist but "most closely" resembled zip codes in Phoenix. Many tax payments may have been routed to Phoenix rather than Jefferson City. See Michael Mansur, "Tax Surcharge for Schools Is Due: Delays are Expected in Court-Ordered Payments," *Kansas City Star*, November 15, 1987, A42.
65 See, for example, "It Had to Be Done," *The Call*, September 18-24, 1987, 20. This editorial did, however, say that Judge Clark's order was "pretty rough."
66 Jeremiah Cameron, "Let's Consider," *The Call*, September 5-11, 1986, 10.
67 Jeremiah Cameron, "Judge Clark's Ruling," *The Call*, October 1-8, 1987, 18.
68 Jeremiah Cameron, "Teachers Must Be Tested," *The Call*, January 8-14, 1988, 10.
69 Edward M. Eveld, "Firms Protest Tax Payments: $4 Million Disputed So Far," *Kansas City Times*, January 7, 1988, A12.
70 Michael Mansur, "KC Business Leaders Back School Tax," *Kansas City Star*, March 15, 1988, A1.
71 Bredemeier interview.
72 *Jenkins v. Missouri et al.*, 855 F.2d 1295 (8th Cir. 1988), Supplemental Brief for

Amici Curiae and applicants for intervention Icelean Clark et al., February 18, 1988.
73 *Jenkins by Agyei v. State of Mo.*, 855 F.2d 1295 (8th Cir. 1988), at 1299.
74 Ibid., at 1310.
75 Ibid., at 1316.
76 Ibid., at 1319.
77 The Supreme Court had already heard one issue surrounding the case on attorneys' fees in *Missouri v. Jenkins I* (491 U.S. 274 [1989]). That decision dealt with technical legal questions about how much money attorneys were entitled to under the Civil Rights Attorney's Fees Awards Act of 1976 (42 U.S.C. 1988). The act allowed courts to award attorney's fees to successful plaintiffs in civil rights cases. Under the act, Clark's initial verdict entitled Benson and the LDF to compensation, but the state of Missouri withheld payment while appealing the case. In turn, Benson and the LDF argued that they were entitled to enhanced compensation because of this delay. They also claimed that they were entitled to more compensation based on the work of their law clerks and paralegals. The Court sided with Benson and the LDF.
78 Michael Mansur and Mary Sanchez, "KC District Is Called the Big Winner," *Kansas City Star*, April 24, 1989, A1.
79 Ibid., A10.
80 Andrew C. Miller, "Justices Question KC School Costs," *Kansas City Star*, October 30, 1989, A1.
81 *Missouri v. Jenkins*, 495 U.S. 33 (1990), at 35.
82 Lynn Horsley, "School Tax Boost Ordered," *Kansas City Star*, July 26, 1990, A1.
83 *Missouri v. Jenkins* (1990), at 77.
84 Justices Harry Blackmun's and Thurgood Marshall's files on the case, the only potential sources on this question until other justices' files are made available, do not contain any notes or comments that would help answer it.
85 Andrew C. Miller, "Plan to Cut Court Power Has Rival: Danforth Seeks Amendment to Bar Judges from Raising Taxes," *Kansas City Star*, April 26, 1990, A6.
86 Lynn Byczynski, "Judge Weathers the Storm: Desire to Do Right Pushes Clark On," *Kansas City Times*, September 23, 1987, A9. Clark also commented that the remedy was left to the experts but that everyone knew what expert witnesses were proposing for single-district remedies.
87 Tim O'Connor, "Clark Says Appeals Court Left Him Little Choice," *Kansas City Star*, July 18, 1990, A10.

Chapter Five

1 Lynn Horsley, "Team Supervising Construction Draws Fire, Praise: Budget Overruns Cited by the Critics of Experts from Outside," *Kansas City Star*, November 18, 1991, A8.
2 Desegregation Monitoring Committee Annual Report, June 30, 1992, 12. All DMC reports are in possession of the author.
3 Lynn Horsley, "Expensive Repairs Were No Guarantee of Survival: Demolition Was

Fate of Paseo, Central Highs and Knots Elementary," *Kansas City Star*, November 17, 1991, A15.
4   Lynn Horsley, "Fine Schools Will Need Years of Expensive Care: Future Taxpayers Face a Maintenance Burden," *Kansas City Star*, November 18, 1991, A1.
5   Tim O'Connor, "Adviser Criticizes Central: Plan for School 'Extravagant' Official Testifies," *Kansas City Times*, March 18, 1989, B1.
6   Author interview with Willie Bowie, principal, Central High School, Kansas City, Mo., January 29, 1998 (hereafter Bowie interview).
7   Dianne Stafford, "Building Less Vital, Magnet Planner Says," *Kansas City Star*, March 17, 1989, A3.
8   Tim O'Connor, "New Central High to Cost $32 Million: Plan for 'Phenomenal' School OK'd," *Kansas City Times*, April 25, 1989, A1.
9   Ibid.
10 Desegregation Monitoring Committee Annual Report to Judge Clark, June 30, 1988, 44.
11 Ibid., June 30, 1989, 34.
12 Author interview with Arthur Benson, plaintiff's attorney, Kansas City, Mo., January 17, 2001 (hereafter Benson interview).
13 Tim O'Connor, "Panel Files Plan to Integrate Suburb Schools: Judge Is Asked to Provide Tuition Vouchers for Blacks," *Kansas City Times*, June 23, 1989, A1.
14 Ibid.
15 Desegregation Monitoring Committee Annual Report to Judge Clark, June 30, 1990, 58.
16 Ibid., June 30, 1991, 39.
17 Lynn Horsley, "Desegregation Costs Far Outpace Progress," *Kansas City Star*, September 23, 1992, C1.
18 Ibid.
19 Lynn Horsley, "Goals Elude KC Magnets: Enrollment and Achievement Lag Despite Years of Effort, Money," *Kansas City Star*, August 10, 1992, A1.
20 Ibid.
21 Lynn Horsley, "The Plan: Ambitiously Unrealistic — Barriers Overcome, but Others Remain," *Kansas City Star*, May 9, 1994, A1.
22 Ibid.
23 Lynn Horsley, "Enrollment of Whites Drops in KC," *Kansas City Star*, November 10, 1995, C1.
24 Lynn Byczynski, "KC School, State Delays Draw Fire: Lack of Progress on Magnet Project Angers Committee," *Kansas City Times*, January 17, 1986, A1.
25 Mary Sanchez, "Desegregation Plan under Fire from Blacks," *Kansas City Star*, September 28, 1988, J2.
26 Desegregation Monitoring Committee Annual Report to Judge Clark, June 30, 1991, 39.
27 Ibid., June 30, 1992, 10.
28 Jack Cashill, "Desegregation Rap: Run! DMC," *Ingram's*, November 1990, 13–15.
29 Ibid.

30. Tim O'Connor, "Critic of School Plan May Lead Ad Effort," *Kansas City Star*, November 20, 1990, B1.
31. Desegregation Monitoring Committee Annual Report to Judge Clark, June 30, 1988, 5–6.
32. See, for example, Lynn Byczynski, "Desegregation Effort Draws Fire from Court Panel," *Kansas City Times*, October 18, 1985, B1, and Byczynski, "KC School, State Delays Draw Fire," A1.
33. Lynn Byczynski, "KC School Board Blasted for Desegregation Delays," *Kansas City Times*, February 21, 1986, B1. See also Lynn Byczynski, "Problems Listed in Desegregation at Panel's Hearing," *Kansas City Times*, March 21, 1986, B1.
34. Lynn Byczynski, "School Panel Decries Lack of Progress," *Kansas City Times*, April 25, 1986, A1. See also Lynn Byczynski, "Desegregation Panel Blasts District, State," *Kansas City Times*, August 22, 1986, A1.
35. Benson interview.
36. Author interview with Eugene Eubanks, former chairman, Desegregation Monitoring Committee; professor, University of Missouri–Kansas City, Kansas City, Mo., January 16, 2001 (hereafter Eubanks interview).
37. Art Brisbane, "District Gets Rap on Knuckles," *Kansas City Star*, December 14, 1990, C1.
38. Desegregation Monitoring Committee Annual Report to Judge Clark, June 30, 1988, 17.
39. Ibid., June 30, 1989, 58.
40. Ibid., June 30, 1990, 72.
41. Tim O'Connor, "KC Offers Good Schools, but Pupils Don't Learn, Panel Says," *Kansas City Star*, August 31, 1991, A1.
42. Horsley, "Desegregation Costs."
43. Ibid.
44. Horsley, "Goals Elude."
45. Ibid.
46. Lynn Horsley, "Magnets' Benefits Doubted: Test Scores by Black Students Don't Show Gains, Experts Testify," *Kansas City Star*, February 25, 1993, C10.
47. Ibid.
48. Stephen W. Winn, "Local Test Scores Prompt Divergent Views on Progress," *Kansas City Star*, March 20, 1994, L1.
49. Ibid.
50. "On the Money," CBS News Transcripts, February 24, 1994.
51. Stephen E. Winn, "Strident Days for KC's Schools," *Kansas City Star*, March 13, 1994, L1.
52. Eubanks interview.
53. Desegregation Monitoring Committee Annual Report to Judge Clark, June 30, 1988, 6.
54. Lynn Horsley, "KC Waivers Prevent Flunking of Students: Board Is Reviewing the Parental Option of Allowing Advancement," *Kansas City Star*, December 4, 1994, A1.

55 Horsley, "The Plan," A1.
56 Benson interview.
57 Eubanks interview.
58 Benson interview.
59 Jeanne S. Chall, "Literacy: Trends and Explanations," *Educational Researcher* (November 1983): 6.
60 David Savage, "Scrutinize Students' Test Scores, and They Might Not Look So Rosy," *American School Board Journal* 171, no. 8 (August 1984): 21–24.
61 Eubanks interview.
62 Rosemary O'Leary and Charles R. Wise, "Public Managers, Judges, and Legislators: Redefining the 'New Partnership,'" *Public Administration Review* 51 (1991): 320.
63 O'Connor, "KC Offers Good Schools."
64 Horsley, "Desegregation Costs."
65 Tim O'Connor, "KC Schools Skip Furniture Saving: Dealing With Area Vendors Could Cost at Least $50,000," *Kansas City Times*, August 2, 1992, A1.
66 Michael Mansur, "State Audit Questions Desegregation Spending," *Kansas City Star*, October 15, 1989, B1.
67 Will Sentell, "Auditor Critical of KC District," *Kansas City Star*, June 27, 1991, C1.
68 Lynn Horsley, "$43,000 was Spent for . . . What?" *Kansas City Star*, August 21, 1992, C1.
69 Desegregation Monitoring Committee Annual Report to Judge Clark, June 30, 1990, 39; Lynn Horsley, "Audit Suggests Possible Savings," *Kansas City Star*, August 1, 1997, C1.
70 Lynn Horsley and Tim O'Connor, "KC District Lacks Leadership and Vision, Report Says," *Kansas City Star*, January 24, 1991, A1.
71 Jerry Heaster, "Raze It? A Lesson Is Better," *Kansas City Star*, May 5, 1990, B1.
72 Ibid.
73 This problem illustrates one of Donald Horowitz's critiques of judicial policymaking: the courts are not compelled to consider economic realities. Considering costs, benefits, and public opinion, which checks unwise government expenditures, does not enter judicial calculations.
74 Benson interview.
75 Tim O'Connor, "Schools Fall Short, KC Watchdog Says: Panel Chairman Foresees Changes," *Kansas City Times*, November 15, 1989, C1.
76 Bill Dalton, "Panel Chairman Challenges Garcia on Low Test Scores: District Leadership Is Now in Question, Eubanks Says on Radio," *Kansas City Star*, September 2, 1990, B5.
77 Benson interview; author interview with Clinton Adams, activist, Kansas City, Mo., January 18, 2001 (hereafter Adams interview).
78 Lynn Horsley, "Superintendent Candidate Meets with School Board," *Kansas City Star*, February 1, 1991, C1.
79 Tim O'Connor, "KC School District's Choice Says No," *Kansas City Star*, February 12, 1991, A1.

80 Tim O'Connor, "California Educator Ran Model Magnet Program," *Kansas City Star*, February 20, 1991, A1.
81 Lynn Horsley, "KC School Committee: Watchdog or Bully? Vigilant Monitors Scold Administrators," *Kansas City Star*, March 13, 1992, A1.
82 Lynn Horsley, "Salesman for KC Schools Walter L. Marks Strives to Persuade Skeptics to Buy into Magnet Dream," *Kansas City Star*, February 22, 1992, E1.
83 "Hello, Goodbye," *Kansas City Star*, June 15, 1996, A14.
84 Adams interview.
85 Benson interview.
86 Ibid.

Chapter Six

1 *Kansas City Star*, May 5, 1994.
2 Author interview with Arthur Benson, plaintiff's attorney, Kansas City, Mo., January 17, 2001 (hereafter Benson interview).
3 Author interview with Clinton Adams, activist, Kansas City, Mo., January 18, 2001 (hereafter Adams interview).
4 Quoted in Paul Ciotti, "Money and School Performance: Lessons from the Kansas City Desegregation Experiment," Cato Policy Analysis No. 298 (March 16, 1998), <<http://www.cato.org/pubs/pas/pa-298.pdf>> (accessed April 23, 2007).
5 Ibid.
6 The *Kansas City Star* originally had both morning and afternoon editions, with the morning edition being called the *Kansas City Times*. The paper abandoned the afternoon edition in 1991 and kept the name *Star* as its title.
7 Adams interview.
8 Phillip O'Connor and Lynn Horsley, "Guardian or Glory Hound: Arthur A. Benson II has been Called Many Things during the KC Schools Case," *Kansas City Star*, July 14, 1996, A1.
9 Regina Akers, "Ministers Use Force to Make Demands Known to Board," *The Call*, August 8–14, 1986, 1.
10 Regina Akers, "Ministers Threaten Boycott If School Board Fires Perkins," *The Call*, August 8–14, 1986, 2.
11 Regina Akers, "Group Continues Pushing for School Board's Resignation; Might Boycott Businesses," *The Call*, August 22–28, 1986, 1.
12 Lynn Byczynski, "Desegregation Panel Blasts District, State," *Kansas City Times*, August 22, 1986, A1.
13 "NAACP Asks Judge Clark for Meeting on Magnets," *Kansas City Times*, December 28, 1988, B2.
14 "Dismal Failure," *Kansas City Star*, December 23, 1988, A5.
15 Tim O'Connor, "Black Leaders Go to Board with Plea," *Kansas City Star*, December 18, 1990, B1.
16 Tim O'Connor, "Black Pupils Want Tuition Vouchers: Nine Sue to Get State Money for Private Schools," *Kansas City Times*, July 15, 1989, A1.

17 Tim O'Connor, "Judge Clark Rejects Lawsuit Requesting Tuition Vouchers," *Kansas City Times*, December 28, 1989, C1.
18 Lynn Horsley and Tim O'Connor, "Has Clark's Ruling Improved Schools?" *Kansas City Star*, June 24, 1990, A1.
19 Jerry Heaster, "Idea: Use Law to Help the People," *Kansas City Star*, September 6, 1988, C5.
20 Adams interview.
21 Author interview with Ed Newsome, former school board president, Kansas City, Mo., January 25, 2001 (hereafter Newsome interview).
22 James S. Kunen, "The End of Integration," *Time*, April 29, 1996, 39.
23 Adams interview.
24 Michael Mansur, "Black Groups Join Attack on Magnet School Quotas," *Kansas City Star*, July 13, 1989, A3.
25 Michael Mansur, "Magnet Quotas Suit Is Rejected," *Kansas City Star*, September 12, 1989, A1.
26 *Jenkins v. Missouri*, 672 F. Supp. 400 (W.D. Mo. 1987), Mark Anthony Nevels et al.'s Motion to Modify Long-Range Magnet School Plan, September 21, 1989, 4.
27 *Jenkins v. Missouri* (1987), Amici Curiae Greater Kansas City Chapter of the Southern Christian Leadership Conference et al.'s Memorandum in Support of Mark Anthony Nevels et al.'s Motion to Modify Long-Range Magnet School Plan, September 21, 1989, 6–7.
28 Tim O'Connor, "Judge Asked to Ease Quotas for Magnets: Guidelines Keeping out Black Students," *Kansas City Star*, October 13, 1989, A1.
29 *Jenkins v. Missouri*, No. 77-0420-CV-W-4, Order of Judge Clark, July 3, 1990.
30 See Lynn Horsley, "School Coalition Devoted: Divisive Group Wants Better KC Schools, but Its Tactics Are Criticized," *Kansas City Star*, September 9, 1993, A1.
31 Phil B. Curls et al., "Critics of Group's Efforts to Improve Schools Have Chosen the Wrong Target," *Kansas City Star*, August 14, 1993, C7.
32 Adams interview.
33 CEEJ, "Retreat Highlights," undated, from the files of Clinton Adams.
34 Lynn Horsley, "Parents Protest Asian Theme Proposed for Holmes School," *Kansas City Star*, June 2, 1992, B1.
35 Lynn Horsley, "Racial Interests Pose Challenge for KC Schools," *Kansas City Star*, June 5, 1992, C1.
36 CEEJ, "Proposal for an African Centered Theme School," June 1992, from the files of Clinton Adams.
37 CEEJ, "Community Based Schools: An Alternative to Expansion of the Long-Range Magnet Plan," Executive Summary (1992): 2, from the files of Clinton Adams.
38 Ibid.
39 Adams interview.
40 George Gurley, "Critics Speak Out on School," *Kansas City Star*, November 5, 1992, C1.
41 Newsome interview.

42. Edward Newsome, speech to the KCMSD School Board, November 23, 1992, from the files of Edward Newsome.
43. "Kansas City School Board," *Kansas City Star*, March 31, 1994, C6.
44. Donna McGuire, "Adams Candidacy Decried," *Kansas City Star*, March 24, 1994, C3.
45. "Kansas City School Board," C6.
46. Rich Hood, "Futures of Our Children at Stake," *Kansas City Star*, March 27, 1994, L5.
47. Julia Hill was a particularly disappointing member of the board for Newsome and Adams. Before being elected president of the board, Hill had been president of the local NAACP and one of the magnet plan's most vocal critics. But she changed her position in 1992, which secured her enough support to become president of the board.
48. *Jenkins v. Missouri*, Suggestions in Support of Motion to Intervene, December 1, 1994, 5. See *Jenkins v. Missouri*, 78 F.3d 1270 (8th Cir. 1996), for the Eighth Circuit's denial of the motion to intervene.
49. Sandler and Schoenbrod, *Democracy by Decree*, 125.
50. Horsley and O'Connor, "Has Clark's Ruling Improved Schools?" A1.

Chapter Seven

1. James S. Kunen, "The End of Integration," *Time*, April 29, 1996, 40.
2. See William L. Christopher, "Ignoring the Soul of *Brown: Board of Education v. Dowell*," *North Carolina Law Review* 70 (1992): 615, and Timothy S. Jost, "The Attorney General's Policy on Consent Decrees and Settlement Agreements," *Administrative Law Review* 39 (1987): 101.
3. *Dowell v. Bd. of Educ. Oklahoma City Pub. Sch.*, 606 F. Supp. 1548 (W.D. Ok. 1985).
4. Ibid.
5. *Dowell v. Okl. City Public Schools*, 677 F. Supp. 1503 (W.D. Ok. 1987), at 1524.
6. *Dowell v. Bd. of Educ. of Okl. City Public Schools*, 890 F.2d 1483 (1989).
7. *Board of Education of Oklahoma City v. Dowell*, 498 U.S. 237 (1991), at 249.
8. *Freeman v. Pitts*, 503 U.S. 467 (1993), at 494. On the *Green* factors, see Chapter 1.
9. Ibid., at 497.
10. Ibid., at 495.
11. "School Tax Irks Residents: Property Owners Don't Like Increase or Its Imposition Without Their Vote," *Kansas City Star*, July 5, 1990, B1.
12. *Jenkins v. Missouri*, No. 77-0420-CV-W-4, Order of Judge Clark, June 25, 1992.
13. *Jenkins v. Missouri*, No. 77-0420-CV-W-4, Order of Judge Clark, June 30, 1993.
14. *Jenkins v. Missouri*, 672 F. Supp. 400 (W.D. Mo. 1987), State's Memorandum in Opposition to Joint Motion of Plaintiffs and KCMSD for Ten-Year Extension and Expansion of Magnet Program, November 13, 1992, 13–14.
15. *Jenkins v. Missouri*, No. 77-0420-CV-W-4, Order of Judge Clark, April 16, 1993, at 2.
16. Rich Hood and Steve Kraske, "Races Create Great Moments—and a Gaffe or Two," *Kansas City Star*, November 8, 1992, A22.
17. *Jenkins by Agyei v. State of Mo.*, 11 F.3d 755 (W.D. Mo. 1993), at 766.

18 Jay Nixon, "Missouri Schools Held to Odd and Unfair Standard," *Kansas City Star*, October 5, 1994, C7.
19 Andrew C. Miller, "Court Hears KC School Appeal: Questions by Justices Suggest a Narrow Ruling," *Kansas City Star*, January 12, 1995, A1.
20 *Missouri v. Jenkins*, 515 U.S. 70 (1995), at 92.
21 Ibid., at 89.
22 Ibid., at 102.
23 Ibid., at 122.
24 Clinton Adams wrote Thomas a letter thanking him for making the same argument that the CEEJ had been making in Kansas City. Otherwise an avowed critic of Thomas on everything from affirmative action to abortion, Adams believed that on desegregation Thomas was entirely correct. See author interview with Clinton Adams, Kansas City, Missouri, January 18, 2001 (hereafter Adams interview).
25 *Missouri v. Jenkins* (1995), at 139, 176.
26 "A Sad Day for Racial Justice," *New York Times*, June 13, 1995, A24.
27 Kunen, "End of Integration," 38.
28 *Jenkins v. Missouri*, 959 F. Supp. 1151 (W.D. Mo. 1997), at 1153.
29 Author interview with Ed Newsome, former school board president, Kansas City, Mo., January 25, 2001 (hereafter Newsome interview).
30 Lynn Horsley and Will Sentell, "KC Board, State Agree to End Aid: Desegregation Payments Would Stop in 1999 If Judge Approves," *Kansas City Star*, May 23, 1996, A1.
31 *Jenkins v. Missouri* (1997), at 1178.
32 Ibid., at 1177.
33 Quoted in Jack Cashill, "Bombs Away," <<http://www.cashill.com/natl_general/bomsaway4.htm>> (accessed April 24, 2007).
34 Phillip O'Connor and Lynn Horsley, "New Judge Chosen to Oversee Desegregation Lawsuit," *Kansas City Star*, March 29, 1997, C8.
35 Phillip O'Connor, "Judge May Appoint KC District Overseer: Whipple's Hint that He Will Assign a Special Master Meets with Criticism," *Kansas City Star*, April 18, 1997, C1.
36 *Jenkins v. Missouri*, Order of Judge Dean Whipple, August 21, 1997.
37 Phillip O'Connor and Lynn Horsley, "KC Board Sets Boundaries for Neighborhood Schools," *Kansas City Star*, March 12, 1998, A14.
38 Newsome interview.
39 Charles R. T. Crumpley and Lynn Horsley, "Who Pays the Price? The Billion-Dollar-Plus Effect Reaches Beyond KC to Burden State Agencies and Other School Districts," *Kansas City Star*, May 10, 1994, A1.
40 Lynn Horsley, "Voters Pass KC School Tax Amendment," *Kansas City Star*, April 8, 1998, A1.
41 Lynn Franey, "4,500 Enroll in Charter Schools Here: KC District's Total Slips, Which Means Less Money," *Kansas City Star*, September 14, 1999, B1.
42 Lynn Franey, "Charter Schools Gaining Ground: Area Enrollment Is Up 30 Percent," *Kansas City Star*, January 25, 2001, B1.

43 Phillip O'Connor, "KC Schools Could Lose Aid: Enrollment Drop Is Attributed to Charters," *Kansas City Star*, September 30, 1999, B1.

44 Phillip O'Connor, "KC Schools Suffer from Staffing Woes: Problems a Result of Charters' Surge, Officials Believe," *Kansas City Star*, October 7, 1999, B1.

45 *Jenkins v. Missouri*, 73 F. Supp. 2d 1058 (W.D. Mo. 1999), at 1074.

46 *Jenkins v. Missouri*, 216 F.3d 720 (8th Cir. 2000).

47 Ibid., at 733.

48 *Chinyere Jenkins et al. v. School District of Kansas City, Missouri et al.*, No. 77-0420-CV-W-DW, Order of Judge Dean Whipple, August 13, 2003, at 29.

49 Phillip O'Connor and Tanika White, "More than Superintendent Stifles KC District: Board Must Overcome Racial and Political Divisions," *Kansas City Star*, October 11, 1998, B1.

50 Phillip O'Connor and Lynn Horsley, "Williams Had Faced Nonstop Skirmishes," *Kansas City Star*, October 17, 1998, A14.

51 Lynn Horsley and Phillip O'Connor, "Board Finishes Budget: Spending Would Be Cut by Millions. Plan Now Goes to Judge," *Kansas City Star*, June 5, 1998, C3.

52 Phillip O'Connor, "Board Ends Williams Era in KC: Vote for Buyout Closes Weeks of Deadlock Over Superintendent," *Kansas City Star*, October 16, 1998, A1.

53 Phillip O'Connor, "Board Seeking Accord with Candidate Demps," *Kansas City Star*, July 16, 1999, A1.

54 Phillip O'Connor, "Judge Warns Demps of Board's 'Bad Record,'" *Kansas City Star*, July 20, 1999, A1.

55 Phillip O'Connor et al., "State Pulls KC School Certification: District Must Lift Test Scores by Mid-2002 to Regain Accreditation," *Kansas City Star*, October 22, 1999, A1.

56 Phillip O'Connor, "Memo Rebukes District Chief: Loewenstein Vents Anger at Demps," *Kansas City Star*, March 30, 2000, B1.

57 Adams interview.

58 Deann Smith, "Demps Seeks Help With Board: Court Official Calls Mediation Hearing," *Kansas City Star*, February 13, 2001, B1.

59 Kit Wagar and Deann Smith, "Demps Urges State to Run KC District: Stunned Board Sets Emergency Session," *Kansas City Star*, February 22, 2001, A1.

60 Deann Smith, "Kansas City District Once Again Without a Superintendent: Demps Fired After 20 Months; Four Members Boycott Meeting," *Kansas City Star*, April 19, 2001, A1.

61 Deann Smith, "U.S. Judge Reinstalls Demps: Superintendent Returns to Work; Board Told Not to Interfere," *Kansas City Star*, April 20, 2001, A1.

62 Deann Smith et al., "Demps Resigns, Denounces KC's 'Fatally Flawed' System; 6 Aides Also Quit; Interim Chief Named," *Kansas City Star*, April 24, 2001, A1.

63 Stephen Winn, "Here's Hoping the School Board Gets Its Wish," *Kansas City Star*, April 29, 2001, B7.

64 Deann Smith, "District Monitor Told to Hire Investigators," *Kansas City Star*, June 20, 2001, A1.

65 Deann Smith, "Study 'Malfeasance,' Judge Tells Board: Court Wants School Personnel Records," *Kansas City Star*, June 28, 2001, B1.
66 Deann Smith, "Benson Says Hearing Wrong: Court Mediation 'On Dangerous Ground,'" *Kansas City Star*, February 15, 2001, B1.
67 Deann Smith, "U.S. Judge Reinstalls Demps," A1.
68 *Chinyere Jenkins et al. v. School District of Kansas City, Missouri et al.*, 73 F. Supp. 2d 1058 (W.D. Mo. 1999), "Suggestions in Support of Joint Motion to Enforce Judgments Incorporating Agreement Involving Dismissal of State Defendants," filed February 22, 2006.
69 *Jenkins et al. v. Missouri et al.*, 2006 U.S. Dist. Lexis 85352.
70 "Tumult, Mistrust in KC Schools," *Kansas City Star*, May 16, 2006, B6.
71 498 U.S. 237 (1991).
72 Gary Orfield and Susan E. Eaton, eds., *Dismantling Desegregation: The Quiet Reversal of Brown v. Board of Education* (New York: New Press), 1996.
73 In some ways, Orfield himself recognizes that substandard education is the most pressing problem. In much of his recent work he argues that segregated minority schools will by and large offer inferior education. Thus, desegregation is necessary for school improvements. But this was the idea behind the remedial plan in Kansas City. The assumption, which black community leaders rejected, was that minority schools must be inferior.

Conclusion

1 For a thorough discussion of the logic and effectiveness of magnet schools, see Christine H. Rossell, *The Carrot or the Stick for Desegregation Policy* (Philadelphia: Temple University Press, 1990).
2 Erika Frankenburg and Chungmei Lee, "Race in American Public Schools: Rapidly Resegregating School Districts," *The Civil Rights Project* (August 8, 2002), <<http://www.civilrightsproject.harvard.edu/research/deseg/Race_in_American_Public_Schools1.pdf>> (accessed April 23, 2007).
3 Malcolm M. Feeley and Edward L. Rubin, *Judicial Policy Making and the Modern State: How the Courts Reformed America's Prisons* (New York: Cambridge University Press, 1998), chap. 7.
4 Author interview with Arthur Benson, plaintiff's attorney, Kansas City, Mo., January 17, 2001 (hereafter Benson interview).
5 This is not to say that money and facilities do not matter. It is hard to imagine how substantial academic improvement could have been made in the squalid facilities the KCMSD operated before the remedial plan. Schools without reliable heat would certainly make the learning process more difficult during a cold midwestern winter. But even if we were to give the KCMSD the benefit of the doubt and assume that its schools' physical deterioration was not caused by mismanagement, it does not follow that it must, therefore, provide lavish facilities in order to teach children how to read and write.
6 Author interview with Clinton Adams, activist, Kansas City, Mo., January 18, 2001.

7 See Richard Hess, *Spinning Wheels: The Politics of Urban School Reform* (Washington, D.C.: Brookings Institution Press, 1999).
8 Edward T. Matheny Jr., one of Southwest's proud alumni of the class of 1940, has written a book documenting the school's uneven history, titled *The Rise and Fall of Excellence: The Story of Southwest High School R.I.P.* (Overland Park, Kans.: Leathers Publishing, 2000).
9 Benson interview.
10 No one has ever denied that Arthur Benson's fundamental goal has always been to help the children of Kansas City, even if they think he has been misguided. As the case has drawn nearer to a close, he has been more than willing to admit his own mistakes and advocate policies that might not be in his personal interest.
11 Although it is plausible that changing to at-large seats could have this effect, one should recall that Ed Newsome, an African American candidate, won an at-large seat in 1994. A black candidate with strong support from the black community always has a good chance of winning an at-large seat when multiple seats are open.
12 Paul Hampel and Steve Giegerich, "State Takeover Could Be Costly for City Schools: St. Louis District Might Face Huge Tuition Bills for Students Transferring to County Schools," *St. Louis Post Dispatch*, April 7, 2007, A19.
13 Missouri Public School Accountability Report, 2005, available at <<http://www.dese.mo.gov/commissioner/statereportcard>> (accessed August 25, 2007).

Bibliography

Note on Sources
The majority of material used in this book came from Arthur Benson's files at the Western Historical Manuscript Collection in Kansas City, Missouri; the archives at U.S. Court for the Western District of Missouri; and the Kansas City, Missouri, Public Library's Missouri Valley Special Collections. Arthur Benson's files are an especially thorough, well-organized, and rich resource. In addition to case briefs, school district records, transcripts, and unreported opinions, they contain a wealth of material on Kansas City's history over the past 100 years. Clinton Adams and Edward Newsome also graciously gave me access to their files from the case, which provided much of the material for Chapter 6.

Chronology of Published Opinions
School Dist. of Kansas City, Mo. v. State of Mo. 438 F. Supp. 830 (W.D. Mo. 1977).
School District of Kansas City v. State of Mo. 460 F. Supp. 421 (W.D. Mo. 1978).
Black v. State of Missouri. 492 F. Supp. 848 (W.D. Mo. 1980).
Jenkins v. State of Mo. 593 F. Supp. 1485 (W.D. Mo. 1984).
Jenkins v. State of Mo. 639 F. Supp. 19 (W.D. Mo. 1985).
Jenkins by Agyei v. State of Mo. 807 F.2d 657 (8th Cir. 1986).
Jenkins v. State of Mo. 672 F. Supp. 400 (W.D. Mo. 1987).
Jenkins by Agyei v. State of Mo. 855 F.2d 1295 (8th Cir. 1988).
Missouri v. Jenkins. 491 U.S. 274 (1989).
Missouri v. Jenkins. 495 U.S. 33 (1990).
Jenkins v. Missouri. 942 F. 2d 487 (8th Cir. 1991).
Jenkins by Agyei v. State of Mo. 11 F.3d 755 (8th Cir. 1993).
Missouri v. Jenkins. 515 U.S. 70 (1995).
Jenkins v. Missouri. 78 F.3d 1270 (8th Cir. 1996).
Jenkins v. Missouri. 959 F. Supp. 1151 (W.D. Mo. 1997).
Jenkins v. Missouri. 965 F. Supp. 1295 (W.D. Mo. 1997).
Jenkins v. Missouri. 122 F.3d 588 (8th Cir. 1997).
Jenkins v. Missouri. 73 F. Supp. 2d 1058 (W.D. Mo. 1999).
Jenkins v. Missouri. 216 F.3d 720 (8th Cir. 2000).

Interviews
All interviews were conducted by the author.
Adams, Clinton. Activist, Kansas City, Mo., January 18, 2001.
Allen, Tracy. Kansas City, Mo., January 16, 2001.
Benson, Arthur. Plaintiff's attorney, Kansas City, Mo., January 17, 2001.
Bowie, Willie. Principal, Central High School, Kansas City, Mo., January 29, 1998.

Bredemeier, Mark. Former attorney, Landmark Legal Foundation, Kansas City, Mo., January 24, 2001.
Bullard, Audrey. Principal, J. S. Chick Elementary School, Kansas City, Mo., January 29, 1998.
Duncan, John. Kansas City, Missouri, School District historian, Kansas City, Mo., January 23, 2001.
Eubanks, Eugene. Former chairman, Desegregation Monitoring Committee; professor, University of Missouri–Kansas City, Kansas City, Mo., January 16, 2001.
Hensley, Darren. Former clerk for Judge Clark, phone interview, March 26, 2001.
Hutchison, Pete. Attorney, Landmark Legal Foundation, Kansas City, Mo., January 23, 2001.
Kirksey, Jessie. Principal, Border Star Elementary School, Kansas City, Mo., January 29, 1998.
Mackinnon, Audrey. Parent, Kansas City, Missouri, School District, Kansas City, Mo., January 16, 2001.
Newsome, Edward. Former school board president, Kansas City, Mo., January 25, 2001.
Rios, John. Former school board president, Kansas City, Mo., January 28, 1998.
Williams, Roger. Principal, Paseo High School, Kansas City, Mo., January 30, 1998.

Books and Articles

Abraham, Henry J., and Barbara A. Perry. *Freedom and The Court: Civil Rights and Liberties in the United States.* New York: Oxford University Press, 1994.
Armor, David J. *Forced Justice: School Desegregation and the Law.* New York: Oxford University Press, 1995.
Beck, Deborah E. "School Choice: A Method for Desegregating an Inner City School District." *California Law Review* 81 (1993): 1029–57.
Ben, James Anthony. "*Missouri v. Jenkins*: Yet Another Complicated Chapter in the Desegregation Saga." *University of Miami Law Review* 51 (1997): 1221–46.
Berger, Raoul. *Government by Judiciary: The Transformation of the Fourteenth Amendment.* Cambridge: Harvard University Press, 1977.
Bickel, Alexander M. *The Supreme Court and the Idea of Progress.* New Haven: Yale University Press, 1978.
Billington, Monroe. "Public School Integration in Missouri, 1954–64." *Journal of Negro Education* 35 (1966): 252–62.
Brocker, Douglas J. "Taxation without Representation: The Judicial Usurpation of the Power to Tax in *Missouri v. Jenkins*." *North Carolina Law Review* 69 (1991): 741–69.
Canon, Bradley C., and Charles A. Johnson. *Judicial Policies: Implementation and Impact.* 2d ed. Washington, D.C.: Congressional Quarterly Press, 1999.
Chayes, Abram. "The Role of the Judge in Public Law Litigation." *Harvard Law Review* 89 (1976): 1281–1316.
Chemerinsky, Erwin. *Interpreting the Constitution.* New York: Praeger, 1987.
Chesler, Mark A., et al. *Social Science in Court: Mobilizing Experts in the School Desegregation Cases.* Madison: University of Wisconsin Press, 1988.

Chubb, John, and Terry Moe. *Politics, Markets, and America's Schools*. Washington, D.C.: Brookings Institution Press, 1990.

Clotfelter, Charles T. *After Brown: The Rise and Retreat of School Desegregation*. Princeton: Princeton University Press, 2004.

Coleman, James S., et al. *Equality of Educational Opportunity*. Washington, D.C.: U.S. Government Printing Office, 1966.

Coleman, James S., Sarah D. Kelley, and John A. Moore. *Trends in School Integration*. Washington, D.C.: Urban Institute, 1975.

Cook, Stuart W. "Social Science and School Desegregation: Did We Mislead the Supreme Court?" *Personality and Social Psychology Bulletin* 5 (1979): 420–37.

Cooper, Phillip J. *Hard Judicial Choices: Federal District Court Judges and State and Local Officials*. New York: Oxford University Press, 1988.

Cox, Archibald. *The Role of the Supreme Court in American Government*. New York: Oxford University Press, 1976.

Devins, Neal. "Judicial Matters." *California Law Review* 80 (1992): 1027–68.

DiIulio, John J., Jr. *Courts, Corrections, and the Constitution: The Impact of Judicial Intervention on Prisons and Jails*. New York: Oxford University Press, 1990.

Douglas, Davison M. *Reading, Writing, and Race: The Desegregation of the Charlotte Schools*. Chapel Hill: University of North Carolina Press, 1995.

Dworkin, Ronald. *Freedom's Law: The Moral Reading of the American Constitution*. Oxford: Oxford University Press, 1996.

———. *Taking Rights Seriously*. Cambridge: Harvard University Press, 1978.

Ely, John Hart. *On Constitutional Ground*. Princeton: Princeton University Press, 1996.

Epstein, Richard A. "The Remote Causes of Affirmative Action, or School Desegregation in Kansas City, Missouri." *California Law Review* 84 (1996): 1101–20.

Erickson, Rosemary J., and Rita J. Simon. *The Use of Social Science Data in Supreme Court Decisions*. Urbana: University of Illinois Press, 1998.

Faigman, David L. *Legal Alchemy: The Use and Misuse of Science in the Law*. New York: W. H. Freeman and Co., 1999.

Feeley, Malcolm M. "Hollow Hopes, Flypapers, and Metaphors." *Law and Social Inquiry* 17 (1992): 745–60.

Feeley, Malcolm M., and Edward L. Rubin. *Judicial Policy Making and the Modern State: How the Courts Reformed America's Prisons*. New York: Cambridge University Press, 1998.

Fife, Brian L. *Desegregation in American Schools: Comparative Intervention Strategies*. New York: Praeger, 1992.

Fiss, Owen M. *The Civil Rights Injunction*. Bloomington: Indiana University Press, 1978.

———. "Foreword: The Forms of Justice." *Harvard Law Review* 91 (1979): 1–58.

Formisano, Ronald P. *Boston Against Busing: Race, Class, and Ethnicity in the 1960s and 1970s*. Chapel Hill: University of North Carolina Press, 2004.

Frankenburg, Erika, and Chungmei Lee. "Race in American Public Schools: Rapidly Resegregating School Districts." *The Civil Rights Project*. August 8, 2002. <<http://www.civilrightsproject.harvard.edu/research/deseg/Race_in_American_Public_Schools1.pdf>>.

BIBLIOGRAPHY

Fuller, Lon. "The Forms and Limits of Adjudication." *Harvard Law Review* 92 (1978): 354–409.

Glazer, Nathan. *The Limits of Social Policy*. Cambridge: Harvard University Press, 1988.

———. "Should Judges Administer Social Services?" *The Public Interest* 50 (1978): 64–80.

Glendon, Mary Ann. *A Nation under Lawyers: How the Crisis in the Legal Profession Is Transforming American Society*. New York: Farrar, Straus and Giroux, 1994.

———. *Rights Talk: The Impoverishment of Political Discourse*. New York: Free Press, 1991.

Halpern, Stephen C. *On the Limits of the Law: The Ironic Legacy of Title VI of the 1964 Civil Rights Act*. Baltimore: Johns Hopkins University Press, 1995.

Hare, Bruce R., and Daniel U. Levine. "Toward Effective Desegregated Schools," United States Department of Education. Washington, D.C.: U.S. Government Printing Office, August 1984.

Hess, Richard. *Spinning Wheels: The Politics of Urban School Reform*. Washington, D.C.: Brookings Institution Press, 1999.

Hofstadter, Richard C. *Anti-Intellectualism in American Life*. New York: Vintage Books, 1963.

Horowitz, Donald L. *The Courts and Social Policy*. Washington, D.C.: Brookings Institution Press, 1977.

Jaffe, Louis L. *Judicial Control of Administrative Action*. Boston: Little, Brown, 1965.

———. "Standing Again." *Harvard Law Review* 84 (1971): 633–38.

Johnson, Charles A., and Bradley C. Canon. *Judicial Policies: Implementation and Impact*. Washington, D.C.: Congressional Quarterly Press, 1984.

Juhnke, Eric. "A City Awakened: The Kansas City Race Riot of 1968." *Gateway Heritage* 20 (Winter 1999–2000): 32–43.

Kagan, Robert A. *Adversarial Legalism: The American Way of Law*. Cambridge: Harvard University Press, 2003.

Kirp, David L. *Just Schools: The Idea of Racial Equality in American Education*. Berkeley: University of California Press, 2002.

Klein, David E., and Robert J. Hume. "Fear of Reversal as an Explanation of Lower Court Compliance." *Law and Society Review* 37 (2003): 579–606.

Kluger, Richard. *Simple Justice: The History of Brown v. Board of Education and Black America's Struggle for Equality*. 2d ed. New York: Vintage Books, 2004.

Levine, Daniel U., and Robert J. Havighurst, eds. *The Future of Big-City Schools: Desegregation Policies and Magnet Alternatives*. Berkeley: McCutchan Publishing Corp., 1977.

Levine, Daniel U., and Jeanie Keeny Meyer. "Level and Rate of Desegregation and White Enrollment Decline in a Big City School System." *Social Problems* 24 (1977): 451–62.

Lukas, J. Anthony, *Common Ground: A Turbulent Decade in the Lives of Three American Families*. New York: Alfred A. Knopf, 1985.

Marshall, Albert P. "Racial Integration in Education in Missouri." *Journal of Negro Education* 25 (1956): 289–98.

McCann, Michael W. *Rights at Work: Pay Equity Reform and the Politics of Legal Mobilization*. Chicago: University of Chicago Press, 1994.
McDowell, Gary L. *Curbing the Courts: The Constitution and the Limits of Judicial Power*. Baton Rouge: Louisiana State University Press, 1988.
———. *Equity and the Constitution: The Supreme Court, Equitable Relief, and Public Policy*. Chicago: University of Chicago Press, 1982.
Melnick, R. Shep. *Between the Lines: Interpreting Welfare Rights*. Washington, D.C.: Brookings Institution Press, 1994.
———. *Regulation and the Courts: The Case of the Clean Air Act*. Washington, D.C.: Brookings Institution Press, 1983.
Moran, Peter William. "Difficult from the Start: Implementing the *Brown* Decision in the Kansas City, Missouri, Public Schools." *Equity and Excellence in Education* 37 (2004): 278–88.
———. *Race, Law, and the Desegregation of Public Schools*. New York: LFB Scholarly Publishing, 2005.
Morantz, Alison. "Money and Choice in Kansas City: Major Investments with Modest Returns." In *Dismantling Desegregation: The Quiet Reversal of Brown v. Board of Education*, edited by Gary Orfield and Susan E. Eaton, 241–64. New York: New Press, 1996.
Myrdal, Gunnar. *An American Dilemma*. New York: Harper and Row, 1944.
Nagel, Robert F. *Constitutional Cultures: The Mentality and Consequences of Judicial Review*. Berkeley: University of California Press, 1989.
———. *Judicial Power and American Character: Censoring Ourselves in an Anxious Age*. New York: Oxford University Press, 1994.
O'Leary, Rosemary, and Charles R. Wise. "Public Managers, Judges, and Legislators: Redefining the 'New Partnership.'" *Public Administration Review* 51 (1991): 316–27.
Orfield, Gary. *Must We Bus? Segregated Schools and National Policy*. Washington, D.C.: Brookings Institution Press, 1978.
Orfield, Gary, and Susan E. Eaton, eds. *Dismantling Desegregation: The Quiet Reversal of Brown v. Board of Education*. New York: New Press, 1996.
Patterson, James T. *Brown v. Board of Education: A Civil Rights Milestone and Its Troubled Legacy*. New York: Oxford University Press, 2001.
Purkey, Stewart C., and Marshall S. Smith. "Effective Schools: A Review." *Elementary School Journal* 83 (1983): 426–52.
Rabkin, Jeremy. *Judicial Compulsions: How Public Law Distorts Public Policy*. New York: Basic Books, 1989.
Report of the United States Commission on Civil Rights, 1959. Washington D.C.: U.S. Government Printing Office, 1959.
Rhodes, Joel. "It Finally Happened Here: The 1968 Riot in Kansas City, Missouri." *Missouri Historical Review* 91 (1997): 295–315.
Rosenberg, Gerald N. *The Hollow Hope: Can Courts Bring About Social Change?* Chicago: University of Chicago Press, 1991.
Rosenholtz, Susan J. "Effective Schools: Interpreting the Evidence." *American Journal of Education* 93 (1985): 352–88.

Rossell, Christine H. *The Carrot or the Stick for Desegregation Policy*. Philadelphia: Temple University Press, 1990.

———. "The Convergence of Black and White Attitudes on School Desegregation Issues." In *Redefining Equality*, edited by Neal Devins and Davison M. Douglas, 120–38. New York: Oxford University Press, 1998.

Ryan, James E., and Michael Heise. "The Political Economy of School Choice." *Yale Law Journal* 111 (2002): 2043–2136.

Sandler, Ross, and David Schoenbrod, *Democracy by Decree: What Happens When Courts Run Government*. New Haven: Yale University Press, 2003.

Sarrat, Reed. *The Ordeal of Desegregation: The First Decade*. New York: Harper and Row, 1966.

Schlegel, John Henry. *American Legal Realism and Empirical Social Science*. Chapel Hill: University of North Carolina Press, 1995.

Schultz, David, and Stephen Gottlieb, eds. *Leveraging the Law: Using the Courts to Achieve Social Change*. New York: Peter Lang, 1998.

Smith, Christopher E. *Courts and Public Policy*. Chicago: Nelson-Hall, 1993.

Sugrue, Thomas J. *The Origins of the Urban Crisis: Race and Inequality in Postwar Detroit*. Princeton: Princeton University Press, 1996.

Thomas, John Clayton, and Dan H. Hoxworth. "The Limits of Judicial Desegregation: Remedies after *Missouri v. Jenkins*." *Publius* (1991): 93–108.

United States Commission on Civil Rights 1963 Staff Report on Public Education. Washington, D.C.: U.S. Government Printing Office, 1963.

United States Commission on Civil Rights 1964 Staff Report on Public Education. Washington, D.C.: U.S. Government Printing Office, 1964.

Viteritti, Joseph P. *Choosing Equality: School Choice, the Constitution, and Civil Society*. Washington, D.C.: Brookings Institution Press, 1999.

Wilkinson, J. Harvie. *From Brown to Bakke: The Supreme Court and School Integration, 1954–1978*. New York: Oxford University Press, 1979.

Wilson, James Q. *Bureaucracy: What Government Agencies Do and Why They Do It*. New York: Basic Books, 1989.

———. *Moral Judgment: Does the Abuse Excuse Threaten Our Legal System?* New York: Basic Books, 1997.

Wolf, Eleanor P. *Trial and Error: The Detroit School Desegregation Case*. Detroit: Wayne State University Press, 1981.

Woodson, Carter G. *The Mis-Education of the Negro*. Trenton, N.J.: Africa World Press, 1990.

Wright, J. Skelly. "Public School Desegregation: Legal Remedies for De Facto Segregation." In *Education and the Law: Cases and Materials on Public Schools*. 2d ed., edited by William R. Hazard, 144–52. New York: Free Press, 1978.

Yoo, John. "Who Measures the Chancellor's Foot? The Inherent Remedial Authority of the Federal Courts." *California Law Review* 84 (1996): 1121–77.

Index

ACLU (American Civil Liberties Union), 52
Adams, Clinton: on superintendents, 135, 136, 176–77; on teachers' unions, 141, 142; on school board politics, 143; on creation of CEEJ, 146–47; opposition to attendance quotas, 149, 150; proposed alternative to magnet-school plan, 153; school board election campaign of, 155–56; definition of desegregation, 157; *Time* interview, 159; on textbook shortage, 186
Adams v. Richardson, 28, 44
AFT (American Federation of Teachers), 163
Alspaugh, John, 126
Amendment 3, 172
American Civil Liberties Union (ACLU), 52
American Federation of Teachers (AFT), 163
Anderson, James, 75
Armor, David, 20
Arnold, Richard, 93, 94
Ashcroft, John, 87
Attendance quotas: black opposition to, 147–50

Beam, Arlen, 173–74
Benson, Arthur: background of, 53–54; relationship with Clark, 57, 76, 78–79; suburban districts, 62, 66, 70–75, 108; legal strategy of, 63–69; remedial plan, 83–97 passim, 103, 116, 129, 137, 144–45, 164; Eighth Circuit, 93–95, 173–74, 178; position on vouchers, 117; and teachers'

unions, 131, 141; conflict with superintendents, 134–38, 175–76; KCMSD School Board, 140, 187–88; positions on quotas, 148–50; opposition to charter schools, 179
Bell, Derrick, 56
Bickel, Alexander, 16, 192 (n. 6)
Black Agenda Group, 135
Black Chamber of Commerce, 148
Black community: opposition movement, 8, 9, 54–56, 140, 146, 150–51, 157, 158; black parents, 8, 34, 43, 46, 47, 52, 85; position on busing, 24, 37, 38; support for neighborhood schools, 37, 38, 171, 189; opposition to school board, 39–41, 140–41, 144; criticism of KCMSD, 60, 150; view of magnet-school plan, 95–97, 120, 129, 137, 139, 143–45, 150, 164; position on tax increases, 104, 105; view of Judge Clark, 134, 139; superintendents, 135–37, 142–43; teachers' unions, 141–42; diversity of, 142; black pastors, 142–44; opposition to quotas, 144–49, 151
Blackmun, Harry, 165
Black United Front, 142, 148
Bluford, Lucille, 71
Board of Education of Oklahoma City v. Dowell, 159–61, 162, 164, 179
Bond, Kit, 87, 88, 110
Bowie, Willie, 115
Bowman, Pasco, 108
Bradley, Cortez, 38
Bredemeier, Mark, 68, 103, 106, 147–48
Brennan, William, 18, 165

Breyer, Stephen, 165
Bright, Myron, 93
Brown v. Board of Education I, 9, 14, 15, 17, 19, 23, 63, 76, 77, 137, 158, 179–81
Brown v. Board of Education II, 15, 18, 23, 76
Burger, Warren, 44
Burkes, Walter, 59, 60
Busing: opposition to in Kansas City, 14, 45–47, 120, 122; as desegregation remedy, 19, 21, 22, 24, 29; intact busing, 37, 74, 75; in St. Louis, 52; Judge Clark's views on, 73, 81, 85, 92, 108; in Oklahoma City, 160

Call, The, 35, 53, 54, 58, 59, 74, 85, 104, 143
Cameron, Jeremiah, 60, 104, 105, 120, 145
Cashill, Jack, 55, 122–23, 174
CEEJ. *See* Coalition for Educational and Economic Justice
Central High School, 35, 38, 39, 42, 100, 114–16, 137
Central Middle School, 114
Chall, Jeanne, 129–30
Charter Schools, 172, 178, 186, 188
Chayes, Abram, 192 (n. 3)
Civic Council of Greater Kansas City, 106
Clark, Russell: and tax increases, 8, 29, 30, 94, 101–7, 110, 159, 163, 179, 185; support for magnet schools, 8, 96–99, 143–45, 152, 164; doctrinal constraints on, 11–13, 78, 79, 82, 86, 87; black community criticism of, 24, 30, 139, 149, 156, 157, 159; and suburban school districts, 29, 73, 74, 83–85; background of, 50, 51; realignment of KCMSD as defendant, 51, 53, 55; certification of KCMSD students as a class, 54; relationship with Arthur Benson, 54, 55; rationale for rulings against KCMSD, 74–79, 82, 168, 170, 174; remedial plan, 80, 91, 113, 130, 137; and DMC, 92, 113; relationship to Eighth Circuit, 93–95, 165–67; on magnet-school themes, 95, 116, 164, 186; and capital improvement plan, 100, 113–16; and Supreme Court, 111, 119, 165–68; opposition to vouchers, 117–18, 187; on student achievement as standard for desegregation, 129, 131, 165; and teachers' unions, 141–42, 163; support for quota system, 146–52, 183; criticism of KCMSD, 169–70; and pay increases, 163, 165
Class actions, 25, 29
Cleaver, Emmanuel, 41, 142, 154, 187
Civil Rights Act: Title IV, 44; Title VI, 16, 18, 28, 41, 45, 74
Coalition for Educational and Economic Justice (CEEJ), 142, 146, 148, 168; political strategy of, 150–53, 154–55; educational positions of, 152–53; legal strategy of, 156–58. *See also* Adams, Clinton; Newsome, Edward
Congress of Racial Equality (CORE), 39
CORE (Congress of Racial Equality), 39
Cortez, Gary H., 102
Curls, Darwin, 155–56

Dalton, John, 33
Danforth, John, 110–11
Dekalb County, Georgia, School System (DCSS), 161–62
Demps, Benjamin, 176–78
Department of Transportation (DOT), 49, 51, 62
Desegregation Monitoring Committee (DMC), 91, 145, 168, 171, 174–75, 177; criticism of KCMSD, 113, 117, 118, 122–24, 131–34, 136; and student achievement, 125–28

DMC. *See* Desegregation Monitoring Committee
Donnelly, Phil, 33
DOT (Department of Transportation), 49, 51, 62
Duncan, John, 43

Eagleton, Thomas, 50
Eaton, Susan, 180
Effective schools, 85, 86, 88, 90, 92
Eighth Circuit, U.S. Court of Appeals: and St. Louis, 53, 63, 67, 87; denial of motion to replace Arthur Benson, 56; as constraint on Judge Clark, 74, 78, 79, 81, 82, 86, 87, 90; support for tax increase, 92–95; composition of, 93, 108; and appeal by Landmark Legal Foundation, 105–8; and appeal on vouchers, 146; on student achievement as standard for desegregation, 164, 165; and appeal of Whipple rulings, 177; interpretation of Supreme Court precedents, 183
Emergent policymaking, 9, 12, 27, 184
Eubanks, Eugene, 85, 100–101, 127, 130, 132, 134–35, 143; and remedial plan, 89, 90, 117; background of, 91; as DMC chair, 91–92, 123, 124; and magnet schools, 98, 129, 145; black community criticism of, 139
Expert witnesses, 10, 12, 21, 38, 64, 65, 86, 88, 89, 167–69

Fagg, George, 93
Federalist Papers: "Federalist No. 78," 5; "Federalist No. 51," 11; "Federalist No. 10," 187
Feeley, Malcolm, 13, 183, 192 (n. 9)
Fields, Edwin, 71
Fields, Michael, 116, 124
Finley, Ronald, 145
Fiss, Owen, 26
Fourteenth Amendment, 14, 44, 68
Freedom Inc., 142, 148, 150, 155

Freedom schools, 43
Freeman v. Pitts, 159, 161–64
Freilich, Robert, 47, 48
Fulson, Sue, 59, 96, 109, 128, 135, 140, 155

Garcia, George, 134–35
Gibson, John, 93, 108
Ginsburg, Ruth Bader, 165, 167
Glazer, Nathan, 192 (n. 6)
Grace, Bill, 147, 151
Grassley, Charles, 111
Green v. New Kent County School Board, 18–20, 22–23, 38, 47, 71, 78, 161, 182

Hale, Phale, 96–97, 144
Hallmark Corporation, 105, 106
Halpern, Stephen C., 193 (n. 23)
Harvard Civil Rights Project, 182
Hazlett, James, 37, 39, 40–42, 141; and "Concepts for Changing Times," 40; and "Hazlett Huts," 41
Health Education and Welfare, Department of (HEW): and Civil Rights Act, 16–18, 28, 29; and KCMSD, 40, 41, 44–47, 49; and Judge Clark, 50, 51; as defendants, 67, 69, 74
Heaney, Gerald, 93, 94, 108
HEW. *See* Health Education and Welfare, Department of
Hill, Julia, 143–44, 156
Honig, Bill, 136
Horowitz, Donald, 10–12, 111, 192 (n. 4)
House Bill (H.B.) 171, 67, 72
House Bill (H.B.) 437, 67, 68, 72
Housing and Urban Development, Department of (HUD), 49, 51, 67, 69, 70, 74
HUD. *See* Housing and Urban Development, Department of
Hudson, Norman, 43
Hutchison, Pete, 78, 79, 101

INDEX

Institutional reform litigation, 9, 10, 24, 26, 27

Jaffe, Louis, 25
Jenkins, Carroll, 54
Jenkins, Craig, 54
Jim Crow laws, 33, 80
Johnson, Herman, 39
Journal of Negro Education, 31, 33, 35
J. S. Chick Magnet School, 189
Judicial activism, 29
Judicial policymaking, 9, 10, 12, 26, 181–85

Kagan, Robert, 26
Kansas City, Missouri, School District (KCMSD): support for tax increases, 8, 110, 171–72; early attempts at integration, 34–38, 40; early suits against, 40, 41, 45, 46; school board, 40, 57, 61, 135, 140–45, 168, 171, 174–79, 182; white flight from, 42; financial mismanagement, 42–45, 88, 89, 131–34, 169–71, 173, 185, 186; teachers' unions, 43, 131, 141, 142, 163; suit against state, 47–50; relationship with Judge Clark, 51–55, 77–79; failures of, 60, 103, 123, 124; neighborhood schools, 65, 66, 175; magnet schools, 80, 95–97, 115–16, 120, 123, 143, 148, 164; capital improvement plan, 113–16, 139; school safety, 123; standardized tests, 125, 129, 130, 165, 188; student achievement, 125–28, 130, 164–65, 168; administration, 127; policy of social promotion, 128; superintendents, 134–37, 141, 142, 175–78, 186, 188; politics of, 140, 143; attendance quotas, 149; support for pay increases, 163, 165; end of state involvement with, 165–70; charter schools, 172, 174; accreditation, 173, 176, 178, 188

Kansas City Star: on history of Kansas City segregation, 31, 36, 43; on KCMSD failure, 58, 131–32, 179; on Judge Clark's rulings, 79, 80; support for tax increases, 102–4, 110; on failure of remedial plan, 118–19, 126–27; on reaction of black community, 135–36, 139, 145, 146, 150–51, 155
Kansas City Times, 92, 98, 102, 103, 112, 117, 123
Kansas City Town Squire, 59
KCMSD. *See* Kansas City, Missouri, School District
Kelly, Margarite, 114
Kennedy, Anthony, 109–10, 116, 161–62, 165
Keyes v. Denver School District No. 1, 20–23, 29, 47, 53, 78, 182
Kilpatrick, A. H., 61

Landmark Legal Foundation, 78–79, 101, 103, 105–7, 108, 147–49
Lay, Donald, 93, 94
LDF (NAACP Legal Defense Fund), 28, 29, 56
Levin, Mark, 148
Levine, Daniel, 47, 72, 85, 86, 88, 89, 90, 96–97
Levinson, Thomas, 104
Liddell v. Caldwell, 52, 63, 67–68, 87
Lindblom, Charles, 13
Lincoln Academy, 137
Lott, Trent, 111

Magnet schools: and KCMSD, 8, 80, 114, 117–28 passim, 163–67; as desegregation remedy, 24, 29, 40, 45, 53, 82, 91–93, 108; themes of, 95–101, 137; financial mismanagement of, 131–34; black opposition to, 139, 143–48, 152–54, 157–58
Maher, John D., 116

Market Information Services, 95
Marks, Walter, 135–37, 152–53, 175
Marshall, Thurgood, 165, 179
Martin Luther King Middle School, 127
Mature policymaking, 9, 11–12, 27, 184
McClain, Charles, 177
McMillian, Theodore, 93–94, 108
Medcalf, Robert, 44
Melnick, R. Shep, 192 (n. 6)
Meredith, James, 52–53, 93
Metro High School, 132
Milliken v. Bradley I, 21–24, 29, 48, 55, 70–71, 74, 81, 83, 108, 166, 182
Milliken v. Bradley II, 22–24
Missouri, state of: educational history of, 32–34; desegregation rulings against, 57, 74–83 passim, 89, 94, 95, 164, 165, 168–70; legal defense of, 71–73; rulings against, 82, 100, 108, 159; proposed remedial plan, 86–89; political motivations of, 87–88; criticism of remedial plan, 98–101; and Eighth Circuit, 106–7, 159; opposition to tax increases, 107–8; and Supreme Court, 109–10, 165–67; opposition to vouchers, 117; settlement agreement, 165–70
Missouri Board of Education, 176
Missouri v. Jenkins: *Jenkins I*, 204 (n. 77); *Jenkins II*, 109–11; *Jenkins III*, 165–68
Montgomery County, Alabama, School District, 169
Murphy, John, 129, 135, 138, 175

NAACP (National Association for the Advancement of Colored People), 38, 41, 52, 135, 165, 190; Kansas City branch of, 39, 52, 142–45, 150; St. Louis branch of, 52–53
NAACP Legal Defense Fund (LDF), 28, 29, 56

National Urban League, 52
Neal, J. McKinley, 72
Neighborhood schools, 19, 35, 38, 46, 65–66, 160, 171, 173, 175
Newsome, Edward, 147; school board election campaign of, 154–56; negotiation with state of Missouri, 168–70; as school board president, 171–72, 175, 188
New York Times, 167
Nixon, Jay, 87–88, 164–65, 169
Nugent, Pete, 143
Nutter, Edward, 154

O'Connor, Sandra Day, 110, 165
Oliver, John D., 49–50
Olson, Phillip, 71
Orfield, Gary, 21, 53, 65, 71, 72, 93, 180

Paseo High School, 42, 134
Perkins, Claude, 95–96, 134, 143–45
Plan E, 45
Plan 6C, 46
Poindexter, Henry, 40, 66
Powell, Justice, 20
Pratt, John H., 28–29, 44, 45
Precedent: role of, 12, 13, 23, 24, 31, 46, 57, 73, 82, 183–84
PMT (Project Management Team), 114–16
Project Management Team (PMT), 114–16
Public law litigation, 10, 25

Rabkin, Jeremy, 26, 27
Rainwater, Art, 152, 154
Rauh, Joseph, 28
Rehnquist, William, 110, 161, 165–67
Residential segregation, 18
Rios, John, 155
Roe, Robert, 41
Roe v. Wade, 181
Roque, Kit Carson, 149
Rosenberg, Gerald, 9–12, 15

226 INDEX

Ross, Donald, 93
Rossell, Christine, 27–28
Rubin, Edward, 13, 183, 192 (n. 9)

St. Louis, Missouri, School District: desegregation of, 52–53. *See also* *Liddell v. Caldwell*
San Antonio v. Rodriguez, 22–24, 29, 73, 83, 85
Sandler, Ross, 26–27
Scalia, Antonin, 109, 165
Schoenbrod, David, 26–27
Segregation: de facto, 13, 19–20, 40–41, 159, 161–62, 165, 167; de jure, 19–20, 40, 66, 159, 161–62, 166, 169, 173
Separate but equal, doctrine of, 14, 32
Shaw, Theodore, 64–65, 165
60 Minutes, 127
Snyder, Allen, 109
Souter, David, 165, 167
SCLC. *See* Southern Christian Leadership Conference
Southern Christian Leadership Conference (SCLC): Kansas City chapter of, 41, 52, 142, 143–45, 148, 150
Southwest High School, 186
Spainhower Commission, 67–68, 72
Springfield, Missouri, School District (SMSD), 170
Stahl, Leslie, 127
Standing, doctrine of, 26–28, 50
Stark, Joyce, 71–72
Swann v. Charlotte-Mecklenburg School Board, 19–23, 28, 29, 44, 78, 182
Stephens, Bob, 143–44
Still, John, 155
Stockton City, California, School District, 169
Struby, Carl, 58
Suburban school districts: defense of, 70–71, 81, 94, 167

Tax increases: Supreme Court and, 8, 9, 108–11; Judge Clark and, 11, 29, 82, 92–94, 188; the KCMSD and, 42, 43, 59–61; constitutional arguments against, 106–8
Taylor, Bernard, 177–78
Teachers' strikes, 43–44, 71
Thedford, Rollie D., 46
Thomas, Clarence, 165–66, 179–80
Thompson, Nelson, 145
Time magazine, 148, 159, 168, 178, 182
Tocqueville, Alexis de, 142
Traditional litigation, 10
Traditional schools, 125–27, 137

U.S. Commission on Civil Rights, 16, 33, 52
U.S. Supreme Court: upholding tax increase, 8, 9, 108–11; and judicial policymaking, 12, 181–83; and desegregation precedents, 13–22, 24, 57, 82, 158; and changing desegregation doctrine, 119, 156, 159–68, 180

Vouchers, 117–18, 146, 187

Wahlberg, Herbert, 88–89, 126
Waiver system, 128
Wallace, George, 22
Waris, Bill, 102
Webster, Ajamu, 136, 147
Webster, William, 87
Wheeler, Robert, 71
Whipple, Dean: reputation of, 170; and case dismissal, 172, 174
White, Byron, 109–10
White flight, 21, 22, 167, 181; from KCMSD, 34, 36, 41, 44, 50, 66, 83–84, 107, 182–83
Williams, Henry, 175–76
Wollman, Roger, 93, 173